Shall Not the Judge of All the Earth
Do What Is Right?

James L. Crenshaw

Shall Not the Judge of All the Earth Do What Is Right?

Studies on the Nature of God in Tribute to James L. Crenshaw

Edited by

DAVID PENCHANSKY and PAUL L. REDDITT

Winona Lake, Indiana
EISENBRAUNS
2000

Cataloging in Publication Data

Shall not the judge of all the earth do what is right? : studies on the nature
of God in tribute to James L. Crenshaw / edited by David Penchansky
and Paul L. Redditt.
    p.   cm.
Includes bibliographical references and indexes.
ISBN 1-57506-043-4 (cloth : alk. paper)
    1. God—Biblical teaching.   2. Bible—Theology.   3. Hidden
God—Biblical teaching.   I. Crenshaw, James L.   II. Penchansky,
David.   III. Redditt, Paul L.
BS544.S53 2000
231—dc21   99-059709
                                                                     CIP

The paper used in this publication meets the minimum requirements of the
American National Standard for Information Sciences—Permanence of Paper for
Printed Library Materials, ANSI Z39.48-1984.⊗™

Contents

Preface

In a time when many people are suspicious of the academic study of religion, it is a pleasure to acknowledge the contributions of the eminent scholar of the Hebrew Bible, Professor James L. Crenshaw, via the publication of this Festschrift. It is presented to him in anticipation of his 65th birthday. It contains essays from scholars on both sides of the Atlantic, who wish to recognize and honor Professor Crenshaw for his decades of teaching and publishing. Many other scholars join in congratulating him and wishing him many more years of scholarly productivity.

A look at Professor Crenshaw's bibliography reveals that he has written ten 15 books, edited 5 more, edited 2 series of monographs, and contributed 125 articles to various publications since 1967. His works have been translated into other languages and have been recognized for special prizes. He has taught at Atlantic Christian College, Mercer University, Vanderbilt University, and now at Duke University, where he is the Robert L. Flowers Professor of Old Testament. Literally thousands of students have sat at his feet for guided tours of the Hebrew Bible or portions thereof. This volume does nothing to enhance his status; it only recognizes and honors his achievements.

The editors are grateful for the opportunity to arrange for and contribute to this Festschrift. We wish to thank the scholars who contributed to it and also James Eisenbraun and his colleagues at Eisenbrauns who prepared it for publication. Above all, we want to thank Professor Crenshaw for his scholarly achievements and for his friendship.

DAVID PENCHANSKY   PAUL L. REDDITT
University of St. Thomas   Georgetown College
Saint Paul, Minnesota   Georgetown, Kentucky

James L. Crenshaw: An Appreciation

DAVID PENCHANSKY

University of St. Thomas

It is my great pleasure to have participated in this volume to honor my teacher, Professor James Crenshaw, and to offer this appreciation. I will here review Crenshaw's remarkable impact on the field of biblical criticism.

Whirlpool of Torment[1] is my favorite book written by any scholar of the Hebrew Bible. In *Whirlpool* Crenshaw looks into the very face of the Bible's presentation of terror before and abandonment by God, a literary world in which God is the hunter and torturer of people. Examining well-known texts such as Abraham's offering of Isaac (the Akedah), Jeremiah's bitter accusations against the deity, and Qoheleth's despair, Crenshaw does not whitewash what he reads.

He uncovers a rich tradition of narrative, legend, and other materials in diverse genres, a tradition that portrays the Israelite God as terrible, dangerous, and capricious—that is, as completely unfair. But these texts in Crenshaw's deft hands never render one hopeless. Rather, in human response to such a God (or perhaps I should say, human response to God so rendered), Crenshaw finds possibilities of redemption, sometimes through a plain realism, sometimes through protest, sometimes through a cleansing despair. In these texts an act of God on human behalf always remains a possibility.

Crenshaw sanctifies this kind of God-talk by rooting it firmly in the texts of the Hebrew Bible. Most commonly, these passages, or entire books in the case of Job and Ecclesiastes, have been explained away by

---

1. J. L. Crenshaw, *A Whirlpool of Torment: Israelite Traditions of God as an Oppressive Presence* (OBT; Philadelphia: Fortress, 1984).

linking them with interpretations that agreed with the standard Jewish
and Christian theological formulations that God is all good, all benevolent, all faithful, dependable, and reliable.

In *Whirlpool*, Crenshaw breathes life into these ancient literary figures (Abraham, Jeremiah, Job, Qoheleth, and the anonymous poet who
wrote Psalm 73), and makes their concerns, their questions, ours. Crenshaw listens to these minority voices in the Hebrew Bible because in
this way Israelite thinkers penned their response to dire pain—the pain
of human disaster and the pain that results from the loss of meaning.
This interest in minority voices creates an added dimension to an understanding of the Hebrew Bible, a dimension lacking in standard formulations and official pronouncements.

Crenshaw gravitates to wisdom literature, which has always stood out
as a distant relative to the rest of the Hebrew Bible. Von Rad, in his *Old
Testament Theology*,[2] tried to make wisdom literature a part of Israel's answer to its experience of the divine covenant, but Crenshaw, in his work
Old Testament Wisdom[3] (which displaced von Rad's *Wisdom in Israel*[4] as a
basic textbook) always allowed wisdom to have its own distinctive voice,
its own distinctive intellectual world. Even the most traditional of wisdom texts (Proverbs 10–21, for instance) claims that human observation
and commonly received traditional proverbs are sources of correct understanding and behavior, rather than direct revelation, as one finds with
Moses and the prophets.

The more marginal expressions of wisdom literature (Job, for instance) are known to have questioned the most deeply held beliefs of the
Israelite people. Throughout the history of ancient Israel, wisdom writings and wisdom teachings provided a counterweight to some of the
other prevailing theological movements in Israel. Whether they originated from a definable class of sages or a commonly held intellectual tradition, Crenshaw does not say, but he leaves no doubt that they offer an
alternative voice. In that voice Crenshaw hears and articulates better
than any other contemporary scholar of the Hebrew Bible the notion of

---

2. G. von Rad, *Old Testament Theology* (2 vols; New York: Harper, 1962–65)
1.355–453.

3. J. L. Crenshaw, *Old Testament Wisdom: An Introduction* (Atlanta: John Knox,
1981).

4. G. von Rad, *Wisdom in Israel* (Nashville: Abingdon, 1972).

sacred doubt. He hears their protests that human suffering is unfair and that something must be done about it. For this reason, Crenshaw once said to me in a discussion that the Panglossian pronouncements in Psalm 37 ("I was young. Now I am old. I have never seen the righteous forsaken or their seed begging bread") is "the song of the blind."

The sages tended to doubt many of the traditional teachings in ancient Israel. Similarly, Crenshaw doubts much in the intellectual tradition of *his* community or field. His work reflects an antipathy to any rigid, global formulation he encounters. Three of his most important contributions specifically undermine commonly assumed notions among the academy of Old Testament / Hebrew Bible scholars. For instance, von Rad in *Wisdom in Israel* suggests that a major intellectual enlightenment took place during the reign of King Solomon. This was for von Rad the social environment in which a class of sage-teachers flourished and wrote much of what we regard as wisdom.[5] Supposedly, this enlightenment was responsible for so-called Royal wisdom and for philosophical/theological wisdom. Crenshaw, in *Old Testament Wisdom*,[6] looks for evidence in the Bible for this enlightenment but finds that von Rad sewed together a patchwork of assumptions from scant evidence. Crenshaw never addresses exactly why von Rad would make such a blunder, but the notion of a Solomonic enlightenment fits very well with nineteenth- and early-twentieth-century German notions of nationhood and the evolution of intellectual advancement. Crenshaw deconstructed von Rad's thesis and, as a result, he changed the way people spoke of the relationship between early Israelite monarchy and wisdom literature.

Second, some scholars in the 1960s and 1970s took a different tack. Rather than trying to make wisdom conform with covenant theology and complaining when it did not, they conformed much of the rest of the Bible to wisdom. They found wisdom everywhere. For instance, they saw it in the Garden of Eden narrative (Genesis 2–3) with its tree of wisdom (the knowledge of good and evil) and its serpent. They saw it in the stories of Joseph and Daniel that were regarded as models of sapiential court behavior. They noted that the book of Hosea employed

---

5. Ibid., 15–16.
6. Crenshaw, *Old Testament Wisdom*, 52.

certain wisdom terms. When Crenshaw examined the specific claims of these scholars, he found in each case that what they regarded as characteristically wisdom was simply part of the general Israelite intellectual pool.

Rather than forcing other parts of the Bible to fit into a wisdom milieu, Crenshaw allowed the wisdom corpus to remain an ambiguous and difficult part of the Hebrew Bible. Further, Crenshaw himself embodied many of the intellectual principles put forth in the sapiential way of thinking, including a willingness to question prevailing assumptions, insisting on measuring them on the basis of human experience and observation. Crenshaw—and the sages—maintained a healthy skepticism against the sweeping claims of others.

Third, Crenshaw also challenged the notion of the presence of formal schools and teachers in ancient Israel. This too has been an attempt to make wisdom fit in with the rest of the Hebrew Bible. Wisdom writings were regarded as the textbooks of the schools, both elementary (portions of Proverbs) and more advanced (the book of Job, Qoheleth).

In each of these three cases (Solomonic enlightenment, wisdom influence, and ancient Israelite schools), Crenshaw affirms the differentness of Wisdom literature, and he decries those who see in the Bible a mirror of their own time. Crenshaw pleads, not for his own specific global reconstruction, but for an acceptance of ambiguity and silence with regard to some of these important questions.

Crenshaw discusses sacred doubt in the wisdom corpus; he chronicles its every permutation. Emotionally and intellectually he was there when Job's experience appeared to deny the law of retribution. Job had conformed to the moral requirements (he was "perfect, upright, fearing God and avoiding evil"), but his life was shattered so that Yahweh might win a bet. Crenshaw was there also in the despair of Qoheleth ("All is emptiness, wind") and Agur ("There is no God at all, and I am powerless" as Crenshaw translates Prov 30:1).[7]

Crenshaw created a safe space for doubt and questions, whereas many other scholars seek to smooth over difficulties and harmonize differences. Yet, there is more to Crenshaw than skepticism. In his recently

---

7. Ibid., 203.

published book of sermons, *Trembling at the Threshold of a Biblical Text*,[8] he consistently affirms the possibility of redemption and transformation in the world and the troubled reality of divine presence.

The editors of any Festschrift hope it will be an expression of the honored scholar's legacy. Crenshaw's legacy is secure. I have arranged the following list of his contributions, in no particular order, in the recognition that it is only representative and that the legacy is still growing:

- He works always in the richness and polyvocality of Scripture.
- He therefore affirms and illuminates the distinctive voices within the wisdom tradition of ancient Israel.
- He elevates the notion of sacred doubt as a central concern of the Hebrew Scriptures. By implication (and some discussion) he validates the possibility of faithful human doubt within the Christian and Jewish traditions, as modeled by certain figures and texts within the Bible.
- He always exhibits a high regard for human dignity, for notions of fairness and graciousness.
- He always seeks to listen to marginalized voices, whether in the text, in his scholarly communities, or in the larger world scene.
- He always exhibits in his writings a high regard for the presence (as well as the absence!) of God in human affairs.

And not least, I must mention his legacy in the love, admiration, and respect he inspires both in his colleagues and his students, and I am certain that all of this great company would want to share with me as we dedicate this volume to Professor Crenshaw.

---

8. Idem, *Trembling at the Threshold of a Biblical Text* (Grand Rapids, Mich.: Eerdmans, 1994).

Introduction

Paul L. Redditt

Georgetown College
Georgetown, Kentucky

This volume is a collection of essays on *theology* in the narrow sense of the word: the doctrine of God. They approach this topic through the avenue of biblical exegesis, and they focus on troubling texts. These are texts in which God says or does things that disturb many readers: for example, orders Abraham to sacrifice his son Isaac, hardens the hearts of people, sends lying spirits to prophets, or turns against Job "for no reason" (Job 2:3). James L. Crenshaw has studied such texts with integrity, refusing to ignore what they say and what they imply. In this volume, some of his colleagues and a few of his students have engaged texts from their own research in the same spirit. The essayists do not always agree with each other or with Professor Crenshaw (such is the state of biblical studies today), but they engage the texts. Even though the authors did not see what any of the other authors wrote, they also appear to engage each other at times.

The volume is arranged to follow the order of the Hebrew Bible. It opens with three essays that make wide-ranging surveys of problematic texts or (in the case of Magne Sæbø) treat a general topic: the hiddenness and nature of God. Articles on the Pentateuch, the Former Prophets, the Latter Prophets, and the Wisdom Literature appear next. The volume closes with an article about the Lord's Prayer as a ritual response to the issue. A brief sketch of each article follows.

R. N. Whybray reviews multiple texts in which God is said to have turned against God's own people without sufficient cause and even with violence. He derives the title of his essay from Gen 18:25, where Abraham rebukes God with the question: "Shall not the Judge of all the earth do what is just?" His essay serves well as a survey of the primary issue in this volume.

Walter Brueggemann examines four texts (Ps 22:1, Lam 5:20, Isa 49:14, and Isa 54:7–8) in which Yahweh is said to have abandoned Israel. Next he surveys five different approaches to these texts, finding all of them defective because they settle theological issues on grounds outside the text. He argues that a better approach is to understand the texts dramatically. His thesis is that "rhetoric constitutes the character of Yahweh." Brueggemann urges readers to assume a "naïvely realistic" view of the text as a script of Yahweh's past, which naïvete "overrides our critical judgments." So, although a " 'truer' picture of Yahweh cast in canonical or theological form has moved beyond these texts," it has not entirely replaced them.

Magne Sæbø reviews the issue of the *dictum* Gerhard von Rad raised in his "Offene Fragen im Umkreis einer Theologie des Alten Testaments" (*TZL* 88 [1963]): "So, it is a serious question whether and in what sense we may still claim to use the title 'Old Testament Theology' in the singular. Where in it is there a center? . . . [W]hat kind of Yahweh is he? Is he not . . . hiding himself . . . from his people?" Sæbø agrees that tradition history research has not uncovered a "center" and faults him for not paying more attention to the "hiddenness" of God. According to Sæbø, von Rad ultimately wished to have in the Old Testament "open windows" to the New and to God's saving act in Christ on the Cross. For von Rad, Old Testament Theology must give way to biblical theology.

Lennart Boström argues that in Abraham, Isaac, and Job one finds two different models of piety. In one model, the hero is commanded to submit to testing by God, primarily for the benefit of other people. In the other model, the hero is allowed to revolt and to challenge God in the face of his pain. The focus of narratives depicting the first model is on the test itself, so the test had to be stringent for the narrative to work dramatically. Boström concludes that these narratives do not intend to "do" theology (and should not be read as though they did) but to offer models of piety to people facing calamity.

Otto Kaiser rejects the picture of the perfect God arrived at through metaphysical speculation in favor of the God of the Bible. The experiences of life teach that innocent people suffer, and this too is problematic. Hence, Kaiser wants to find "some mediation between the actions of the revealed God and those of the hidden God, between those of the *deus absconditus* and those of the *deus revelatus.*" To explore the issue Kaiser studies three difficult passages (Gen 22:1–19, 32:23–33; and Exod 4:24–26). He concludes that the passages remind the reader that temptation and tribulation are part of faith and that behind suffering one may see God's instruction in steadfastness and God's call to self-surrender.

Lou H. Silberman notes that the question of the hiddenness of God appears in Exod 33:12–23 and becomes the focus of rabbinic inquiry in *Exodus Rabba* 2 (chapters 12–40). This tradition testifies that Moses may have spoken to the Divine face to face, but he "never uncovered the mystery of the face that would have shown him . . . the darkened way of the Divine in the world." Moses sought justice but found instead the grace that lies beyond it.

Douglas A. Knight notes that Professor Crenshaw was among the earliest scholars to appreciate the religious diversity that existed among the Israelite people, some of whom held points of view at variance with the orthodoxy enshrined in the biblical literature. Knight argues that Deuteronomic laws constitute one example of a conflict between what is written and the reality behind it. He says that these laws not only inculcate the religious concerns of their authors but also were constructed to benefit materially the levitical group that promulgated them.

Ronald E. Clements studies the episode of Achan's sin as a tragic story with a confusing ethical message resting on assumptions at variance with legal prescriptions found elsewhere in the Old Testament. In short, he finds no residual merit or moral lesson in the narrative, except for this negative warning: "That faith can promote hatred, intolerance, and a guilt-ridden savagery, as well as love, joy, and peace remains a necessary warning to every serious-minded exegete of the Old Testament."

Marti Steussy studies how God is characterized in 1 and 2 Samuel as this characterization appears in explicitly reported feelings and motivations of God, actions of God reported by the narrator, sayings of God reported by the narrator or by prophets, and the comments human beings make about God. Narrative reports "depict a passionate, labile God, whose feelings and motives are more often negative than positive." Reports of God's actions may well depict God solving problems, but they are likely to be problems of God's own making, with positive actions of God comprising less than a fifth of the cases. Prophets conveying messages explicitly said to be God's word or instructions show no consistent relationship between God's willingness to talk to persons (or bless them) and their ethical behavior, and God punishes and rejects (and sometimes even misguides) more often than God elects and blesses. Finally, the comments made about God "depict a God who can bless as well as punish but a God with whom it is pointless to argue. . . ." Steussy then raises the question of whether these characterizations deliberately darken the picture of God due to a "deep-seated grudge of the narrator against Yahweh." She concludes that a canonical reading might ameliorate some of these conclusions.

In a study of the lament found in Isa 62:7–64:12, Walter Harrelson engages a text that blames God at least partially for the plight of the people of Israel in exile. By extending his study to include 65:1, Harrelson is able to say that God invites just the kind of outpouring of anger, grief, and remorse expressed here. In addition, the response also presupposes the implicit faith of the poet that the deity hidden is, at heart, merciful, compassionate, and One who will surely come to save.

Paul L. Redditt begins his essay with an exploration of Mal 1:2b–3a, which attributes to God the sentence: "I have loved Jacob, but Esau I have hated." Redditt reviews various explanations of the sentence and understands it in terms of God's fidelity to Israel within the context of their covenant. Redditt is more interested, however, in the question of how to do a theology of the Hebrew Bible. He argues for a theology that is corrected by and corrects the theology of metaphysical speculation spurned by Kaiser. As convinced as Brueggemann is that one should retain these characterizations of God in one's theology albeit in a "second naïvete," Redditt argues that the theological statements must be evaluated for what they are: characterizations ultimately unacceptable for the God of the whole world."

Roland Murphy revisits a disagreement between himself and Professor Crenshaw, which Crenshaw summarized as follows: the crucial difference between them is whether ancient sages accepted the world view of Yahwism; Murphy thinks they did, Crenshaw thinks they did not. Murphy first questions the use of the Exodus-Sinai revelation as the criterion by which other forms of Yahwism are to be judged. Second, he doubts that the presence of outside influences in wisdom literature disqualifies it as Yahwistic, since much of the Hebrew Bible does battle against the influence of Canaanite religion. Accordingly, he emphasizes the traditionally "Israelite" origins of wisdom traditions in Israel. Third, Murphy speculates "that behind the separation of Yahwism and wisdom lies a modern presupposition, the distinction between revelation and natural theology." The entire Hebrew Bible, including wisdom literature, knows no such distinction but speaks of "the one order of things." Fourth, the book of Proverbs makes continual references to Yahweh. Finally, it is in wisdom literature more than elsewhere that one finds expressions of the agony and grief of Israel before Yahweh.

Leo G. Perdue reviews four scholars who have addressed the problem of revelation in wisdom literature: J. Coert Rylaarsdam, Gerhard von Rad, Roland Murphy, and James L. Crenshaw. He constructs a typology for their views under four headings. (1) Rylaarsdam traced three stages in the understanding of revelation in wisdom literature: natural reason, irrationality, and the nationalization of wisdom. (2) Rylaarsdam further examined the relationship between reason and revelation, arguing that "revelation in wisdom literature finally came to be viewed as a combination of salvation history, cultic theophany, and sapiential observation, but only after a period of significant struggle and doubt evidenced in the writings of Job and Qoheleth." (3) Von Rad introduced the new category of intellectual eros, "that is, wisdom was the meaning of reality, hidden at first, that became both the voice of God . . . and the alluring representation of divine mystery. . . ." Murphy parted company from von Rad by arguing that in wisdom literature "creation" is understood both as "beginning" and as the "context" of living human life. In Ben Sira the revelation of the divine word is one and the same with the revelation of the witness of creation. (4) Crenshaw has emphasized the hiddenness of God in wisdom literature—that is, the sages' recognition that human experience did not always easily correlate with the idea of retribution. The attack on divine justice was only partially quieted by Qoheleth's teaching that God was ultimately mysterious and hidden, a Being to be feared.

David Penchansky asks what one is to make of Job's wife. Is she an evil woman doing the work of the Satan, is she a feminist saint bringing a breath of fresh air to the stifling piety of Job 1 and 2, or is she a woman who meant well but was misunderstood? Penchansky offers a new reading, a feminist one, in which Job's wife is seen as slighted in the protrayal of her as an unnamed, minor character though she had suffered everything Job suffered. She was also unwilling to bow down in her pain and reacted by rejecting the norms of her society. Penchansky thinks she attacked Job, thus personifying the universe that had turned against him. His pain was intensified through her abuse so that he did blaspheme God. In doing so he found his integrity.

Antoon Schoors examines the 49 occurrences of the verb *hāyâ* in the book of Qoheleth. What he finds is that quite often it has the meaning 'to happen'. This finding has implications for Qoheleth's philosophy. Qoheleth turns out to be more interested in human life than in ontology. His problem, though, is that despite all his wisdom he "cannot fathom in a satisfactory way . . . [that] the God who has preordained human life 'under the sun' belongs to the metaphysical world."

Bernhard Lang studies the Lord's Prayer as a response to the hiddenness of God in the Hebrew Bible. He argues that the prayer is more attuned to the message of John the Baptist than to the message of Jesus. Its essential petition asks for the coming of the kingdom of God—that is, the reestablishment of the Israelite state. It was originally used as a prayer in ritual assemblies in which the Baptist announced the coming of this kingdom and contributed to that state by baptizing its new citizens into citizenship. The Baptist expected God to inaugurate a new era of divine blessings, outlined in seven requests. These hopes were no longer shared by the Christian evangelists, but its words "transcend and survive the context in which they originated."

In these essays, exegesis often turns into theology, and this is as it should be. Though the issues and the answers these scholars have discussed vary widely, they join together in an attempt to think seriously about the presentation of God in the Hebrew Bible rather than simply to ignore disturbing texts. The authors also join in saluting James L. Crenshaw for his pioneering work on similar issues and present these essays to him in honor of his 65th birthday.

Publications of James L. Crenshaw

COMPILED BY DAVID A. MILLS

1967

A "The Influence of the Wise upon Amos." *Zeitschrift für die Alttestamentliche Wissenschaft* 79: 42–52.

1968

A "Amos and the Theophanic Tradition." *Zeitschrift für die Alttestamentliche Wissenschaft* 80: 203–15.

1969

A "Method in Determining Wisdom Influence upon 'Historical' Literature." *Journal of Biblical Literature* 88: 129–42.

A "Yʜwʜ ṣᵉbāʾôt šᵉʿmô: A Form Critical Analysis." *Zeitschrift für die Alttestamentliche Wissenschaft* 81: 156–75.

R Review of *Old Testament Life and Literature*, by G. A. Larue; and *Introduction to the Old Testament* (rev. ed.), by E. Sellin and G. Fohrer. *Journal of the American Academy of Religion* 37: 300–302.

R Review of *Jesus and the Historian, Written in Honor of Ernest Cadman Colwell*, edited by F. T. Trotter. *Religion in Life* 38: 468–69.

1970

A "Popular Questioning of the Justice of God in Ancient Israel." *Zeitschrift für die Alttestamentliche Wissenschaft* 82: 380–95.

R Review of *The Prophets*, by E. G. H. Kraeling. *Religion in Life* 39: 471.

R Review of *Amos: A Commentary*, by J. L. Mays. *Religion in Life* 39: 313–14.

1971

B *Prophetic Conflict*. Beihefte zur Zeitschrift für die Alttestamentliche Wissenschaft 124. Berlin: de Gruyter.

Sigla used:
A = Article
B = Book
R = Review
E = Editor

A "A Liturgy of Wasted Opportunity: Am. 4:6–12; Isa. 9:7–10:4." *Semitics* 1: 27–37.

1972

A "*Wᵉdōrek ʿal bamotê ʾareṣ.*" *Catholic Biblical Quarterly* 34: 39–53.

R Review of *Weisheit im Wandel: Untersuchungen zur Weisheitstheologie bei Ben Sira*, by J. Marbock. *Journal of Biblical Literature* 91: 543–44.

R Review of *American Judaism: Adventures in Modernity*, by J. Neusner; and *There We Sat Down: Talmudic Judaism in the Making*, by J. Neusner. *Religion in Life* 41: 574–75.

R Review of *Isaiah and Wisdom*, by J. W. Whedbee. *Interpretation* 26: 74–77.

1973

R Review of *Translating and Understanding the Old Testament: Essays in Honor of Herbert Gordon May*, edited by H. T. Frank and W. L. Reed. *Journal of the American Academy of Religion* 41: 467–68.

R Review of *The Way of Wisdom in the Old Testament*, by R. B. Y. Scott. *Journal of Biblical Literature* 92: 442–43.

1974

A "The Eternal Gospel (Eccles. 3:11)." Pp. 23–55 in *Essays in Old Testament Ethics*, edited by J. L. Crenshaw et al. New York: KTAV.

A "The Samson Saga: Filial Devotion or Erotic Attachment?" *Zeitschrift für die Alttestamentliche Wissenschaft* 86: 470–504.

A "Wisdom." Pp. 225–64 in *Old Testament Form Criticism*, edited by J. Hayes. Trinity University Monograph Series 2. San Antonio: Trinity University Press.

R Review of *From Politics to Piety: The Emergence of Pharisaic Judaism*, by J. Neusner. *Perspectives in Religious Studies* 1: 196–97.

1975

B *Hymnic Affirmation of Divine Justice*. Society of Biblical Literature Dissertation Series 24. Missoula, Montana: Scholars Press.

A "The Problem of Theodicy in Sirach: On Human Bondage." *Journal of Biblical Literature* 94: 47–64.

A "Journey into Oblivion (A Structural Analysis of Gen. 22:1–19)." *Soundings* 58: 243–56. [Reprinted by Pittsburgh Theological Monograph Series]

1976

E *Studies in Ancient Israelite Wisdom*, edited by J. L. Crenshaw. Library of Biblical Studies. New York: KTAV.

A "The Human Dilemma and Literature of Dissent." Pp. 235–58 in *Tradition and Theology in the Old Testament*, edited by D. A. Knight. Philadelphia: Fortress. [French translation, 1982: "Le dilemme humain et la littérature contestataire," in *Tradition et théologie dans l'ancien Testament*. Lectio Divina 108. Paris: Du Cerf / Desclée, 1982.]

A Introduction and Annotations to Job, Proverbs, and Ecclesiastes. *Oxford New English Bible: A Study Edition*.

A "Response to Dan O. Via." Pp. 47–56 in *Semiology and Parables*, edited by Daniel Patte. Pittsburgh Theological Monograph Series 9. Pittsburgh: Pickwick.

A "Wisdom." "Theodicy." "Riddles." "False Prophecy." Pp. 701–2, 749–50, 895–96, 952–56, respectively, in *The Interpreter's Dictionary of the Bible, Supplementary Volume*, edited by Keith Crim et al. Nashville: Abingdon.

R Review of *Die sogenannten Hymnenfragmente im Amosbuch*, by W. Berg. *Catholic Biblical Quarterly* 38: 213–14.

R Review of *Wisdom in Israel*, by G. von Rad. *Religious Studies Review* 2: 6–12.

R Review of *Ecclesiasticus or the Wisdom of Jesus the Son of Sirach*, by J. G. Snaith. *Journal of Biblical Literature* 95: 298–300.

1977

A "In Search of Divine Presence." *Review and Expositor* 74: 353–69.

A "Job as Drama: A Response to Louis Alonso-Schökel." *Semeia* 7 (*Studies in the Book of Job*, edited by R. Polzin and D. Robertson; Missoula, Mont.: Scholars Press): 64–69.

R Review of *Job: An Introduction and Commentary*, by F. I. Andersen. *Catholic Biblical Quarterly* 39: 255–57.

R Review of *Frau Weisheit: Deutung einer biblischen Gestalt*, by B. Lang. *Journal of Biblical Literature* 96: 436–37.

1978

B *Samson: A Secret Betrayed, a Vow Ignored.* Atlanta: John Knox / London: SPCK. Reprinted, Macon, Georgia: Mercer University Press, 1982.

B *Gerhard von Rad.* Waco, Texas: Word. [German translation, Munich: Kaiser, 1979]

R Review of *Vom rechten Reden und Schweigen: Studien zu Proverbien 10–31*, by W. Bühlmann. *Journal of Biblical Literature* 97: 286–87.

R Review of *The Message of Jonah*, by T. E. Fretheim. *Catholic Biblical Quarterly* 40: 240–41.

R Review of *Jeremia und die Falschen Propheten*, by I. Meyer. *Journal for the Study of the Old Testament* 5: 71–73.

1979

A   "The Shadow of Death in Qoheleth." Pp. 205–16 in *Israelite Wisdom: Theological and Literary Essays in Honor of Samuel Terrien*, edited by J. G. Gammie et al. Missoula, Mont.: Scholars Press.

A   "Questions, Dictons et Epreuves Impossibles." Translated by Aline Patte. Pp. 96–111 in *La Sagesse de l'Ancien Testament*. Bibliotheca ephemeridum theologicarum lovaniensium 51. Louvain: Duculot.

R   Review of *Der Ausschliesslichkeitsanspruch Jahwes*, by M. Rose. *Catholic Biblical Quarterly* 41: 321–22.

1980

A   "The Birth of Skepticism in Ancient Israel." Pp. 1–20 in *The Divine Helmsman*, edited by J. L. Crenshaw and S. Sandmel. New York: KTAV.

A   "Impossible Questions, Sayings, and Tasks." *Semeia* 17 (*Gnomic Wisdom*, edited by J. Crossan; Chico, Calif.: Scholars Press): 19–34.

R   Review of *I Samuel: A New Translation with Introduction and Commentary*, by P. K. McCarter, Jr. *Religion in Life* 49: 387–89.

R   Review of *Philo of Alexandria: An Introduction*, by S. Sandmel. *Perspectives in Religious Studies* 7: 78–79.

R   Review of *Das Buch Jona*, by G. Vanoni and *Das Buch Jona*, by H. Witzenrath. *Journal of Biblical Literature* 99: 607–8.

1981

B   *Old Testament Wisdom: An Introduction*. Atlanta: John Knox / London: SCM. [Japanese translation, 1987; Korean translation, 1993]

A   "The Contest of Darius' Guards in I Esdras 3:1–5:3." Pp. 74–88 in *Images of Man and God: The Old Testament Short Story in Literary Focus*, edited by B. Long. Sheffield: Almond.

A   "Wisdom and Authority: Sapiential Rhetoric and Its Warrants." Pp. 10–29 in *Congress Volume: Vienna, 1980*. Vetus Testamentum Supplements 32. Leiden: Brill.

R   Review of *When Prophecy Failed*, by R. P. Carroll. *Journal for the Study of the Old Testament* 19: 116–18.

R   Review of *Zefanjastudien: Motiv- und Traditionskritik + Kompositions- und Redaktionskritik*, by G. Krinetzki. *Catholic Biblical Quarterly* 43: 111–12.

1982

R   Review of *Amos's Oracles against the Nations*, by J. Barton. *Catholic Biblical Quarterly* 44: 475–77.

1983

B   *Proverbs, Ecclesiastes, Song of Songs*. 2 volumes. Nashville: Graded Press.

A "The Shift from Theodicy to Anthropodicy." Pp. 1–16 in *Theodicy in the Old Testament*, edited by J. L. Crenshaw. Philadelphia: Fortress / London: SPCK.

A "A Living Tradition: The Book of Jeremiah in Current Research." *Interpretation* 37: 117–29. [Reprinted on pp. 100–112 in *Interpreting the Prophets*, edited by J. L. Mays and P. J. Achtemeier. Philadelphia: Fortress, 1987]

A "Qoheleth in Current Research." *Hebrew Annual Review* 7: 41–56.

R Review of *Seek the Lord: A Study of the Meaning and Function of the Exhortations in Amos, Hosea, Isaiah, Micah, and Zephaniah*, by A. V. Hunter. *Catholic Biblical Quarterly* 45: 459–60.

R Review of *Those Who Ponder Proverbs: Aphoristic Thinking and Biblical Literature*, by J. G. Williams. *Biblical Theology Bulletin* 13: 67.

1984

B *A Whirlpool of Torment: Israelite Traditions of God as an Oppressive Presence.* Philadelphia: Fortress.

R Review of *Les écoles et la formation de la Bible dans l'ancien Israël*, by A. Lemaire. *Journal of Biblical Literature* 103: 630–32.

R Review of *Wisdom Literature: Job, Proverbs, Ruth, Canticles, Ecclesiastes, Esther*, by R. E. Murphy. *Journal of Biblical Literature* 103: 444–45.

1985

A "Burden." "Counsel." "Counsellor." "Education." "Eunuch." "Goad." "Israelite." "Othniel." "Prince." "Samson." "Son." "Uzziah." "Wrestle." *Harper's Bible Dictionary.* San Francisco: Harper & Row.

A "Education in Ancient Israel." *Journal of Biblical Literature* 104: 601–15.

A "The Wisdom Literature." Pp. 369–407 in *The Hebrew Bible and Its Modern Interpreters*, edited by D. Knight and G. Tucker. Philadelphia: Fortress / Chico, California: Scholars Press.

A "Wisdom Literature, Biblical Books." Pp. 401–9 in volume 15 of *The Encyclopedia of Religion.* New York: Macmillan and Free Press.

R Review of *Ecclesiastes*, by M. A. Eaton. *Catholic Biblical Quarterly* 47: 119–21.

1986

B *Story and Faith: A Guide to the Old Testament.* New York: Macmillan. [Reprinted, Peabody, Massachusetts: Hendrickson, 1992]

A "Pentateuch." "Psalms." "Dream." "Genesis." "Kings." "Righteousness." "Eschatology." "God." "Joshua, Book of." "Samuel, Books of." "Amos, Book of." "Amos." "Wisdom Literature." "Proverbs." "Theodicy."

"Job." "Ecclesiastes." "Job, Book of." "Samson." "Jeremiah." "Jeremiah, Book of." *Illustrated Dictionary and Concordance of the Bible.* New York: Macmillan / Jerusalem Publishing House.

A   "The Expression *Mî yôdēaʿ* in the Hebrew Bible." *Vetus Testamentum* 36: 274–88.

A   "Megillot." "Ecclesiastes." "Creation, Old Testament." Volume 2, cols. 1303–5; volume 3, cols. 356–57; and volume 4, cols. 97–100, respectively, in *Evangelisches Kirchenlexikon.* Göttingen: Vandenhoeck & Ruprecht.

A   "Youth and Old Age in Qoheleth." *Hebrew Annual Review* 10: 1–13.

1987

B   *Ecclesiastes.* Old Testament Library. Philadelphia: Westminster / London: SCM.

A   "The Acquisition of Knowledge in Israelite Wisdom Literature." *Word and World* 7: 245–52.

A   "The High Cost of Preserving God's Honor." *The World and I* (December): 375–82.

A   "Murphy's Axiom: Every Gnomic Saying Needs a Balancing Corrective." Pp. 1–17 in *The Listening Heart,* edited by Kenneth G. Hoglund et al. Journal for the Study of the Old Testament Supplement Series 58. Sheffield: JSOT Press.

R   Review of *The Book of Job: A Commentary,* by N. C. Habel. *Hebrew Studies* 28: 182–83.

1988

E   *Perspectives on the Hebrew Bible,* edited by J. L. Crenshaw. Macon, Georgia: Mercer University Press.

A   "Ecclesiastes." "Sirach." Pp. 518–24, 836–54, respectively, in *The Harper Bible Commentary.* New York: Harper & Row.

A   "A Mother's Instruction to Her Son (Prov. 31:19)." *Perspectives in Religious Studies* 15: 9–22.

A   "Walter Harrelson: Scholar and Believer." *Perspectives in Religious Studies* 15: 5–7.

1989

A   "Clanging Symbols." Pp. 51–64 in *Justice and the Holy: Essays in Honor of Walter Harrelson,* edited by D. Knight and P. Paris. Philadelphia: Fortress.

A   "Poverty and Punishment in the Book of Proverbs." *Quarterly Review* 9: 30–43.

A   "Proverbs." Pp. 223–30 in *The Books of the Bible,* edited by B. W. Anderson. New York: Scribner's.

A "What Does One Need to Know to Understand the Bible?" *Books and Religion* 16: 6–11.

R Review of *The Literary Guide to the Bible*, edited by R. Alter and F. Kermode. *Books and Religion* 16: 6–11.

R Review of *Underdogs and Tricksters: A Prelude to Biblical Folklore*, by S. Niditch. *Journal of the American Academy of Religion* 57: 663–66.

R Review of *The Wisdom of Ben Sira*, by P. W. Skehan and A. A. Di Lella. *Books and Religion* 16: 6–11.

1990

A "Ecclesiastes: Odd Book In." *Bible Review* 6: 28–33.

A "The Sage in Proverbs." Pp. 205–16 in *The Sage in Israel and the Ancient Near East*, edited by J. Gammie and L. G. Perdue. Winona Lake, Indiana: Eisenbrauns.

A "Literature, Bible as." "Riddle." "Samson." "Wisdom." "Wisdom Literature." Pp. 515–19, 764, 791–92, 961–95, respectively, in *The Mercer Dictionary of the Bible*. Macon, Georgia: Mercer University Press.

R Review of *Qoheleth and His Contradictions*, by M. V. Fox. *Journal of Biblical Literature* 109: 712–15.

R Review of *Qoheleth*, by G. S. Ogden. *Journal of Theological Studies* 41: 149–52.

1991

R Review of *The God of the Sages: The Portrayal of God in the Book of Proverbs*, by L. Boström. *Journal of Theological Studies* 42: 628–30.

1992

A Annotations to Proverbs, Job, and Ecclesiastes. *The Oxford Study Bible*. Revised English Bible. New York: Oxford University Press.

A "Prohibitions in Proverbs and Qoheleth." Pp. 115–24 in *Priests, Prophets and Scribes*, edited by E. Ulrich et al. Journal for the Study of the Old Testament Supplement Series 149. Sheffield: JSOT Press.

A "Ecclesiastes, Book of" [2.271–80]. "Job, Book of" [3.858–68]. "Proverbs, Book of" [5.513–20]. "Riddles" [5.721–23]. "Samson" [5.950–54]. "Theodicy" [6.444–47]. In *The Anchor Bible Dictionary*, edited by. D. N. Freedman. 6 volumes. New York: Doubleday.

A "When Form and Content Clash: The Theology of Job 38:1–40:5." Pp. 70–84 in *Creation in the Biblical Traditions*, edited by R. J. Clifford and J. J. Collins. Catholic Biblical Quarterly Monograph Series 24. Washington: Catholic Biblical Association.

R Review of *Biblical Poetry through Medieval Jewish Eyes*, by A. Berlin. *Christianity and Literature* 41: 206–8.

R Review of *Wisdom and Worship*, by R. Davidson. *Interpretation* 46: 193–94.
R Review of *Job the Silent: A Study in Historical Counterpoint*, by B. Zuckerman. *Hebrew Studies* 33: 174–81.

1993

A Annotations to Job. Pp. 749–96 in *The Harper Collins Study Bible*. San
Francisco: HarperCollins.
A "The Concept of God in Old Testament Wisdom." Pp. 1–18 in *In Search
of Wisdom*, edited by L. G. Perdue, B. B. Scott, and W. J. Wiseman.
Louisville: Westminster/John Knox.
A "Wisdom Literature: Retrospect and Prospect." Pp. 161–78 in *Of Proph-
ets' Visions and the Wisdom of Sages: Essays in Honour of R. Norman Why-
bray on His Seventieth Birthday*, edited by H. A. McKay and D. J. A.
Clines. Journal for the Study of the Old Testament Supplement Series
162. Sheffield: Sheffield Academic Press.
R Review of *A Study of Job 4–5 in the Light of Contemporary Literary Theory*,
by D. W. Cotter. *Journal of Biblical Literature* 112: 707–9.
R Review of *The Bible, Violence, and the Sacred*, by J. G. Williams. *Theology
Today* 49: 566–69.

1994

B *Trembling at the Threshold of a Biblical Text*. Grand Rapids, Michigan: Eerd-
mans.
A "Reflections on Three Decades of Research." *Religious Studies Review* 20:
111–12.
A "Wisdom and the Sage: On Knowing and Not Knowing." Pp. 137–44 in
Proceedings of the Eleventh World Congress of Jewish Studies, Division A:
The Bible and Its World. Jerusalem: World Union of Jewish Studies.
A "Trembling at the Threshold: On Reading a Biblical Text." *Perspectives* 9:
22–24.

1995

B *Urgent Advice and Probing Questions: Collected Writings on Old Testament Wis-
dom*. Macon, Georgia: Mercer University Press.
B *Joel*. Anchor Bible 24C. New York: Doubleday.
A "The Contemplative Life in the Ancient Near East." Pp. 2445–58 in vol-
ume 4 of *Civilizations of the Ancient Near East*, edited by J. Sasson et al.
New York: Scribner's.
A "Psalms." Pp. 391–93 in *Concise Encyclopedia of Preaching*, edited by W. H.
Willimon and R. Lischer. Louisville: Westminster/John Knox.

A "Who Knows What YHWH Will Do? The Character of God in the Book of Joel." Pp. 185–96 in *Fortunate the Eyes That See: Essays in Honor of David Noel Freedman*, edited by A. Beck et al. Grand Rapids, Michigan: Eerdmans.

R Review of *Toward a Grammar of Biblical Poetics: Tales of the Prophets*, by H. C. Brichto. *Journal of the American Academy of Religion* 63: 612–15.

R Review of *The Hebrew Bible, the Old Testament, and Historical Criticism: Jews and Christians in Biblical Studies*, by J. D. Levenson. *Journal of Religion* 75: 260–61.

1996

A "Sirach, Wisdom of." "Wisdom Literature." Pp. 589 and 672, respectively, in *Dictionary of Judaism in the Biblical Period*, edited by J. Neusner. New York: Macmillan.

A "A Reply to Douglas, *In the Wilderness: The Doctrine of Defilement in the Book of Numbers*." *Religion* 26 (January): 73–77.

R Review of *The Leopard's Spots: Biblical and African Wisdom in Proverbs*, by F. W. Golka. *Journal of Semitic Studies* 41: 328-30.

R Review of *The School Tradition of the Old Testament*, by E. W. Heaton. *Journal of Religion* 76: 102–3.

R Review of *Wisdom and Creation: The Theology of Wisdom Literature*, by L. G. Perdue. *Theology Today* 52: 544–45.

R Review of *Wealth and Poverty in the Instruction of Amenemope and the Hebrew Proverbs*, by H. C. Washington. *Journal of Biblical Literature* 115: 734–36.

R Review of *Early Israelite Wisdom*, by S. Weeks. *Journal of Biblical Literature* 115: 130–32.

1997

A "Sirach." *New Interpreter's Bible* 5.601–867. Nashville: Abingdon.

A "Freeing the Imagination: The Conclusion to the Book of Joel." Pp. 129–47 in *Prophecy and Poets*, edited by Y. Gitay. Society of Biblical Literature Semeia Studies 32. Atlanta: Scholars Press.

A "The Primacy of Listening in Ben Sira's Pedagogy." Pp. 172–87 in *Wisdom, You Are My Sister: Studies in Honor of Roland E. Murphy, O. Carm., on the Occasion of His Eightieth Birthday*, edited by M. L. Barré. Catholic Biblical Quarterly Monograph Series 29. Washington, D.C.: Catholic Biblical Association.

A "The Missing Voice." Pp. 133–43 in *A Biblical Itinerary: In Search of Method, Form and Content—Essays in Honor of George W. Coats*, edited by E. E. Carpenter. Journal for the Study of the Old Testament Supplement Series 240. Sheffield: Sheffield Academic Press.

A   "The Restraint of Reason: The Humility of Prayer." Pp. 81–97 in *Echoes of Many Texts: Reflections on Jewish and Christian Traditions—Essays in Honor of Lou H. Silberman*, edited by W. G. Dever and J. E. Wright. Brown Judaic Studies 313. Atlanta: Scholars Press.

A   "A Scribe's Prayer." P. vii in *Echoes of Many Texts: Reflections on Jewish and Christian Traditions—Essays in Honor of Lou H. Silberman*, edited by W. G. Dever and J. E. Wright. Brown Judaic Studies 313. Atlanta: Scholars Press.

R   Review of *Character in Crisis: A Fresh Approach to the Wisdom Literature of the Old Testament*, by W. P. Brown. *Interpretation* 51: 423–26.

R   Review of *Vorwurf gegen Gott: Ein religiöses Motiv im Alten Orient (Ägypten und Mesopotamien)*, by D. Sitzler. *Journal of Biblical Literature* 116: 327–29.

R   Review of *Rhetorical Criticism and the Poetry of the Book of Job*, by P. van der Lugt. *Journal of Biblical Literature* 116: 342–44.

R   Review of *Roots of Wisdom: The Oldest Proverbs of Israel and Other Peoples*, by C. Westermann. *Journal of the American Oriental Society* 117: 603.

1998

B   *Education in Ancient Israel: Across the Deadening Silence*. Anchor Bible Reference Library. New York: Doubleday.

B   *Old Testament Wisdom*. Revised and enlarged. Louisville: Westminster John Knox.

A   "Gerhard von Rad." Pp. 526-31 in *Historical Handbook of Major Biblical Interpreters*, edited by D. K. McKim. Downer's Grove, Illinois: InterVarsity.

A   "A Good Man's Code of Ethics (Job 31)." Pp. 221–23 in *The Family Handbook*, edited by H. Anderson, M. S. van Leeuwen, I. S. Evison, and D. S. Browning. Louisville: Westminster/John Knox.

A   "Joel's Silence and the Interpreters' Readiness to Indict the Innocent." Pp. 255–59 in *Lässt uns Brücken bauen . . . ,*" edited by K.-D. Schunck and M. Augustin. Beiträge zur Erforschung des Alten Testament und des antiken Judentums 42. Berlin: Peter Lang.

A   "Qoheleth's Understanding of Intellectual Inquiry." Pp. 205–24 in *Qoheleth in the Context of Wisdom*, edited by A. Schoors. Bibliotheca ephemeridum theologicarum lovaniensium 136. Leuven: Leuven University Press.

A   "The Sojourner Has Come to Play the Judge: Theodicy on Trial." Pp. 83–92 in *God in the Fray: A Tribute to Walter Brueggemann*, edited by T. Linafelt and T. K. Beal. Minneapolis: Fortress.

R Review of *Leiden und Gerechtigkeit: Studien zu Theologie und Textgeschichte des Sirachbuches*, by L. Schrader. *Journal of the American Oriental Society* 118: 77–79.

1999

A "Flirting with the Language of Prayer (Job 14:13-17)." Pp. 110–23 in *Worship in the Hebrew Bible: Essays in Honor of John T. Willis*, edited by M. Patrick Graham, Rick R. Marrs, and Steven L. McKenzie. Journal for the Study of the Old Testament Supplement Series 284. Sheffield: Sheffield Academic Press.

A "The Deuteronomist and the Writings." Pp. 145–58 in *Those Elusive Deuteronomists: The Phenomenon of Pan-Deuteronomism*, edited by L. Schearing and S. McKenzie. Journal for the Study of the Old Testament Supplement Series 268. Sheffield: Sheffield Academic Press.

In Press

A "Job, Book of," in *The Oxford Bible Commentary*, edited by J. Barton and J. Muddiman. Oxford: Oxford University Press.

A "Psalms," in *Eerdmans Dictionary of the Bible*, edited by D. N. Freedman. Grand Rapids, Michigan: Eerdmans.

A "Introduction, Annotations, and Translation of Jonah." *New American Bible* (Old Testament). Washington, D.C.: Catholic Biblical Association.

A "Love Is Stronger Than Death: Intimations of Life beyond the Grave," in *Resurrection in the Bible*, edited by W. Willis and W. P. Weaver. Philadelphia: Trinity.

A "Teaching the Bible in Christian Seminaries." *When You Lie Down and When You Rise Up: Teaching Bible in Postsecondary Academic Settings*, edited by R. Lowery and L. Humphreys. Atlanta: Scholars Press.

A "Unresolved Issues in Wisdom Literature," in Festschrift volume (secret).

A "Latter Prophets: The Minor Prophets," in *Companion to the Hebrew Bible*, edited by L. G. Perdue. Oxford: Blackwell.

A "Transmitting Prophecy across Generations," in *Writings and Speech in Israelite and Ancient Near Eastern Prophecy*, edited by E. Ben Zvi and M. Floyd.

A "Sirach" (revised), in *Harper Bible Commentary*, ed. J. L. Mays. San Francisco: HarperCollins.

A "Ecclesiastes, Book of," in volume 2 of *Encyclopedia of Christianity*. Grand Rapids: Eerdmans/Leiden: Brill.

Series Editor, Society of Biblical Literature Monograph Series (Scholars Press)

Jenks, Alan. *The Elohist and North Israelite Traditions.*
Petersen, David. *Late Israelite Prophecy.*

Brownlee, William. *The Midrash Pesher of Habakkuk.*
Miller, Patrick. *Sin and Retribution in the Prophets.*
Sanders, Jack. *Ben Sira and Demotic Wisdom.*
Halpern, Baruch. *The Emergence of Israel in Canaan.*
Fraade, Steven. *Enosh and His Generation.*

Series Editor, Personalities of the Old Testament
(University of South Carolina Press)

Lacocque, André. *Daniel in His Time.*
Humphreys, W. L. *Joseph and His Family.*
Klein, Ralph. *Ezekiel: The Prophet and His Message.*
Bailey, Lloyd. *Noah.*
Lacocque, A., and P. E. Lacocque. *Jonah: A Psycho-Religious Approach to the Prophet.*
Fox, Michael. *Character and Ideology in the Book of Esther.*
VanderKam, James. *Enoch: A Man for All Generations.*
Steussy, Marti. *David: Biblical Portraits of Power.*

Abbreviations

General

ANE	Ancient Near East
BH	Biblical Hebrew
LXX	Septuagint
MT	Masoretic Text
NAB	New American Bible
NEB	New English Bible
NJB	H. Wansbrough (ed.), New Jerusalem Bible
NJPSV	New Jewish Publication Society Version
NRSV	New Revised Standard Version
OT	Old Testament
RSV	Revised Standard Version
Sym	Symmachus
Syr	Syriac version (Peshiṭta)
Tg.	Targum
Vg	Vulgate

Reference Works

AB	Anchor Bible
ABD	D. N. Freedman (editor). *Anchor Bible Dictionary*. 6 Vols. New York: Doubleday, 1992
ATD	Das Alte Testament Deutsch
BBB	Bonner biblische Beiträge
BDB	F. Brown, S. R. Driver, and C. A. Briggs (editors). *Hebrew and English Lexicon of the Old Testament*. Oxford: Clarendon, 1907
BHS	*Biblia Hebraica Stuttgartensia*
BHT	Beiträge zur historischen Theologie
Bib	*Biblica*
BibLeb	*Bibel und Leben*
BibRev	*Bible Review*
BJRL	*Bulletin of the John Rylands University Library of Manchester*
BKAT	Biblischer Kommentar: Altes Testament
BN	*Biblische Notizen*
BTZ	*Berliner Theologische Zeitschrift*
BWANT	Beiträge zur Wissenschaft vom Alten und Neuen Testament
BZAW	Beihefte zur ZAW

CBQ	*Catholic Biblical Quarterly*
ConBOT	Coniectanea Biblica, Old Testament
ÉBib	Études bibliques
EvT	*Evangelische Theologie*
FRLANT	Forschungen zur Religion und Literatur des Alten und Neuen Testaments
GCS	Die griechischen christlichen Schriftsteller der ersten Jahrhunderte
HALAT	L. Koehler and W. Baumgartner et al. (editors). *Hebräisches und aramäisches Lexikon zum Alten Testament.* 4 Vols. Leiden: Brill, 1967–90
HAT	Handbuch zum Alten Testament
HTR	*Harvard Theological Review*
IB	*Interpreter's Bible*
ICC	International Critical Commentary
JANES	*Journal of the Ancient Near Eastern Society*
JBL	*Journal of Biblical Literature*
JJS	*Journal of Jewish Studies*
JQR	*Jewish Quarterly Review*
JSOT	*Journal for the Study of the Old Testament*
JSOTSup	Journal for the Study of the Old Testament Supplement Series
JTS	*Journal of Theological Studies*
KAT	Kommentar zum Alten Testament
KB	L. Koehler and W. Baumgartner (editors). *Lexicon in Veteris Testamenti libros.* Leiden: Brill, 1958
KEHAT	Kurzgefasstes exegetisches Handbuch zum Alten Testament
KHC	Kurzer Hand-Commentar zum Alten Testament
LAI	Library of Ancient Israel
LCL	Loeb Classical Library
NCB	New Century Bible Commentary
NICOT	New International Commentary on the Old Testament
NovT	*Novum Testamentum*
NTS	*New Testament Studies*
OBO	Orbis biblicus et orientalis
OBT	Overtures to Biblical Theology
OLA	Orientalia Lovaniensia Analecta
OTL	Old Testament Library
PG	J.-P. Migne (editor). Patrologia graeca
RelSRev	*Religious Studies Review*
RevExp	*Review and Expositor*
SAT	Die Schriften des Alten Testaments
SBB	Stuttgarter biblische Beiträge
SBT	Studies in Biblical Theology
SC	Sources chrétiennes
SWBA	The Social World of Biblical Antiquity
TBü	Theologische Bücherei
TDOT	G. J. Botterweck and H. Ringgren (editors). *Theological Dictionary of the Old Testament.* Grand Rapids, Mich.: Eerdmans
ThStud	Theologische Studien

TLZ	*Theologische Literaturzeitung*
TWAT	G. J. Botterweck and H. Ringgren (editors). *Theologisches Wörterbuch zum Alten Testament.* Stuttgart: Kohlhammer, 1973
TZ	*Theologische Zeitschrift*
UCOP	University of Cambridge Oriental Publications
VC	*Vigiliae christianae*
VD	*Verbum Domini*
VF	*Verkündigung und Forschung*
VT	*Vetus Testamentum*
VTSup	Vetus Testamentum Supplements
WBC	Word Biblical Commentary
WC	Westminster Commentaries
WMANT	Wissenschaftliche Monographien zum Alten und Neuen Testament
ZAW	*Zeitschrift für die alttestamentliche Wissenschaft*
ZNW	*Zeitschrift für die neutestamentliche Wissenschaft*
ZTK	*Zeitschrift für Theologie und Kirche*

"Shall Not the Judge of All the Earth Do What Is Just?"

God's Oppression of the Innocent in the Old Testament

R. N. WHYBRAY†

University of Hull

The "light" and the "dark" sides of God are briefly defined in the Decalogue:

> I, Yahweh your God, am a jealous God, punishing children for the iniquity of their parents to the third and fourth generation of those who reject me, but showing steadfast love towards thousands of those who love me and keep my commandments. (Exod 20:5–6, Deut 5:9–10)

That God should love those who love him ought to be taken for granted; conversely, that he should punish those who disobey him is hardly surprising; but is this an accurate summary of what he is represented as actually doing in the Old Testament? Does he, in fact, always show love towards those who love him and faithfully serve him? It is this question that I want to explore in this essay. I am here mainly concerned, not with God's punishment of those who clearly deserve his punishment nor with his hostile actions against Israel's declared enemies, but rather with a not insignificant number of passages in the Old Testament where it could be said that he turns against his own people or members of that people, attacking them *without cause*, or at least with excessive violence—that is, where it can be argued that there is a demonic or vicious side to his nature.

Author's note: I count it a privilege to have been invited to contribute to this volume in honor of my old friend Jim Crenshaw, who has made each a notable contribution to the discussion of the darker side of God in the Old Testament as well as to the study of Israelite wisdom as a whole, and to wish him many more years of scholarly research.

1

I

The dark side of God is a subject that has received astonishingly little attention from Old Testament scholars. The standard Old Testament theologies, monographs about the Old Testament doctrine of God, articles about particular passages, even commentaries are almost completely silent on the matter.[1] Only a handful of recent articles, mainly of a deconstructionist tendency, have given serious attention to it. It is almost as though there is a scholarly consensus that any criticism of God's character in the Old Testament is inconceivable.[2]

Most commentaries, though theoretically committed to the exposition of all significant features of the text, have ignored the implications of such passages; even those that make some reference to them have tended to play down their implications or sought to explain them away with a variety of arguments. To take examples only from Genesis 2–3, it has been variously alleged that a relevant text does not in fact have the meaning that would most naturally be attributed to it;[3] that a particular passage reflects a "primitive" concept of God that was subsequently corrected in the later literature;[4] that the negative view of God that is found in isolated passages is a regrettable but untypical feature which must be acknowledged but which is a mystery that we ought not to try to understand;[5] that it is important to recognize that the grace of God is

---

1. C. Westermann (*What Does the Old Testament Say about God?* [London: SPCK, 1979] 1) asserts that "it is the task of a theology of the Old Testament to describe and view together what the Old Testament as a whole, in all its sections, says about God"; but in fact he does not deal with this particular aspect.

2. J. L. Crenshaw, as the title of the present volume suggests, is a notable exception. He first treated the subject in an article, "Popular Questioning of the Justice of God in Ancient Israel," *ZAW* 82 (1970) 380–85 (reprinted in *Studies in Ancient Israelite Wisdom* [ed. J. L. Crenshaw; New York: Ktav, 1976] 289–304); subsequently in the introduction to *Theodicy in the Old Testament* (Philadelphia: Fortress / London: SPCK, 1983) 1–16; and in *Whirlpool of Torment: Israelite Traditions of God as an Oppressive Presence* (Philadelphia: Fortress, 1984).

3. E.g., (on Gen 2:17) B. Holzinger, *Genesis* (KHC; Freiburg: Mohr, 1898); G. J. Wenham, *Genesis 1–15* (WBC; Waco, Texas: Word, 1987); cf. also R.W. L. Moberly, "Did the Serpent Get It Right?" *JTS* n.s. 39 (1988) 1–27.

4. E.g., L. Derousseaux, *La crainte de Dieu dans l'Ancien Testament* (Lectio Divina 63; Paris: du Cerf, 1970) 141, on 2 Sam 6:6–9.

5. E.g., H. Gunkel, *Genesis* (SAT; Göttingen: Vandenhoeck & Ruprecht, 1910) 10; C. Westermann, *Genesis 1–11* (London: SPCK, 1976) on Genesis 2–3; 4:45.

often demonstrated in a mitigation of the suffering that he inflicts;[6] that it is necessary that God should test human beings and cause them to suffer so that their character and faith may thereby be strengthened;[7] that there is an essentially evil element in human nature such that punitive action by God is always justified;[8] that the verses in question are incidental to their contexts and that the point of the stories lies elsewhere;[9] that belief in a sole deity necessarily involves his sending evil as well as good upon mankind;[10] that the narratives in question are *fundamentally* positive in their portrayal, and that it is the grace of God that ultimately prevails.[11] It has been maintained that God himself shares the suffering that he inflicts;[12] and in Gen 18:23–32, a text in which God proposes to destroy a city (Sodom) irrespective of individual guilt, it has been argued that this is a purely abstract theological discussion in which there is never any question that God is contemplating an injustice.[13]

Despite such arguments, the fact remains that a number of Old Testament texts *seem* to state or imply that God sometimes attacks, or threatens to attack, his own people or individual members of it unjustly, cruelly, and without cause; and that this matter ought to be investigated more thoroughly than it has been. It is appropriate in a volume honoring James Crenshaw to mention that his work is one of the few exceptions to the general neglect of the question.

Genesis 1–11

These chapters, of course, are not ostensibly about God's dealings with Israel. They concern his dealings with humanity as a whole; however, they undoubtedly have lessons to teach the Israelite reader. The

---

6. Crenshaw, *A Whirlpool of Torment*, 111–19.

7. E.g., S. R. Driver, *The Book of Genesis* (WC; London: Methuen, 1905) 56.

8. So apparently A. H. J. Gunneweg, "Urgeschichte und Protevangelion," in *Sola Scriptura* (ed. P. Höffken; Göttingen: Vandenhoeck & Ruprecht, 1983) 83–95, in an exposition of the Yahwist's theology.

9. E.g., G. von Rad, *Genesis* (OTL; London: SCM, 1972) on Genesis 22; Westermann, *Genesis 1–11* on Gen 3:4.

10. E.g., Crenshaw, *Theodicy*, 2.

11. E.g., Gunkel, *Genesis* on Genesis 22; von Rad, *Genesis*, on Gen 3:19.

12. T. E. Fretheim, *The Suffering of God: An Old Testament Perspective* (OBT 14; Philadelphia: Fortress Press, 1984) esp. chap. 7.

13. E. Ben Zvi, "The Dialogue between Abraham and Y_HWH_ in Gen. 18,23–32: A Historical-Critical Analysis," *JSOT* 53 (1992) 27–46; Gunkel, *Genesis*.

God who is depicted here is a God who is curiously unsure of himself. Although he is apparently the omnipotent creator of the world and of everything that it contains, he shows himself to be afraid of his own human creatures and to be constantly taking steps to ensure that they do not deprive him of his authority and put themselves on an equality with him. In the first place, although the reason why he forbade the man and the woman whom he placed in the garden to eat of the fruit of the tree of the knowledge of good and evil on pain of immediate death is not stated (2:17), it cannot reasonably be denied that the story represents the snake (3:1–5) as in the right,[14] since later, in his own reflection on the matter, God *does* reveal his motive: "The man has become like one of us." He had in some measure acquired the divine status that God had intended to withhold from him. Moreover, God is afraid that this is only the first step toward full divine status. Using the knowledge that he has now acquired, the man could complete the process by eating of the other tree, the tree of life, and so gain immortality (3:22). For this reason, God banishes him from the garden and so places the cherubim and a flashing sword to ensure that he will never reenter it (3:23).

The man and the woman were guilty, of course; they had disobeyed God's explicit command. They had been persuaded to do so by the most subtle and persuasive of God's own creatures (3:1), who had assured them that God had lied to them and that the tree's fruit was eminently desirable. Nor did God make an allowance for their naivete or their weakness when he meted out their punishment. It is also true that God had failed in his purpose: he had been unable to prevent what had happened; his authority had been challenged by his own creatures; and he had lost the services of the man whom he had placed in his garden to work there and keep it in order.

Is there not, however, something more sinister in the portrayal of God here than a simple failure to control his creatures? In order to preserve his authority he told a lie (there is no reason to suppose that "in the day that . . ." is not to be taken literally or that "die" in 2:17 has

---

14. Moberly ("Serpent," 13) admits that the snake appears to be telling the truth and God to be lying, but shies away from this interpretation on the grounds that "it is inconceivable that the Genesis writer could have allowed it." He takes refuge in a different meaning of the word *bĕyôm* 'in the day that . . .' in 2:17, but this is a strange way of arguing.

anything other than its usual meaning); and it is at least arguable that his prohibition was itself a deliberate temptation, a testing of man's obedience—in fact, a snare that resulted in misery for those who fell into it.

The portrayal of God in Genesis 2–3 is confirmed in the narratives that follow. In 6:3 God takes a further measure to ensure human mortality and restricts human life to 120 years. In 6:6–7, faced with the spread of human wickedness, God determines to destroy the human race altogether, being forced to regret that he had created such a dangerous species. This determination is revoked only because of the existence of a single righteous individual, Noah, which enables him to make a fresh start after his calamitous failure. In 11:19 the challenge to God's authority comes once again to the fore. Faced with the attempt by human beings to "make a name" for themselves by building a city and a tower reaching to the heavens, God is fearful[15] that there will be no end to their ambition: "Nothing that they purpose to do will be impossible for them" (v. 6). God therefore intervenes with further punishment, confusing their speech and scattering them throughout the world so that they will be unable to unite and overthrow him.

Genesis 18 and 22

Two other incidents in Genesis call for consideration here. Gen 18:23–32, a dialogue in which God and Abraham discuss the question of the number of righteous persons in Sodom that would be sufficient to save the city from destruction at God's hands, may well be an academic theological discussion inserted into an earlier story; but it raises a serious question about God's justice. God has determined to destroy Sodom because of its wickedness. Its inhabitants are described in 13:13 without differentiation as wicked and "very great sinners against Yahweh." God does in fact destroy the city (19:24) but decides first to tell Abraham what he is going to do (18:17–18). Abraham thereupon speaks to God, raising a question about the matter: "Will you indeed sweep away the righteous together with the wicked?" (v. 23). In v. 25 he goes further: "Far be it from you to do such a thing, to kill the righteous together with the wicked, so that the fate of the righteous will be the same as that

---

15. Gunkel, *Genesis*, recognizes that vv. 5–7 might be so interpreted but rejects this interpretation.

of the wicked! Far be that from you! Should not the Judge of all the earth act justly?"

This last sentence can hardly be construed as other than a direct rebuke;[16] and Abraham is aware of his temerity in rebuking God; he is fearful of offending the deity (vv. 27, 30, 31, 32). His words contain an implied accusation that God has given no thought to the possibility that the city may contain a number of innocent people. The initiative is entirely Abraham's; and although he does not succeed in reducing the number of righteous persons sufficient to justify the sparing of the city beyond ten (v. 32), God implicitly admits the justice of the rebuke. The dialogue is thus not simply an academic one; it is assumed that God would have been ready to perform an action that might kill innocent persons. (In 19:4 we are told there were *no* righteous inhabitants of Sodom. Only the innocent travelers, Lot and his family, were saved.)

Genesis 22 is principally a story about the faith of Abraham rather than about the character of God. But the implications of God's command to Abraham to kill his son Isaac and to offer him to God as a burnt offering cannot be dismissed as irrelevant. True, the reader is informed at the outset (v. 1) that God's purpose was to *test* Abraham and that, as becomes clear at the end of the story, God never intended to let Abraham carry out his initial command, but such intentions do not excuse God's behavior.

Abraham's distress is not directly mentioned in the story; but, as has rightly been pointed out, this is poignantly suggested by the style of the narrative itself: not only in the phrase "your son, your only son Isaac, whom you love" (v. 2) and in the verbal exchange between Abraham and Isaac (vv. 7–8), but also in the labored and immensely detailed account of the journey to the appointed place of sacrifice and the preparations for the sacrifice itself.[17] Further, Sarah, Isaac's mother, is not

---

16. Westermann (*Genesis 1–11*), however, regarded the passage as a *vindication* of God's justice: Abraham "is the one who approaches God in order to receive from God himself confirmation of the divine righteousness against any possible doubt." See also von Rad, who held that the passage is a revelation of God's righteousness.

17. J. Skinner, *Genesis* (ICC; Edinburgh: T. & T. Clark, 1930) simply remarks that the absence of reference to Abraham's distress is typical of such legends. Crenshaw (*Whirlpool*, 12) speaks of a "dreadful story" in which God's compassion can hardly be discerned, and of a "real ordeal" for Abraham. He also notes the inexplicable failure to mention Sarah.

mentioned in the chapter at all; but later interpreters have rightly insisted that a proper understanding of the story is bound to take into account the intense distress of both parents. However important the story may have been in the mind of its author as a proof of Abraham's unwavering and unquestioning faith and trust in God's purposes, the callous deception practiced by God and his indifference to human suffering cannot have failed to impress the original readers.

Exodus–Numbers

Early in the book of Exodus, Moses, who has been living in Midian after his flight from Egypt, returns to that country with the full approval of God and accompanied by his wife and family (4:18–20). Indeed, he has been commanded to make the journey in order to confront Pharaoh and demand the release of his fellowIsraelites (vv. 21–23). But while he is on the way there, we are told quite abruptly, Yahweh met him and tried (literally, "sought") to kill him (v. 24). No reason is given for this extraordinary attempt.[18] The following two verses describe some action of Moses' wife, Zipporah, involving circumcision, the significance of which still remains a mystery but the result of which was that he let him alone (v. 26). Whether Yahweh's failure to carry out his intention was because he had somehow received satisfaction or because he was frustrated by Zipporah's action and unable to do what he had intended to do we are not told. No further reference is made to this incident; Moses continues on his way, and the narrative moves on.

The only story in the Old Testament with which this narrative has been compared is the equally mysterious one of Jacob's wrestling with the "man" at the ford of the Jabbok (Gen 32:22–32). In fact there are no significant similarities between the two stories apart from their mysterious character. Exod 4:24–26, however, does have some affinity with the rest of Exodus and Numbers in that it is the first in a long series of incidents that depict God as a destroying God, a God of violence. God kills many people in these books, mainly enemies of Israel or Israelite rebels

---

18. Various suggestions have been made to account for the incident. For example, W. H. Propp ("That Bloody Bridegroom [Exodus iv 24–26]," *VT* 43 [1993] 495–518) suggests that it was a propitiatory rite to atone for Moses' guilt in killing the Egyptian (Exod 2:12) and subsequently escaping to Midian to avoid suffering the death penalty for murder. But the text of 4:24–26 in fact offers no explanation whatever.

against God or Moses, who presumably may be said to have deserved
their fate. But it is worth noting that the numbers of Israelites slain by
God are often extremely large: 14,700 in Num 17:14[16:49];[19] the
Egyptian dead are even more numerous: the eldest son of every Egyptian
family. Numbers especially is an extremely "bloodthirsty" book.

Three dialogues between God and Moses in these books throw further light on the narrator's view of God. In both Exod 32:10 and Num
14:12 God has lost patience with his people (over the making of the
golden calf in the first case and over the people's rejection of the leadership of Moses and Aaron and their determination to return to Egypt
under new leadership in the second). In Exodus 32 the furious Yahweh
tells Moses that he will now destroy this whole people and instead make
Moses himself the founder of a new chosen people and a great nation.
Moses pleads with God to change his mind and advances two reasons
why he should refrain from his proposed course of action—reasons, it
is implied, of which Yahweh is unaware. First, he argues that the Egyp-
tians, when they hear what has happened, will attribute his taking the
people into the wilderness to an evil intention to destroy them (v. 12).
Second, he reminds Yahweh of his own oath that he had sworn to Abraham, Isaac, and Israel (Jacob) to make their descendants into a great and
numerous people and to give them the land of promise forever (v. 13).
This amounts to a severe rebuke, which Yahweh meekly accepts, and
"change[s] his mind about the disaster that he had planned to bring on
his people" (v. 14).

The second dialogue (Num 14:13–20) is concerned with a similar
situation. God again tells Moses that he intends to destroy his people
and replace them with a new people of whom Moses himself is to be
the founder (vv. 11–12). Moses again warns him about the consequences of such an action as regards his reputation among the surrounding peoples; but this time it is not his motives that will be questioned,
but his power: it will be supposed that he has destroyed his people because he was unable to carry out his oath to give them the promised
land (v. 16). Moses himself does not doubt God's power, but he pleads

---

19. R. C. Culley speaks of "punishment followed by mitigation." See "Five Tales of
Punishment in the Book of Numbers," in *Text and Tradition: The Hebrew Bible and Folklore* (ed. S. Niditch; Atlanta: Scholars Press, 1990) 25–34. But in Num 17:14, at least,
there was no mitigation for those who had already died of the plague sent by Yahweh.

that he will exercise this power in accordance with his own earlier assurance that he is "slow to anger and abounding in steadfast love, forgiving iniquity and transgression." As he has pardoned the people's sins in the past, so he ought to pardon them now (vv. 13–19). Yahweh again heeds Moses' plea and promises to forgive them one time more, though he will still inflict the lesser punishment that the present generation will be excluded from the land (vv. 20–24).

The third dialogue (Num 11:11–17) is of a somewhat different kind, though it also is associated with God's anger. The people had complained of their meager diet of manna, contrasting it with the excellent dishes that they had supposedly enjoyed in Egypt (vv. 4–6). Moses loses his patience and violently accuses God of treating him badly by unreasonably laying the entire responsibility of leadership on him as if it were he who had given birth to the whole people. It is God, now angered by the people's lack of trust, who ought to take the responsibility. Finally, Moses asks God to kill him at once if he is not to be given some relief. God does not directly answer the whole of Moses' complaint, but he goes some way in giving Moses relief by directing that his burden is to be shared to some extent by the appointment of a group of seventy elders (vv. 16–17). As with some of the earlier incidents in Genesis and Numbers, these dialogues, whether this was the narrator's intention or not, give the impression of a violent and over-impetuous God who needs to be guided by the advice of his own servants.

The Deuteronomistic History

The Deuteronomistic History is a work whose aim is to justify God's punitive behavior toward his people. Viewed from a standpoint subsequent to 587 B.C., Israel has sinned and rejected Yahweh; and its punishment, which took the form of material destruction, foreign rule, and exile, has been inflicted only after many warnings. Hence, it was fully justified. According to this view there was nothing demonic about Yahweh in his dealings with his people; he did not act arbitrarily against them. The situation is different, however, when it comes to his treatment of individual Israelites. There are a number of stories incorporated into this work where it is not difficult to demonstrate unfair treatment of individuals and some in which God is represented as making innocent persons suffer.

In Judges 11 Jephthah kills his own daughter and offers her as a sacrifice to Yahweh in order to fulfill a vow that he had made to him, probably in the knowledge that the first person to greet him after his victory would be she (v. 31). That this act was regarded by the narrator as shocking is indicated by the way in which the story is told and by the reference to an annual custom of commemorating the girl's death. Yet although human sacrifice is forbidden elsewhere in the Old Testament and regarded as abominable, there is no mention here of God's intervention to prevent it as in Genesis 22 and no indication of his disapproval of an act done in his name.[20]

In 1 Samuel, the behavior of Eli's sons is not only punished by Yahweh's total rejection of his family's hereditary priesthood, it also leads to Eli's death and that of his sons (4:11–18). Although Eli had attempted to correct the behavior of his sons that was the cause of Yahweh's displeasure (2:22–25), he is condemned for not restraining them (3:13). But 2:25 gives a more sinister reason for Yahweh's action: he deliberately prevented the sons from listening to their father, since "it was Yahweh's purpose to kill them." (No reason for this murderous intention is given.) It is equally strange that when later Samuel's own sons behave badly, taking bribes and perverting justice, no punishment is meted out to them; in fact, their behavior is mentioned only as a contributory factor to the people's demand for a king rather than continued rule by Samuel's family.

The rejection of Saul as king may appear to modern readers to be without adequate justification. His offenses were that he had not waited for Samuel to arrive before offering sacrifice in an emergency (13:8–9) and he had not exterminated the defeated Amalekite king or the Amalekites' livestock (15:8–33). God's actions also appear to have won the disapproval of Samuel, who "was angry, and cried aloud to Yahweh all night" (15:11) and "lamented over Saul," whom he was not to meet again alive (15:35).[21]

---

20. R. G. Boling, *Judges* (AB 6A; New York: Doubleday, 1975) calls Jephthah's conduct "exemplary." By contrast, J. A. Soggin (*Judges* [OTL; London: SCM, 1981]) thinks the story offers a glimpse of early preprophetic Israelite religion, which had much in common with Canaanite religion.

21. D. M. Gunn (*The Fate of King Saul* [JSOTSup 14; Sheffield: JSOT Press, 1980] 129–31) takes the view that the main cause of Saul's fall was that God (that is, "the dark side") was against him from the beginning.

The striking death of Uzzah when he touched the Ark of God (2 Sam 6:6–7) no doubt corresponds to what might have been expected in view of contemporary options of the divine holiness; nevertheless, David "was angry because Yahweh had broken out" in this way on what had been intended to be a particularly auspicious occasion (v. 8) and "was afraid of Yahweh that day" (v. 9). David's was a real terror in the face of a terrifying and utterly unpredictable God, despite the opinion of some scholars that the "fear of God (or of Yahweh)" never has this meaning.[22]

The plague sent by Yahweh as punishment for David's taking a census (2 Samuel 24) also earns a rebuke from David. David admits his personal fault but believes that it is wrong that innocent Israelites should be so "punished" because of what he had done: "But these sheep, what have *they* done?" Some commentators appear to justify Yahweh here either because he "mitigated" the massacre, making the destroying angel stay his hand, or because it all "turns out well" with the founding of the altar; but it is surely a tardy mitigation that occurs after 70,000 innocent Israelites have already been slaughtered!

The story of the man of God from Judah and the old prophet of Bethel (1 Kgs 13:11–32) is notoriously difficult to interpret. But the death of the Judean man of God in an attack by a lion (v. 24) is the fulfilment of a genuine oracle of God (vv. 21–22) pronounced against him because of his disobedience to Yahweh's earlier command (vv. 8–9, 17). He is thus condemned to death by Yahweh although his disobedience is not intentional but due to a failure to detect a first oracle countermanding a previous one.

The story of Micaiah (1 Kgs 22:5–23) takes the reader to the heavenly court to reveal Yahweh's method of dealing with human situations. Yahweh sanctions the sending of a "lying spirit" into the mouths of the prophets advising the king of Israel (v. 22) so that the king may be enticed into a military action in which Yahweh has decided (vv. 20, 23) that he is to be defeated and killed.

---

22. W. Zimmerli (*Old Testament Theology in Outline* [Atlanta: John Knox, 1978] 146) comments: "It is a striking fact that, in all its talk of the fear of Yahweh, the faith of the Old Testament never was diverted into a mere trepidation before God" (translated from *Grundriss der alttestamntlichen Theologie* [Stuttgart: Kohlhammer, 1975] 127). Derousseaux (*La crainte Dieu*, 141) speaks of a "primitive conception of Yahweh" here.

In 2 Kgs 2:23–24 an incident is recorded that has been described by one commentator as "in every respect a puerile tale" but one which "borders on blasphemy."[23] The attack by bears on forty-two boys was the consequence of the curse pronounced by Elisha "in the name of Yahweh." Though the purpose of the narrator was presumably to present Elisha as a prophet who was an effective instrument of Yahweh, the incident also presents the reader with a Yahweh who does not scruple to cause the death of small children simply because they have shown disrespect to his prophet.

Is the shocking and unexpected death of King Josiah (2 Kgs 23:29) further evidence of the "dark" side of God? This was an occurrence completely at variance with the principle followed elsewhere in the books of Kings that those who did what was good in the sight of God were appropriately rewarded; so the premature death of a king who had behaved perfectly in that respect all his life (22:2) was inexplicable to the narrator who, however, could hardly avoid recording it. In the context, however, Josiah's death is clearly intended to be understood as a particular act of God that was not only unjust but was a personal and national tragedy that hastened the demise of the kingdom of Judah.[24]

The Prophetic Literature

In the prophetic books in general, as in the Deuteronomistic History, the calamities that Yahweh inflicts, or threatens to inflict, on Israel are held to be richly deserved. In a number of scattered passages, however, his justice is questioned, especially in the book of Jeremiah (for example, 15:18; 20:7–9). Here we find a quite different situation from that of the historical books. Instead of statements by personally uninvolved narrators that God performed certain actions that could be interpreted as brutal or unfair, we have purportedly the anguished laments, addressed to God, of an individual whose life has been devoted to God's service but who now accuses God of deceiving him and making his life intolerable. These are presented to the reader as part of a series of private conversations between Jeremiah and God; and they do not break the relationship between them but end with expressions of renewed confi-

---

23. J. Gray, *I & II Kings* (OTL; London: SCM, 1970) 429.

24. See especially S. B. Frost, "The Death of Josiah: A Conspiracy of Silence," *JBL* 87 (1968) 369–82.

dence and hope on the part of the prophet. These so-called "confessions" are thus hardly characteristic expressions of an Old Testament view of the cruelty of God; on the contrary, Jeremiah has even been seen as God's "suffering servant," exemplifying the principle that innocent suffering is a "cross" to be borne, an integral element in the service of God. But this is a notion that lies outside the scope of the present investigation.

Ezek 20:25–26 has been described by one commentator as "a curious piece of casuistry, only intelligible on the writer's assumptions," which were that God's treatment of his people, however immoral it might appear to be, needs no justification and that the only consideration of paramount importance to him is the preservation of his "name" or "honor."[25] God had at first given his people laws that gave them "life"; but when they rejected these he reversed his practice, tricking them into sin by giving them laws that were "not good" (v. 25), laws that led them to practice human sacrifice, by offering up their own firstborn children. According to this tortured argument, which forms part of an oracle spoken by Yahweh himself, the purpose, if not the method, had been a good one: it was that the people should ultimately be so horrified by what they had done that they would abandon these practices and come to know Yahweh! This notion of God's devious behavior is untypical of Ezekiel, who elsewhere (chapter 18, especially vv. 25 and 29) vigorously defends God against a charge that he has acted unfairly.

Mal 2:17 is also concerned with a complaint that God is unfair. This complaint is also found in the lamentations in the Psalms and in the book of Job in the complaint that the wicked prosper while the righteous do not. The accusation is not specifically denied; but in the verses that follow, swift action by God's messenger or by God himself is promised, to bring the wicked to judgment and so to give the lie to the complainants.

The Book of Job and the Psalms

Complaints about God's treatment either of the nation or of individuals are most persistent, and indeed most vociferous and anguished, in these two books. Yet the fact that the complaints are addressed to God

---

25. G. A. Cooke, *Ezekiel* (ICC; Edinburgh: T. & T. Clark, 1936) 218.

in prayer shows that whether God is guilty of unfairness or not, there is always hope for better things in the future. These lamentations are most eloquent witnesses to human distress; but in the case of the Psalms lament often turns to thanksgiving, and the complaints and accusations of Job, however justified, are silenced when Job after his confrontation with God admits that he himself is in the wrong (42:1–6). Neither the speaker in the lamentations in the Psalms nor Job in his distress ends by denying the goodness of God. The same is true of the "confessions" of Jeremiah and the book of Lamentations; it is also true of Qoheleth, of which it has been argued that its portrait of God is primarily of his "dark" side.[26] Although all these books testify to the fact that faith is not easy, they are not to be understood in the end as indictments of a cruel God.

But in the prologue to Job (chapters 1 and 2), where the reader is taken behind the scenes (compare with 1 Kings 22) to a session of the heavenly court, Job's later accusations against God in chapters 3–21 before his final "conversion" are seen to be fully justified. First, Job's unblemished and indeed saintly character is stressed (1:8, 2:3). Against this background we are told of a series of calamities that befell him: the annihilation of his family and his wealth and the infliction of a loathsome disease that makes him unrecognizable to his friends (2:12). These calamities were actually inflicted by one of the 'sons of God' (*běnê haʾĕlōhîm*) referred to as 'the Satan' (*haśśāṭān*), a member of the heavenly court (compare with 1 Kgs 22:21), but it is made clear in the narrative that the Satan, though argumentative, is simply one of God's servants. None of his actions is undertaken on his own initiative; they are in each case carried out in obedience to God's express command (1:12, 2:6).[27] God alone (it is important to note that in these chapters he is identified as Yahweh) is responsible for causing excruciating physical and mental suffering on the best of human beings and his family. Job himself, though unaware of the reason for his affliction, is in no doubt that this is so (2:10).

---

26. Crenshaw (*Whirlpool of Torment*, 77–92) includes Qoheleth among his examples of texts in which God is an "oppressive presence," but I cannot agree with his judgment that for Qoheleth God is "wholly indifferent to goodness." See my *Ecclesiastes* (NCB; Grand Rapids: Eerdmans / London: Marshall, Morgan and Scott, 1989) 22–30.

27. See L. K. Handy, "The Authorization of Divine Power and the Guilt of God in the Book of Job: Useful Ugaritic Parallels," *JSOT* 60 (1993) 107–18.

But it is the reason for these actions that particularly justifies the accusation (not made in these chapters by Job or, indeed, by the "neutral" narrator) of God's immorality: the decision to test the sincerity of Job's piety arises from a conversation between God and the Satan, who challenges God's opinion of Job (1:8–12, 2:3–6). God's decision to test Job could be for any of a number of reasons: to gain the information about Job's character that he lacked; to salvage his dignity and reputation for omniscience; or for idle entertainment.[28] In any case, the picture presented of God in these chapters is hardly a flattering one.

II

The above examples, which are by no means exhaustive, are drawn from a great variety of literary types and from very different periods. No attempt has been made here to differentiate them along either literary or religiohistorical lines. This synchronic approach is, I believe, justified by the fact that what may appear to the modern reader to be an inadequate and even distasteful view of God was not suppressed by the final editors and compilers of the Old Testament books but was retained by them and so appears in the final form of the text. This permits the modern scholar to observe that despite marked differences of literary type, theological level, and period of origin all these passages share a common topic and to conclude that this negative view of an aspect of the divine nature was a remarkably persistent one that was not confined to any one particular social or religious group.

Various attempts have been made by scholars to mitigate the harshness of the theme. It has, for example, been rightly pointed out that these passages constitute only a very small minority of the totality of passages describing or reflecting on the nature of the God of Israel. God's righteousness, grace, and mercy are the sides of his nature that dominate the Old Testament. But this does not alter the fact that the Old Testament writers were conscious of the other, darker side. They were, if only dimly, aware of the complexity and the apparent contradictions experienced by the Israelite people in their encounters with this God.

---

28. Cf. D. J. A. Clines, "Deconstructing the Book of Job," in *What Does Eve Do to Help? and Other Readerly Questions to the Old Testament* (JSOTSup 94; Sheffield: JSOT Press, 1990) 106–23, especially 117–18; also Crenshaw's chapter "Murder without Cause," in *A Whirlpool of Torment*, 57–75.

It has also been pointed out that in many, at least, of the cases in which God inflicts pain or death on the innocent, his behavior is not the "point" of the incident in question; that frequently the narrator appears to be almost unaware that he is presenting God, as it were, "in a bad light." But this argument hardly touches the problem. It suggests that the narrator took God's cruelty for granted: that he regarded it as "normal," as a side of God's nature that is not unexpected but is in conformity with his apprehension of God. It would seem, therefore, that these cases, though infrequent, are not to be seen as exceptional: their very rarity adds significance to them.

Nor is it cogent to argue, despite the conclusion of the "patient" Job in 2:10 ("Shall we receive the good at the hand of God, and not receive the bad?"), that in a religion which recognizes only one God who is responsible for all that happens, he is "inevitably" the cause of the "bad" as well as the "good." Job's wife understands that truth better than Job; she urges him to curse God (2:9). In this case at least 'the bad' (*hārā*ʿ) that is received, as the reader knows (but Job does not) is not just a "natural" calamity but something that God has deliberately chosen to inflict on a particular person for a specific, though hardly defensible, reason. In this as in other cases there is no "impersonal" mixing of good and bad things in the life of a human being but a deliberate intention to do harm.

A further argument that has been presented to account for God's behavior is that it is due in some way to the character of the special relationship between the God of Israel and his chosen people (Job, in the prologue, is a worshiper of Yahweh), which accounts for Yahweh's continual *testing* of the people to see whether they will obey and trust him. This is an extremely weak argument. As has been shown above, it does not explain a number of the cases in question. It has, I think, to be accepted that human beings are sometimes treated by God as pawns or puppets—as beings whose lives and emotions are of no account for God, though in some cases they may be used as instruments serving some great and good purpose. This is true, for example, of his treatment of Abraham and Isaac and his lack of concern for the surprisingly absent Sarah in Genesis 22. In other cases there seems to be no great and good purpose. The story of the forty-two boys in 2 Kgs 2:23–24 may have something to do with the importance of preserving the reputation of prophets, but it is difficult to discern any purpose in God's behavior in Job 1–2. Moreover, in Job 42:13–15 the fate of Job's first family appears to be completely forgotten and his "replacement family" to be considered an adequate compensation. In Genesis 3 and 11 God's overriding concern is with his own power and status rather than with the fates of human beings.

It should be pointed out that a concern with the value of human lives is not a purely modern one. That the problem was recognized at least in late antiquity is shown by the anxiety of some rabbinic writers to conceal these divine "faults" or to defend God against the imputation of them. Another attempt to mitigate the indictment against God consists of the idea that God shares the suffering of his people even while punishing them. The Old Testament passages in which this theme appears are extremely few, and those that have been cited above in this essay are not among them. Finally, it has been suggested that the narratives in which the "darker" side of God appears are "just stories"—that is, that they are unconnected anecdotes that do not necessarily represent what their narrators actually believed. This argument also is extremely improbable. None of the narrative books of the Old Testament (or parts of books) is a collection of anecdotes. Whatever may have been the origins of particular stories, each was composed or edited with a theological purpose. Even the story of the forty-two boys in 2 Kings 2 now forms part of a series of narratives that exalts the God-given powers of Elisha as Yahweh's prophet. This series, in turn, is intended to demonstrate the power of Yahweh and the role of Elisha in upholding faith in Yahweh in the kingdom of Israel, so contributing to the general message of the books of Kings and of the Deuteronomic History. Similarly, the stories in Genesis 1–11, however naive they may appear to be, have a clear theological and teaching purpose.

III

It was, at least in part, those aspects of the character of God in the Old Testament to which attention has been drawn in this essay that led Marcion in the second century A.D. to reject the Old Testament as Christian scripture and to deny the identity of its God with the Christian God. It is hardly surprising that it is also these aspects of the Old Testament God that have encouraged a modern Marcionism and have also led modern commentators to pass over or to seek to minimize them or explain them away. That they are present in the text cannot be denied. Nor can it be denied that they constituted a part, albeit a minor one, of the beliefs of ancient Israel, whose God, while essentially a God of love toward his chosen people, nevertheless had a "dark" side. This must be admitted. A task that remains for Old Testament scholars to investigate more thoroughly is why this should have been so.

Professor Crenshaw has drawn attention to the fact that the questioning of God's motives in the Old Testament is not an exclusive feature of the wisdom books but that it had its origin in what he would call a "popular religion," traces of which are especially to be found in quotations in the prophetic books of orally expressed objections to the prophets' confident defense of God's righteousness.[29] Such protests would have been the consequence of ordinary people's experience of injustices or undeserved misfortunes that they had encountered in their lives—experiences that they attributed to faults in the divine governance of human affairs. Similar questionings had been voiced earlier in other parts of the ancient Near East and had eventually been expressed in the literatures of Egypt and Mesopotamia. In other words, the "official" dogma that "all is for the best in the best of all possible worlds" (of which in the Old Testament Ps 37:25 is the clearest expression) was never accepted by all Israelites, especially not by the less fortunate. While this may well be so, the wide spread of texts in which negative views of God occur shows that such views were fairly generally entertained, often by people who seem not to have been fully aware that they were not consistent with the "orthodox" position to which, in general, they conformed.

It is significant that this component of popular belief was not suppressed by the editors and compilers of the books of the Old Testament, which in its final form is largely a creation of the postexilic period. As has been noted by some scholars, this may be due to the editors' desire to impress on a generation of readers living in an age of uncertainty about what the future would bring, that God is and remains sovereign and unpredictable.[30]

---

29. Crenshaw, "Popular Questioning."
30. See, for example, Ben Zvi, "Dialogue."

In 587 B.C. God permitted, or caused, the destruction of the kingdom of Judah together with the Davidic dynasty, the Jerusalem Temple
and other institutions, and many of the inhabitants of Judah and Jerusalem were killed. Although the "official" explanation of these events
given both in the Deuteronomistic History and in the books of the
prophets was that this was a fully deserved punishment for the nation's
rejection of Yahweh, it is significant that in the book of Lamentations,
a book mainly concerned with these events, there are traces of a feeling
that the punishment has been unnecessarily severe, and also that it has
been imposed indiscriminately without regard to the guilt or innocence
of individuals (for example, Lam 2:20, 3:34–36, 4:13).[31] The theme of
the wholesale slaughter of many of the people in the wilderness stories
of Exodus and Numbers, on the assumption of universal guilt, together
with the accounts of Moses' questioning of God's decisions, would also
have had an immediate relevance to a postexilic generation and would
have provided further food for thought about his self-proclaimed merciful nature.

---

31. See the discussion in I. Provan, *Lamentations* (NCB; London: Marshall Picker-
ing / Grand Rapids: Eerdmans, 1991) 20–25.

Texts That Linger, Not Yet Overcome

WALTER BRUEGGEMANN

Columbia Theological Seminary

It is clear that God, as rendered in the Bible, is a continually unsettled character and consequently an unending problem for theology, as
theology has been conventionally done in the Christian West. The profound tension between the textual rendering of God and conventional
theological settlements constitutes an on-going interpretive problem for
any who move between text and a Christian interpretive community.[1]
No one has written more passionately or effectively on this issue than
has James Crenshaw, and I have come to believe that his careful, critical
work has an intentional thrust against reductionist theological conven-
tions.[2] The problematic character of God in the text may be treated variously under the topics of wrath, anger, capriciousness, hiddenness, and
so on. Here I shall seek to advance the direction of Crenshaw's acute interest in the issue in one small way by addressing the question of God's
abandoning absence.[3]

---

1. I regard this as especially a problem for Christians and will so discuss the matter.
This is partly because there is an inherent propensity in Christianity to give closure to
its thought and partly because of the long history of Christianity as a dominant cultural
power. It is not, however, a peculiarly Christian problem. Thus, for example, see Jon D.
Levenson, *Creation and the Persistence of Evil: The Jewish Drama of Divine Omnipotence* (San
Francisco: Harper & Row, 1988) 3, and his reference to Yehezkel Kaufmann, who exhibits something like the same propensity to closure.

2. On this aspect of Crenshaw's work, see my "James L. Crenshaw: Faith Lingering
at the Edges," *RelSRev* 20/2 (April, 1994) 103–10. See Crenshaw's comments in the
same issue, which agree with this assessment.

3. This problem has received much more attention from Jewish thinkers than from
Christian, no doubt because of the Christian eagerness to give closure, as acknowledged
in n. 1. Thus, for example, we may refer to Martin Buber's "Eclipse," André Neher's
"exile" and "silence," and the several articulations of Emil Fackenheim.

I

We may begin our discussion by focusing on four texts, all of which ponder the absence of God by the strong use of the verb *ʿāzab*.
(1) Perhaps the obvious place to begin is Ps 22:2[1]:[4]

> My God, my God, why have you *forsaken* me?
> Why are you so far from helping me,
> from the words of my groaning?

This characteristic complaint voices an accusation against God, suggesting that God's (seeming?) absence is unreasonable, unexpected, and inexcusable, and in fact reflects God's untrustworthiness. As is well known this psalm, with a series of "motivations," expresses a series of petitions that urge Yahweh's presence and active intervention (vv. 11, 19–21a) and culminates in a celebration of rescue.[5] That is, by the end of the poem this abandoning absence of God is overcome and God is decisively present. We cannot, however, permit the resolution at the end of the poem to nullify the experience and expression of absence at the beginning.[6] Moreover, no hint of fault, blame, or sin on the part of the speaker is expressed, as though the speaker's conduct justified the absence of God. It is clear that God is culpable in the intention of the speaker.

The accusation of v. 1, because it is a complaint, is of course in the mouth of the human (Israelite) speaker. Thus it is possible to say that the human voice has it wrong, that God is not absent but "seems" to be absent (on which see below). For Christians, of course, this accusation against God takes on additional gravity when it occurs on the lips of Jesus (Matt 27:46; Mark 15:34). It is a common theological strategy

---

4. The English and Hebrew versification differ in this psalm. I will be using the English versification throughout the rest of this essay.

5. There is of course a vast literature on Psalm 22. Among the more recent and most helpful are Ellen F. Davis, "Exploding the Limits: Form and Function in Psalm 22," *JSOT* 53 (1992) 93–105; and John S. Kselman, " 'Why Have You Abandoned Me?' A Rhetorical Study of Psalm 22," in *Art and Meaning: Rhetoric in Biblical Literature* (ed. David J. A. Clines et al.; JSOTSup 19; Sheffield: JSOT Press, 1982) 172–98.

6. For the phrase "experience and expression," I refer to Paul Ricoeur ("Biblical Hermeneutics," *Paul Ricoeur in Biblical Hermeneutics* [*Semeia* 4; 1975] 107–45) and his notions of "limit experience" and "limit expression." These texts of unsettling dimension are "limit expressions" that give Israel access to its "limit experiences."

among Christians to explain away the abrasion of the opening lines of the psalm by observing that the line quoted in the Gospel narratives only introduces the whole implied psalm, again as though the implied ending nullifies the expressed beginning. In an important exception to this conventional Christian strategy, Jürgen Moltmann takes the Gospel reiteration of Ps 22:1 with theological seriousness.[7] God is absent and is said to be absent. The narrative of the crucifixion of Jesus is a Christian articulation of that absence of God which causes the world to revert to chaos.[8]

(2) The capacity to explain Ps 22:1 away, because it is a human articulation of absence that may be a misperception of God, is an equally possible strategy in Lam 5:20:

> Why have you forgotten us completely?
> Why have you forsaken (*'āzab*) us these many days?

Whereas Psalm 22 deals with an unspecified situation, Lam 5:20 is context specific. The verse pertains to the collapse of the symbolic (as well as political) world of Jerusalem (and of Judaism) over which Israel grieved massively.[9] The physical loss entailed by Jews in the crisis of 587 B.C.E. is matched by the powerful sense of intimate, personal, religious loss. The destruction of Jerusalem signifies God's absence and happens as a consequence of God's (unwarranted?) absence.[10] The interrogative form of v. 20 is the same as in Ps 22:1 with *lāmâ*. The speaker does not question that God has abandoned. The abandonment by Yahweh is

---

7. J. Moltmann, *The Crucified God: The Cross of Christ as the Foundation and Criticism of Christian Theology* (San Francisco: Harper & Row, 1974) 146–51, 207, 218, and passim.

8. On the cross of Jesus as an enactment of the unsettling dimension, see the powerful statement of D. J. Hall, *Toward an Indigenous Theology of the Cross* (Philadelphia: Westminster, 1976). Moltmann (*The Crucified God*, 243) has a very nice phrase for the significance of the cross: "The Fatherlessness of the Son is matched by the Sonlessness of the Father. . . ."

9. On grief over the destruction of Jerusalem as paradigmatic grief for Jews, see A. Mintz, *Hurban: Responses to Catastrophe in Hebrew Literature* (New York: Columbia University Press, 1984). See especially his programmatic statement on p. 2.

10. This sense of God's absence is very different from the conventional Deuteronomic notion that God's absence is a result of Israel's sin. On the tension Lamentations has with both Deuteronomic and Zion traditions, see the discussion of B. Albrektson, *Studies in the Text and Theology of the Book of Lamentations* (Studia Theologica Lundensia 21; Lund: CWK Gleerup, 1963).

taken as a given. In asking "why," the speaker does not seek an explanation from God but seeks to assert that the absence of God is inexplicable and inexcusable.

Verse 20 is framed in the last strophe of vv. 19–22 by three striking assertions, each of which functions in relation to the desperate accusation of v. 20. In v. 19, the speaker utters a wondrous doxology, appealing to the enthronement liturgies, acknowledging God's sovereign power. The effect of this verse is to make the absence of v. 20 all the more scandalous, for the one who "reigns forever" can hardly be absent. Verse 21 looks behind v. 20 to v. 19, and on the basis of the doxology issues an urgent imperative for God's action, thus characteristically following complaint with petition.[11] In spite of the doxology and petition, however, the final verse (v. 22) returns to and reasserts the conclusion of v. 20:

> But instead you have completely rejected us;
> You have been very angry with us.[12]

And thus the poem ends. The accusatory verbs of v. 20 ("forget, abandon") are reinforced by "reject, be angry" (v. 22). Unlike Ps 22:1, there is no resolution in this dread-filled complaint. The poem ends abruptly and without any response from God. The effect is to confirm God's absence, a fickle absence, and to leave the words "forget, abandon" ringing in Israel's exilic ears.

(3) The enduring echo of "forget, abandon" in the exilic literature apparently takes on liturgic form as evidenced in Isa 49:15. This verse is introduced by the rubric "But Zion said. . . ." This is presumably a stylized, often reiterated liturgic complaint. Indeed, this usage is plausibly a reference back to and quotation of Lam 5:20, given the propensity of exilic Isaiah to be a response to Lamentations.[13] To be sure, the two defining terms, *ʿāzab* and *šākaḥ*, are here in reverse order, but the intention is the same. The complaint, which we have seen already in Lam 5:20 as well as Ps 22:1, is that Yahweh is unfaithful and neglectful.

---

11. On complaint and petition, see E. Gerstenberger, *Der bittende Mensch* (WMANT 51: Neukirchen-Vluyn: Neukirchener, 1980).

12. The translation is that of D. R. Hillers, *Lamentations: A New Translation with Introduction and Commentary* (AB 7A; Garden City, N.Y.: Doubleday, 1972) 96. See his comments on pp. 100–101.

13. See Mintz, *Hurban*, 41–46, on the relation of Lamentations and Second Isaiah. My student, T. Linafelt, has begun important work on this connection.

Moreover, it is Yahweh's failure to be faithfully present in Israel that results in the suffering and shame of the exile.

The statement of v. 14, however, is lodged in the midst of a proclamation of salvation, whereby the assurance of Yahweh intends to dispute and overcome the accusatory claim of Israel. Thus, in v. 13 Yahweh is assigned two recurring words of assurance, 'comfort' (*nhm*) and 'compassion' (*rhm*). In direct response to the complaint of v. 14, Yahweh now speaks in the first person, using the term "compassion" and three times "forget" by way of denying the accusation of v. 13. It is worth noting, though perhaps not important, that Yahweh's response does not use a word to negate the accusation of *ʿāzab*. The accent is placed on "forget" in the denial of Yahweh.

Given the assurance of Yahweh in the third person (v. 13) and in the first person (v. 15), it is not completely clear how the assurances are related to the complaint. It is easiest to take the assurance as a refutation and denial of the complaint. That is, Israel seemed to be forgotten and forsaken but was not. On this reading, the complaint of Lam 5:20 was mistaken. A possible alternative is that Israel is momentarily forgotten by Yahweh, but finally, in the end, Yahweh does not forget. Such a reading points us to our fourth and final text.

(4) Thus far, all three texts (Ps 22:1; Lam 5:20; Isa 49:14) have been on the lips of Israel. This fact still allows for the claim that Yahweh "seemed" to Israel to abandon, that Israel "experienced" abandonment, but in fact Israel had it wrong and was not abandoned by Yahweh. Such a reading is of course possible, but it goes well beyond the plain sense of the text, which offers no qualification or ambiguity about the accusation.

In our fourth text, Isa 54:7–8, that possible "protection" of Yahweh from the accusation of Israel is excluded, for now the word *ʿāzab* is on the lips of Yahweh.[14] The poetry utilizes the image of barren wife, abandoned wife, and widow.[15] Already in v. 6, the term *ʿāzab* is used

---

14. On this text, see my "Shattered Transcendence? Exile and Restoration," in *Problems and Prospects in Biblical Theology* (ed. B. C. Ollenburger; Nashville: Abingdon, forthcoming).

15. Mintz (*Hurban*, 23–25) suggests that the use of the image of raped, dying woman rather than dead woman is used in order that the suffering, pain, and grief may be on-going and not yet (or ever) terminated: "The raped and defiled woman who survives . . . is a living witness to a pain that knows no release."

parallel to 'cast off' (*mā'as*), both terms as passive participles, affirming that Yahweh has taken the disruptive actions.

In vv. 7–8, Yahweh continues to speak in the first person:

> For a brief moment I abandoned you (*'ăzabtîk*) . . .
> In overflowing wrath, for a moment I hid my face (*histartî*) from you.

The two terms ("abandoned, hid") are straightforward and unambiguous. Yahweh did abandon! Yahweh has abandoned Israel and readily admits it. In these verses, moreover, no blame is assigned to Israel as cause of the abandonment, though Yahweh says, "in overflowing wrath." From the text itself, this "wrath" could as well be capriciousness on the part of Yahweh as righteous, warranted indignation.

To be sure, these two admissions whereby Yahweh concedes that Israel has been abandoned are promptly countered by two assurances:

> . . . with great compassion (*raḥămîm*) I will gather you . . . with everlasting love (*ḥesed 'ôlām*) I will have compassion on you (*riḥamtîk*).

It is profoundly important that the two positives do not nullify the two negatives, as the positive may nullify the negative in 49:14–15. Here the statements refer to a sequence of actions and experiences, whereby compassion comes after an acknowledged abandonment. This is reinforced by the term 'again' (*'ôd*) in v. 9 which admits one abandonment but assures that there will not be a second one. This use of *'ôd* is closely paralleled to its use in Gen 8:21, 9:11, which admits that there has indeed been one angry flood, but there will not be another (cf. Isa 54:10).

This fourth text, Isa 54:7–8, belongs in the same theological horizon as Ps 22:1, Lam 5:20, and Isa 49:14, all of which are preoccupied with Israel's experience of bereftment caused by Yahweh's unwarranted inattentiveness. This fourth text, however, is of another sort, because it is in Yahweh's own mouth and because Yahweh concedes that compassion and everlasting love come *after* the abandonment.

Now all of this is commonplace and well established in Crenshaw's work. My intent is not to establish an exegetical point that is already amply recognized by readers of Israel's text. It is rather to inquire about what to do with such texts in reading communities that want to override them with sweeping assurances about Yahweh's presence, fidelity, and graciousness. Thus my study is an exercise in adjudicating the tension between large theological claims and the awkward specificity of texts.

II

There is no doubt that these assertions about Yahweh's abandoning activity are problematic for any theology that wants finally to assert the unambiguous fidelity of God. A variety of interpretive strategies are available and much practiced whereby these troublesome texts can be overcome, but in each case the alternative strategy does not appear to take the direct statement of the text with full seriousness. They may be regarded as adequate resolutions of the problem, unless one is intensely committed to facing the concreteness of the text, a commitment that we may take to be important for any responsible reading of the text.

We may identify five such strategies that are frequently employed:

(1) It is easiest and most common simply to *disregard such texts*. It is for the most part impossible to make use of all texts in any interpretive reading, or all texts at once, and surely impossible to attend to all of them if one wants to present a "seamless" reading, for the text itself is disjointed and disruptive and filled with contradictions, ambiguities, and incongruities. They render the text as a whole "unreadable" on our usual theological readings.[16]

On the basis of that "unreadable" textual reality, reading communities of every kind, including church communities (but also academic communities), tend to be selective. Indeed, it is my judgment that serious readers tend to be "selective fundamentalists," whether theological readers liberal or conservative, or critical readers. That is, readers pick out texts on the basis of hidden or explicit criteria, take those texts with great attentiveness or even urgency, and let the other texts drop out of the working repertoire. An easy example, of course, is the church's lectionary, which operates around such principles that even some verses in the chosen texts are habitually silenced. Part of recent hermeneutical activity is the insistence that those silenced, dismissed texts must be sounded again.

(2) The unsettling character of Yahweh is justified by *the sin of Israel*, thus suggesting that God's silence, absence, wrath, or infidelity is

---

16. On our "usual theological readings" that render texts "unreadable," see S. A. Handelman, *The Slayers of Moses: The Emergence of Rabbinic Interpretation in Modern Literary Theory* (Albany: State University of New York Press, 1982). Handelman's study informs much of the argument of my paper.

warranted in light of Israel's sin and disobedience.[17] This interpretive posture posits a tight moral structure, so that Yahweh responds with precision to moral affront.[18] There are of course many texts that support such a view.

There are other texts, however, including those that we have cited, which do not claim such an exact calculus or even suggest Israel's culpability. Moreover, there are texts (such as Job) that voice an unsettling response of Yahweh that is disproportionate to any available affront. There are sufficient texts to warrant the judgment that there is a wild dimension to Yahweh's unsettled character that runs well beyond any tight moral equation. Israel's experience of Yahweh's unsettled character runs well beyond moral justification when the texts are taken seriously.

(3) There is a great propensity to explain away the unsettling aspect of Yahweh (in our case, abandonment) by claiming that the accusation made against Yahweh and the desperate plea for presence addressed to God are a case of *human misperception and mistakenness*. That is, God "seems" to be abandoning but in truth is not. Such a human "experience" is asserted by Israel in good faith, and there may be a "subjective" dimension of reality to this claim, but it is theologically not true. It is only in the eyes of the beholder.

This is of course not as difficult to claim in our first three cases (Ps 22:1, Lam 5:20, Isa 49:14) because the statements are all on the lips of Israel, and no data is offered beyond the "sense" of the speaker. Thus resort is often taken to the stratagem that claims that this is only "human speech," which is not finally reliable. The case is more difficult in Isa 54:7–8, where the utterance is Yahweh's own—that is, an oracle that purports to be God's utterance. Even here, of course, critical awareness

---

17. This is, for example, the affirmation of the hymn "Holy, Holy, Holy" by R. Heber:

Holy, holy, holy! though the darkness hide thee,
Though the eye of sinful man thy glory may not see. . . .

On that assumption, God is not absent but only unseen because of sin.

18. On such a "tight moral structure," see K. Koch, "Gibt es ein Vergeltungsdogma im Alten Testament?" *ZTK* 52 (1955) 1–42, and an abridged English translation, "Is There a Doctrine of Retribution in the Old Testament?" in *Theodicy in the Old Testament* (ed. J. L. Crenshaw; Issues in Religion and Theology 4; Philadelphia: Fortress, 1983) 57–87; and the more nuanced discussion of P. D. Miller, Jr., *Sin and Judgment in the Prophets: A Stylistic and Theological Analysis* (Chico, Calif.: Scholars Press, 1982).

can readily claim that this speech is "human speech," done by a human author, in this case "Second Isaiah," so that even this more insistent affirmation is explained away as not theologically reliable.[19]

This common interpretive procedure, however, is deeply problematic. It appeals to theological-dogmatic convictions nowhere grounded in the particular texts but imposed upon the text in order to dismiss a reading that on the face of it is not in doubt. Moreover, if one explains away as "human and mistaken" such self-assertions made by Yahweh, one is hard put to draw the line and treat with seriousness the textual self-disclosures of Yahweh that one prefers. It may be claimed that the dismissal of the assertion is "canonical"—that is, read in relation to many other texts that say otherwise and are judged to be more central.[20] Such a claim, however, is characteristically reductionist and flattens the dialectic that, in my judgment, belongs properly to canonical reading.[21]

(4) A more subtle approach to this same "subjective" verdict voiced in the text is the logical, philosophical claim that even though Yahweh is genuinely "experienced" as one who abandons, the experience of God's abandoning contains within it an assumption of cosmic, primordial presence, thus giving us a *dialectical notion of "presence in absence" or "absence in presence."*[22] That is, even speculation about God's abandoning

---

19. This is from time to time the strategy of John Calvin. On these verses, Calvin (*Commentary on the Book of the Prophet Isaiah* [Calvin's Commentaries 8; Grand Rapids: Baker, 1979] 140) writes:

> When he says that he *forsook* his people, it is a sort of admission of the fact. We are adopted by God in such a manner that we cannot be rejected by him on account of the treachery of men; for he is faithful, so that he will not cast off or abandon his people. What the Prophet says in this passage must therefore refer to our feelings and to outward appearance, because we seem to be rejected by God when we do not perceive his presence and protection. And it is necessary that we should thus feel God's wrath. . . . But we must also perceive his mercy; and because it is infinite and eternal, we shall find that all afflictions in comparison of it are light and momentary.

20. This is the perspective of B. S. Childs, *Biblical Theology of the Old and New Testaments: Theological Reflection on the Christian Bible* (Minneapolis: Fortress, 1992).

21. The whole matter of a "canonical reading" is not obvious in its meaning. Childs himself has, over time, suggested a variety of different dimensions to the notion of "canonical" and, as far as I am aware, only in his most recent book, *Biblical Theology*, has he concluded that "canonical" means according to a theological "rule of faith."

22. I am grateful to my colleague, Shirley Guthrie, for clarifying this point for me. He and I have had fruitful exchanges about this matter. In the end, I suspect we do not

absence (which never posits God's nonexistence) affirms God's "background" presence in experienced absence. This is, I take it, a quite sophisticated form of a "subjective-objective" distinction, which seeks to honor fully the *lived experience* of Israel, while at the same time guarding against an *ontological* dismissal of God that Israel would not countenance. This strategy is based on the theological affirmation that there would be no world without God, no world in which to issue complaint and accusation against God, for the world is "held into existence" by God.

This is a powerful and logically coherent position, and I have no desire to combat it. I suggest only that (a) it is a way of reasoning that is subtle in ways that Israel would not entertain, and (b) it requires a judgment that is against the clear, uncomplicated, and unreserved statement of the text. As a result, even after this argument, we are still left with our guiding question: what shall one do with texts such as these?

(5) Finally, a popular stratagem is an appeal to the "evolution" of "the religion of Israel," which includes the *"evolution" of Yahweh*, the subject of that religion. This hypothesis proposes that Israel's religion and Israel's God "developed" from primitivism to the nobility of "ethical monotheism," culminating, perhaps, in Second Isaiah. Thus there may have been a time when Yahwism (and Yahweh) were understood in quite primitive terms. There may have been a time when Yahweh was excessively unsettling in terms of capriciousness, infidelity, violence, absence, and silence. But Yahweh has "evolved" toward fidelity, peaceable generosity, justice, and forgiveness.

This hypothesis of course has been duly critiqued as a reflection of Hegelianism or a reflection of a nineteenth-century milieu dominated by something like Darwinism.[23] Nonetheless, there is of course something substantive to the hypothesis, as there regularly is in any hypothesis that captures scholarly imagination over a long period of time. It is the case that there are important changes in the character of Yahweh. Moreover, given a certain literary analysis, one can insist on a direc-

---

agree. Nonetheless I have come to understand better because of his instruction and am able to rethink matters in ways reflective of his persuasive and gentle influence.

23. For a recent critical assessment of Wellhausen, see *Julius Wellhauser and His Prolegomana to the History of Israel* (ed. D. A. Knight; *Semeia* 25; 1983). On the world of Darwin and the tensions between nineteenth-century science and conventional religion, see A. Desmond and J. Moore, *Darwin* (New York: Warner, 1991).

tional inclination to that change. It is the most standard critique of the hypothesis that the change is said to be progressive and unilaterally developmental. In addition to that claim, the critique that is most important for our purposes is the correlative of progressive developmentalism, that as each *novum* appears in the character of Yahweh, the previous portrayals of the character of Yahweh may be sloughed off as now irrelevant and "superseded."

I shall want to insist in what follows that textually there is no supersessionism but that what has transpired in the life of Yahweh endures as text and therefore as data for theological understanding. This remembered character of Yahweh continues to exercise important influence over the whole of Israel's articulation of Yahweh. Specifically, because Israel has texts of God's abandoning, which it evidently has, the character of Yahweh never outgrows or supersedes that remembered reality, which continues to be present textually and therefore substantively both for Yahweh and the community of Yahweh. As a consequence, neither Yahweh nor the interpreters of Yahweh may pretend that such behavior has not happened in the on-going life of Yahweh with Israel and may not act as though these textual markings do not continue to be present and available to Yahweh in Yahweh's life with Israel.[24]

Thus I suggest that all five strategies—disregarding such texts, justification through sin, judgment that it only "seems so," philosophical subtlety, and evolutionary supersessionism—are unpersuasive approaches to the problem. Each of these attempts arises from a theological impetus that lies outside the horizon of the text itself, and each of them imports a conviction that is contrary to the unmistakable claim of the text itself. All of these inadequate strategies seek to protect the character of Yahweh from the passionate experience and conviction of Israel with Yahweh. Israel is clear that Yahweh need not and cannot be protected; Yahweh must run the risks that belong to Yahweh's way of being present/absent in the memory and life of Israel.

---

24. For a dramatic understanding of Yahweh that moves in a postcritical direction, see D. Patrick, *The Rendering of God in the Old Testament* (OBT; Philadelphia: Fortress, 1981).

III

I propose now to suggest an alternative interpretive response to these texts of abandonment and, by implication, to all texts that testify to Yahweh's unsettling character.

(1) An alternative approach to these unsettling texts will need to move from a *metaphysical* to a *dramatic* approach to interpretation. A conventional approach to Christian theology that posits a "nature of God" with which to challenge these texts apparently operates with a notion of a God "out there" who exists independent of these texts.[25] Such a view may be plausible from some other perspective, but it is of little help in taking the specificity of the biblical text seriously. Such a posited "nature" outside of the text stands as a criterion with which to justify or explain away a text without facing its concrete claim seriously. Indeed, such an approach cannot take such texts with theological seriousness, because matters are settled on grounds other than the text and in other arenas.

A consequence of such an approach is that we are still left with the problem: what to do with the text. An alternative approach that shuns the escape of a metaphysical criterion is to take the texts in a dramatic way, as a script for a drama.[26] The biblical text then becomes "the real thing" in terms of plot and character, and there is no appeal behind the text or elsewhere. On such a perspective, when God asserts, "For a brief moment I have abandoned you," we have a God who abandons Israel for a brief moment. That is what Yahweh says, what Yahweh does, and who Yahweh is.

The move toward a dramatic sense of the text permits the reading community to stay with the terms of the text, even with its contradictions, incongruities, and unwelcome lines. Thus the text is "unreadable," not because of a poor redactional outcome, but because the subject and character who dominates the plot does not conform to our

---

25. It is my impression that in his most recent work, *Biblical Theology*, Childs attends to the problem of referentiality in a way that results in a God "out there."

26. On a dramatic mode of theological interpretation, see, in addition to Patrick, the work of H. Frei and W. Brueggemann, *Texts under Negotiation: The Bible and Postmodern Imagination* (Minneapolis: Fortress, 1993). Most broadly, see H. U. von Balthasar, *Theo-Drama: Theological Dramatic Theory I—Prolegomena* (San Francisco: Ignatius, 1988), *II—The Dramatis Personae: Man in God* (San Francisco: Ignatius, 1990).

flattened reading propensity, theological or critical. The character who has once uttered these lines and committed these acts remains always the character who has once uttered these lines and committed these acts. There is more to this character than these particular lines, but these lines become inescapably part of who this character is, no matter what other renderings, actions, and utterances may follow. That is, this approach comes to the text prepared to treat the text "realistically" and "literally," if "literal" means not "factual," not canonically reduced, but according to the concrete utterance of the text.[27]

(2) But consider what it means to take the text "realistically." I have found Richard Lanham's distinction between *homo seriosus* and *homo rhetoricus* enormously helpful.[28] Lanham characterizes the model interpreter in this way:

> The serious man possesses a central self, an irreducible identity. These selves combine into a single, homogeneously real society which constitutes a referent reality. . . . This referent society is in turn contained in a physical nature itself referential, standing "out there," independent of man.[29]

By contrast,

> Rhetorical man is an actor; his reality public, dramatic. His sense of identity, his self, depends on the reassurance of daily histrionic reenactment. He is thus centered in time and concrete local event. The lowest common denominator of his life is a social situation. And his motivations must be characteristically lucid, agonistic. . . . He is thus committed to no single construction of the world; much rather, to prevailing in the game at hand.[30]

The important difference is that the "serious man" appeals to an "out there" reference. It is a curious fact that common cause in this category

---

27. B. S. Childs ("The Sensus Literalis of Scripture: An Ancient and Modern Problem," in *Beiträge zur Alttestamentlichen Theologie: Festschrift für Walther Zimmerli zum 70 Geburtstag* [ed. Herbert Donner et al.; Göttingen: Vandenhoeck & Ruprecht, 1977] 80–93) has offered a most provocative understanding of "literal sense." Childs of course knows that his view is not without problem and is not uncontested.

28. R. A. Lanham, *The Motives of Eloquence: Literary Rhetoric in the Renaissance* (New Haven: Yale University Press, 1976).

29. Ibid., 1.

30. Ibid., 4.

includes those who grasp at metaphysics and the "historical critics" who assess the rhetoric of the text in terms of an outside historical reference. Both metaphysicians and historical critics trim and shave the rhetoric of the text to fit some other criterion. By contrast, those who value rhetoric in a central way recognize that speech constitutes reality in some decisive way. The world of "rhetorical man" is

> teeming with roles, situations, strategies, interventions, but . . . no master role, no situation of situations, no strategy for outflanking all strategies . . . no neutral point of rationality from the vantage point of which the "merely rhetorical" can be identified and held in check.[31]

It is clear that this dispute is as old as Plato's and Aristotle's dispute with the Sophists. And it is clear that our dominant educational, intellectual tradition is a powerful advocacy toward Plato and Aristotle and a facile dismissal of the Sophists, without attending to the powerful ways in which even Plato and Aristotle are rhetoricians.[32] Thus the critique of Fish goes further than that of Lanham. It suggests that even the "serious man" in fact makes a claim for reality in terms of the effectiveness of utterance.

What to do with the unsettling texts depends on where one is in this dispute between rhetoric and "seriousness." If one seriously assumes a reference out there, then these texts must be disregarded, toned down, justified, or explained away in order to suit that outside reference. If we take rhetoric as constitutive, however, then the reference "inside the drama" must yield to these texts and take them with defining seriousness. Richard Rorty makes this distinction:

> There are two ways of thinking about various things. . . . The first . . . thinks of truth as a vertical relationship between representations and what is represented. The second . . . thinks of truth horizontally—as the culminating reinterpretation of our predecessors' reinterpretation of their predecessors' reinterpretation. . . . It is the difference between regarding truth, goodness, and beauty as eternal objects which we try to

---

31. S. Fish, "Rhetoric," in *Critical Terms for Literary Study* (ed. F. Lentricchia and T. McLaughlin; Chicago: University of Chicago Press, 1990) 215.

32. For a recent reconsideration of the Sophists, see S. C. Jarratt, *Rereading the Sophists: Classical Rhetoric Refigured* (Carbondale: Southern Illinois University Press, 1991). I am grateful to P. Daniel for this reference and for suggesting this line of reflection to me.

locate and reveal, and regarding them as artifacts whose fundamental design we often have to alter.[33]

Fish concludes, of Rorty's verdict,

> It is the difference between serious and rhetorical man. It is the difference that remains.[34]

My argument here, which seems to me inescapable if the texts are to be taken seriously and if Crenshaw is correct about the persuasive intentionality of speech, is that rhetoric constitutes the character of Yahweh.[35] And so the Yahweh of the Bible is indeed an unsettling character who does abandon and who acts sometimes in unfaithfulness. Focus on the text rather than on a reference "out there" gives us no character other than this one.

(3) But we are not yet agreed on what it means to take the text seriously or how to take the text seriously. I cite two interpreters who well articulate what I regard as two quite distinct alternative approaches.

In his "canonical approach" to the text, Brevard Childs is a "serious" reader who does indeed take the text seriously. That is beyond question. In a series of books, Childs has pondered "canonical" reading.[36] In his most recent and most mature book, it is now more clear than in his earlier work, that Childs means by "canonical" reading the text according to Christian doctrinal norms and categories.[37]

> It is one thing to suggest that biblical scholars have not adequately resolved the problem of biblical referentiality; it is quite another to suggest that it is a non-issue. Moreover, I would argue that the attempt of many literary critics to by-pass the problem of biblical reality and refuse to distinguish between text and the reality of its subject matter severely

---

33. R. Rorty, *Consequences of Pragmatism* (Minneapolis: University of Minnesota Press, 1982) 92, quoted by Fish, "Rhetoric," 221.

34. Fish, "Rhetoric," 222.

35. J. L. Crenshaw, "Wisdom and Authority: Sapiential Rhetoric and Its Warrants," in *Congress Volume: Vienna, 1980* (VTSup 32; Leiden: Brill, 1981) 10–29. On the constitutive power of speech, see my *Israel's Praise: Doxology against Idolatry and Ideology* (Philadelphia: Fortress, 1988) 1–53.

36. B. S. Childs, *Biblical Theology in Crisis* (Philadelphia: Westminster, 1970); *The Book of Exodus: A Critical, Theological Commentary* (OTL; Philadelphia: Westminster, 1974); *Old Testament Theology in a Canonical Context* (Philadelphia: Fortress, 1985); and *Biblical Theology of the Old Testament and New Testament.*

37. Ibid., 20, 67, 724, and passim.

cripples the theological enterprise of Biblical Theology. It is basic to Christian theology to reckon with an extra-biblical reality, namely with the resurrected Christ who evoked the New Testament Witness. When H. Frei, in one of his last essays, spoke of "midrash" as a text-creating reality, he moved in a direction, in my opinion, which for Christian theology can only end in failure.[38]

In his response to Stanley Hauerwas and James Barr, Childs concludes that "narrative interpretation"

> avoids for a time the difficult problems of referentiality involved in the term history. . . . In a word, the term "story" is not strong enough to support the function assigned to the Bible. Indeed Christians have always believed that we are not saved by a text or by a narrative, but by the life, death, and resurrection of Jesus Christ in time and space.[39]

It becomes clear that Childs's understanding of God in the text, an "extrabiblical reality," is not construed or nuanced according to the detail of the text but is a reference that is known apart from and at times over against the text. This theological reference must move "from a description of the biblical witnesses to the object toward which these witnesses point, that is, to their subject matter, substance, or *res.*"[40]

Childs's comments following this statement indicate that he is aware of the dangers in what he suggests, but he proceeds on that basis. Childs is interested in "the reality constitutive of these biblical witnesses."[41] That "reality" is not only "testified to in the Bible." It is "that living reality known and experienced as the exalted Christ through the Holy Spirit within the present community of faith."[42]

---

38. Ibid., 20. On the problem of "reference" with particular attention to H. Frei, see Frei, *The Eclipse of Biblical Narrative: A Study in Eighteenth and Nineteenth Century Hermeneutics* (New Haven: Yale University Press, 1974); and "The 'Literal Reading' of Biblical Narrative in the Christian Tradition: Does It Stretch or Will It Break?" in *The Bible and the Narrative Tradition* (ed. Frank McConnell; New York: Oxford University Press, 1986) 36–77. On Frei's work vis-à-vis Childs, see G. T. Sheppard, *The Future of the Bible: Beyond Liberalism and Literalism* (Toronto: United Church Publishing House, 1990) 41–42; and C. L. Campbell, *Preaching Jesus: Hans Frei's Theology and the Contours of a Postliberal Homiletic* (Ph.D. dissertation, Duke University, 1993).
39. Childs, *Biblical Theology of the Old Testament and New Testament*, 665.
40. Ibid., 80.
41. Ibid., 83.
42. Ibid., 86.

In a Christological formulation of the kind that Childs makes central to his perspective, the text as such is subordinated to other claims. A consequence is that the unsettling texts exercise almost no influence on Childs's interpretation and argument.

A sharp contrast to the approach of Childs occurs in the powerful work of David Blumenthal, who takes his beginning points from the brutality of the holocaust.[43] In contrast to the "canonical reading" of Childs, Blumenthal reads texts "*seriatim* . . . one after another, one by one in succession, which matches the way we live. We live *seriatim*."[44] This approach yields an accent upon "Caesura, Fragmentedness, Irruption"—of course, the very matters that Childs wants to exclude.[45]

With relentless determination, Blumenthal insists on attending to all of the texts.

> By contrast, I choose to engage seriously the texts as we have received them. . . . There is, thus, for me, a certain sacredness to the tradition, *prima facie*, and I try to work within it. For this reason, I reject attempts to "clean up" the Psalms, to interpret away the rage, to make them more "pious."[46]

Blumenthal mentions, as I have also, that historicism and an assumption of moral evolution are two ways to dispose of parts of the text with which one does not agree.[47] Of course, he rejects any such maneuver. By attending *seriatim* to all of the texts, Blumenthal comes to the interpretive conclusion that the God of the Bible "is abusive, but not always."[48] In any case, he makes much room for unsettling texts that Childs drops from purview.

It is important that both Blumenthal and Childs allow for plurivocity in the text. Blumenthal judges,

> In the end, the text has more than one meaning, the reader reads on more than one level, and the teacher teaches more than one meaning. Text and life itself are multifaceted; interpretation is multidimensional.

---

43. D. R. Blumenthal, *Facing the Abusing God: A Theology of Protest* (Louisville: Westminster/John Knox, 1993).

44. Ibid., 47–48.

45. Ibid., 9.

46. Ibid., 239.

47. Ibid.

48. Ibid., 247–48.

> Plurivocity is normal; not hierarchy, not the single authoritative teaching. . . . Plurivocity is, thus, not only normal; it is normative, it is what the norm should be.[49]

Childs agrees, "There is a 'reader response' required by any responsible theological reflection."[50] But Childs of course qualifies such an allowance.

> Yet it is crucial to theological reflection that canonical restraints be used and that reader response be critically tested in the light of different witnesses of the whole Bible. . . . There is a biblical rule of faith which sets the standard for family resemblance. . . . Once the task of discerning the kerygmatic content of the witnesses has been pursued, it is fully in order to offer an analogical extension of this kerygmatic message by means of a modern reader response.[51]

This qualification of course causes Childs to part decisively from Blumenthal, in the end, concerning unsettling texts.

IV

This still leaves us with the question, what to do with these texts that are there, as Blumenthal insists, but texts that are enormously problematic, as Childs insists. My suggestion is that we take a "naively realistic" view of the text as a "script" of Yahweh's past. Such naiveté, for this purpose, overrides our critical judgments. Without a hypothesis of moral evolution, it is clear that Yahweh "moves on" as a character in the text, as any character surely will move on in the drama.[52] Thus these texts are in Yahweh's *past*, but they are at the same time assuredly *in* Yahweh's past. I propose, with an analogue from "the enduring power of the past" in therapeutic categories, that these "past texts" are enduringly painful memories still available to the character of Yahweh, mostly not operative, but continuing to work even in the present. They must therefore be taken seriously even in the canonical, "final form" of the text.

This means that a "truer" picture of Yahweh cast in canonical or theological form has moved beyond these texts but has not superseded

---

49. Ibid., 239.
50. Childs, *Biblical Theology of the Old Testament and New Testament*, 335.
51. Ibid., 335–36.
52. See Patrick, *The Rendering of God*, 28–60.

these texts, just as no human person understood in depth ever supersedes or scuttles or outgrows such ancient and powerful memories. There lingers in the character of Yahweh ancient memories (texts) that belong to the density of Yahweh and that form a crucial residue of Yahweh's character. Yahweh may not be, in a "truer" "canonical" understanding, a God who abandons. But this past marking of Yahweh is still potentially available in the current life of Yahweh (for the text lingers) and must in any case be taken as a crucial part of the career of Yahweh. Yahweh cannot simply will away this past, nor can the interpreters of Yahweh.

For the interpreting community (especially for the religious communities of interpretation but also for the academic community) that intends to face the fullness of the text, the witness to Yahweh and the interpreters of the witness must take into full account that past and those memories that are in important ways still present, available, and potentially operative. This in turn suggests that it is faithful to the text and healthy for the reading community that there is in this shared, read past an unsettling dimension that has wounded, troubled, and betrayed those with whom Yahweh has to do. This past of wound, trouble, and betrayal, moreover, still tells in the present. I suggest that such a recovery of the past is not like "critical excavation," for it is not a past that is over or finished but a past that persists like any such held script.[53] Full embrace of these texts permits the interpretive community to embrace fully its theological past, which is marked by abandonment (and other dimensions). It is not necessary to claim that such an unsettling dimension is normative or presently operative but only that it has been there in the past and continues to be present in the present. Thus the God of "steadfast love and mercy" is at the same time also the God who has abandoned, and all current steadfastness bears the wounding mark of that ancient, undenied reality.

Such an interpretive strategy affirms that the canonical text is indeed the full telling of the tale of Yahweh, a tale that has odd and unpleasant dimensions to it.

(1) As an interpretive perspective, such a procedure permits some thematic closure in the direction that Childs wants to go but not such

---

53. See the comment of R. Alter, *The World of Biblical Literature* (New York: Basic Books, 1992) 133, on "excavative" reading.

closure that it eliminates the candor of the text itself, which has generated the candor of Blumenthal. It occurs to me that while many historical critics insistently resist Childs's closure, they finally make common
cause with Childs, though for very different reasons. Childs tends to
shave the text to fit "the creed," whereas historical critics have tended to
shave the text to fit Enlightenment reasonableness that wants to eliminate disruption and incongruity in the text. Neither "canonical" nor
"critical" readers entertain the naiveté to permit a rendering of the text
as the dramatic reality of this God with this people.

(2) But my main concern is not interpretive theory. Rather my
concern is pastoral responsibility, the kind of pastoral responsibility that
belongs to any "classic" read in a theologically serious interpretive community.[54] First, I propose that seeing these texts as a past pertinent to the
present, even if now suppressed or denied, permits the interpretive
community to see fully who Yahweh has been and potentially is. There
is no cover-up of who this God is, no notion that this character can be
made to conform to our preferred Enlightenment or orthodox categories of reading. A "second naiveté" permits the reading community to
take this God with theological seriousness in all of Yahweh's consternat-
ing Jewishness, in all of Yahweh's refusal of domestication.[55]

Second, if this character be understood as a real live agent who concerns the life of the reader or the reading community, the reader is
thereby authorized and permitted to entertain unsettling dimensions of
one's own life (or one's community) as palpable theological dimensions
of reality. Both canonical and critical reading that fend off the unsettling
texts encourage denial and cover-up of the intimate savageness of life.
But when the reading community can see that brutality, abusiveness,
and abandonment are live and present in the past of this God, it is credible to take the same dimension in one's own life as past realities that
continue to have potential power in the present.

---

54. D. Tracy (*The Analogical Imagination: Christian Theology and the Culture of Pluralism* [New York: Crossroad, 1981]) has explored a notion of "classic" as a category for religious texts.

55. The term "second naiveté" is Ricoeur's. See M. I. Wallace, *The Second Naiveté:
Barth, Ricoeur, and the New Yale Theology* (Studies in American Biblical Hermeneutics 6;
Macon, Ga.: Mercer University Press, 1990).

It is not at all my intention to take a therapeutic or instrumental approach to the character of Yahweh. Nonetheless, theological, interpretive, textual candor does have important pastoral consequences. The only way beyond such woundedness is through such woundedness. This ancient woundedness perdures in text and in life. But when voiced and accepted, as the text invites us to do, the ancient woundedness is robbed of its present authority. As long as one pretends that these texts are not "back there," a terrible denial is required, which denies movement into a healing present and a healed future.

It is a delight to honor James Crenshaw, who has thought and written most persistently and most honestly about this unsettling side of the text and its God. Crenshaw has indeed shown us that critical analysis and pastoral realism can live close together. Together they can make a pact to engage in denial and cover-up. But they need not. This text, when read without too many protections (canonical or critical), does not protect in such ways. A refusal to deny or censure invites the movement of this Character and the reading community into new dimensions of peaceableness.

Yahweh as Deus absconditus
Some Remarks on a Dictum by Gerhard von Rad

MAGNE SÆBØ

Oslo, Norway

I

The Jubilarian has shown a particular interest in the research and theology of Gerhard von Rad (1901–71), who in many ways revitalized the study of the Old Testament and will remain one of the most distinguished Old Testament scholars of this century.[1] It may be appropriate, on this occasion, to discuss briefly some basic points of his reflections on the theology of the Old Testament, especially as far as the hiddenness of Yahweh, the God of Israel, is concerned. The two-volume *Theologie des Alten Testaments* that von Rad published in 1957–60[2] not only differed from all previous works in the field but also generated a more intense and variegated debate on the issue than ever before.[3] A prime aspect of the actual debate was the question whether there is a theological "center"

---

1. J. L. Crenshaw, *Gerhard von Rad* (Makers of the Modern Theological Mind; Waco, Tex.: Word, 1978; German trans.: *Gerhard von Rad: Grundlinien seines theologischen Werks* [Munich: Kaiser, 1979]).

2. On this occasion, the English translation is used: *Old Testament Theology*, vols. 1–2 (London: SCM, 1975).

3. Among many assessments of his theology and the extensive discussion of it, see especially D. G. Spriggs, *Two Old Testament Theologies: A Comparative Evaluation of the Contributions of Eichrodt and von Rad to Our Understanding of the Nature of Old Testament Theology* (SBT 2/30; London: SCM, 1974); G. F. Hasel, *Old Testament Theology: Basic Issues in the Current Debate* (rev. ed.; Grand Rapids, Mich.: Eerdmans, 1975) esp. 46–49 and 57ff.; cf. also W. H. Schmidt, " 'Theologie des Alten Testaments' vor und nach Gerhard von Rad," *VF* 17 (1972) 1–25; L. Schmidt, "Die Einheit zwischen Altem und Neuem Testament im Streit zwischen Friedrich Baumgärtel und Gerhard von Rad," *EvT* 25 (1975) 119–39.

(German: *Mitte*) in the Old Testament.[4] Von Rad denied its existence, in general, and formulated a dictum in 1963 that will be discussed here. It runs as follows:

> So, it is a serious question whether and in what sense we may still claim to use the title "Old Testament Theology" in the singular. Where in it is there a center? It may, of course, be said that Yahweh is the center of the Old Testament. But just here starts the real question: for what kind of Yahweh is he? Is he not a Yahweh who from time to time in his self-revelation is hiding himself more and more deeply from his people?[5]

The most remarkable point in von Rad's argument is his denial of the existence of a theological "center" in the Old Testament by referring to the growing hiddenness of Yahweh from his people. This statement really deserves a closer examination.[6] In order to understand it properly, we must also keep in mind that he made his statement in the context of a sharp debate and that under these circumstances he worded his posi-

---

4. See, among others, R. Smend, *Die Mitte des Alten Testaments* (ThStud 101; Zurich: TVZ, 1970); also in idem, *Gesammelte Studien* (with the same title) (Munich: Kaiser, 1986) 1.40–84; G. F. Hasel, "The Problem of the Center in the Old Testament Theology Debate," *ZAW* 86 (1974) 65–82; idem, *OT Theology*, 77–103; W. Zimmerli, "Zum Problem der 'Mitte des Alten Testaments,'" *EvT* 35 (1975) 97–118; H. Graf Reventlow, *Problems of Old Testament Theology in the Twentieth Century* (London: SCM, 1985) 125–33 (and further literature there); J. H. Hayes and F. C. Prussner, *Old Testament Theology: Its History and Development* (London: SCM, 1985) 257–60. In von Rad, *OT Theology*, 2.362–63, 415, Stalker translates *Mitte* 'focal-point' and 'focal point', which is criticized by Hasel, "The Problem of the Center," 73 n. 56.

5. In his argumentive article "Offene Fragen im Umkreis einer Theologie des Alten Testaments," *TLZ* 88 (1963) 401–16 (repr. in von Rad, *Gesammelte Studien zum Alten Testament* [TBü 48; Munich: Kaiser, 1973] 2.289–312; trans. Stalker in idem, *OT Theology*, postscript, 2.410–29), cols. 405–6, resp. p. 294: "So ist es eine ernste Frage, ob und in welchem Sinne wir die singularische Bezeichnung 'Theologie des Alten Testaments' noch in Anspruch nehmen dürfen. Wo ist da eine Mitte? Natürlich kann man sagen, Jahwe sei die Mitte des Alten Testaments [with reference to H. Graf Reventlow, *Theologische Zeitschrift* (1961) 96]. Aber hier beginnt doch erst die Frage: Was ist das denn für ein Jahwe? Ist es nicht ein Jahwe, der sich von Mal zu Mal in seinen Selbstoffenbarungen vor seinem Volk tiefer und tiefer verbirgt?" Compare the somewhat different translations by Stalker, *OT Theology*, 2.415, and by Hasel, "The Problem of the Center," 75.

6. In the following, much of what will be commented on may represent a commonplace to those who know von Rad's writings well. To the youngest generation of Old Testament scholars, however, it may not be as familiar.

tion forcefully, perhaps even more forcefully than he otherwise would have. Be that as it may, he seems to have made his matter of concern clear and noteworthy. The main point of his dictum was apparently an assumed theological "center" of the Old Testament. This key point has been connected with one, singular Old Testament theology—that is, the question of its theological unity. It has also been connected with a specific definition of the alleged "center"—here, presumably, Yahweh. Closely connected to these two points is the theme of a God who is hiding himself from his people. The three points are closely interwoven. It is also significant whether von Rad's dictum is compatible or consonant with other matters of this kind that he has maintained in his many writings—primarily in his *Theology*, the real "storm center" of the actual debate.

II

The intricate question before us is how and why Yahweh is hiding himself from his people[7] or, to cite the well-known phrase from the Vulgate of Isa 45:15, why Yahweh is described as *Deus absconditus*. As was just shown, this question is intimately connected with the view that Yahweh must be regarded as the theological "center" of the Old Testament, and this notion again is associated with the problem of the Old Testament's theological unity. This last topic was actually the starting point of the dispute centering on von Rad's *Old Testament Theology*.

It is well known that, prior to von Rad's *Theology*, scholarly studies on the history and religion of ancient Israel as well as on the theology of the Old Testament displayed for the most part a tension between two extremes—if the two extremes were not combined in one way or another. One perspective was more or less occupied only with a great plurality of religious phenomena in ancient Israel: the history of its religion. The other perspective assumed a theological unity of the Old Testament, preferably of a doctrinal character. In other words, there was a deep tension between what was considered "history" and what was considered "theology" in the Old Testament, as well as considerable disagreement

---

7. Cf. S. E. Balentine, *The Hidden God: The Hiding of the Face of God in the Old Testament* (Oxford: Oxford University Press, 1983).

about the relationship between them. The key question here, then, is what effect this dual tendency in modern Old Testament studies may have had on the issue under discussion.

For von Rad, it was obviously a primary concern to overcome the traditional discrepancy between "history" and "theology" and the foundational axioms underlying this discrepancy; he did this by attacking the traditional understanding of both of them.

First of all, von Rad was very much opposed to any attempt to define the theological unity of the Old Testament in some doctrinal way, such as the conventional dogmatic tripartite scheme, theology-anthropology-soteriology,[8] or even by some overarching conceptual idea from the Old Testament itself, such as God's covenant (*bĕrît*) with Israel (see W. Eichrodt's use of covenant in structuring his theology, in his well-known *Theologie des Alten Testaments*).[9] Breaking with this long and diversely conceived doctrinal tradition of unifying principles, von Rad structured his presentation of Old Testament theology in close relation to modern exegetical and isagogical studies (not least his own).[10] Thus, methodically and substantially, he managed to give the discipline of Old Testament theology a completely new setting and character.

Von Rad's fresh approach, making the discipline of Old Testament theology basically dependent on the disciplines of Old Testament exegesis and isagogics,[11] had various consequences. One effect, which may perhaps be deemed positive, pertains to the structuring principles for an Old Testament theology. Instead of using "imported" or "foreign" principles or procedures, von Rad's method made it easier (even in comparison with the presentation of Eichrodt) to "let the Old Testament

---

8. Among others, L. Koehler, *Theologie des Alten Testaments* (Tübingen: Mohr, 1936; 4th ed., 1966); cf. further Reventlow, *Problems*, 44–58.

9. W. Eichrodt, *Theologie des Alten Testaments* (3 vols.; Stuttgart: Klotz, 1933–39; rev. [5th] ed. vol. 1, 1957; rev. [4th] ed. vols. 2–3 [in one], 1961); English trans. J. A. Baker: *Theology of the Old Testament* (2 vols.; London: SCM 1961–67). Cf. Spriggs, *Two OT Theologies*; Hasel, *OT Theology*, 42–46; Hayes and Prussner, *OT Theology*, 179–84; and Reventlow, *Problems*.

10. First of all, his study *Das formgeschichtliche Problem des Hexateuch* (Stuttgart: Kohlhammer, 1938; reprinted in von Rad, *Gesammelte Studien zum Alten Testament* [2 vols.; TBü 8; Munich: Kaiser, 1971] 1.9–86).

11. There is a great similarity between von Rad's position and that of J. P. Gabler, the alleged father of biblical theology; cf. my "Johann Philipp Gablers Bedeutung für die biblische Theologie: Zum 200-jährigen Jubiläum seiner Antrittsrede vom 30. März 1787," *ZAW* 99 (1987) 1–16.

itself speak out."[12] Conversely, another effect may be considered negative: theology's dependence on exegetical and historical scrutiny of the various books and blocks of writings in the Old Testament led to more-or-less different *theologies,* relative to the different literary units. Inevitably, therefore, the theological pluriformity of individual parts of the Old Testament had caused a remarkable fragmentation of its theology as a whole, not to speak of its unity. Thus, it is not surprising that a vehement debate quickly broke out over the unity—or "center"—of Old Testament theology as a result of von Rad's exegetical-theological approach. Furthermore, von Rad's focus on the exegetical and isagogical scrutiny of the Old Testament, including its theological implications, generated new perspectives on the concept of "history." Modern critical studies of the Old Testament, especially its "historical books," to a large extent had concentrated on the political history of Israel, understanding the latter term in a wide sense. As a result, a new critical understanding and presentation of the "history of Israel" was established and has survived, though with considerable variations.

For von Rad, however, this "general" or "ordinary" history of Israel, though founded in criticism and scholarship, was theologically not fully adequate or sufficient. Furthermore, to him the Old Testament certainly was "a historical book," but in a different sense, for in an idiosyncratic way it presented "a history that is caused by the word of God."[13] Thus von Rad shifted the theological interest from the "general" history of Israel to a history in which Yahweh, through the generations of the people, communicated with them and acted for them; at the same time, it was a history of the people's faith and confession (*Glaubensgeschichte*).

Further, von Rad, in his own way, revived the old and theologically freighted concept of a divine 'salvation history' (*Heilsgeschichte*).[14] The

---

12. In an answer to criticism of his *Theology,* von Rad said: "ging ich von der Annahme aus, dass es verheissungsvoll sein könnte, das Alte Testament noch mehr, als es bisher geschehen ist, ausreden und seine Sache selbst sagen zu lassen, statt ihm dauernd ins Wort zu fallen," *Theologie,* 2.11 ('I proceed from the assumption that it could be promising once again, more than usually has been the case, to let the Old Testament have its say and to speak for itself, instead of continuing to interrupt it'—trans. P. L. R.).

13. Cf. von Rad, "Das Alte Testament ist ein Geschichtsbuch," in *Probleme alttestamentlicher Hermeneutik* (ed. C. Westermann; TBü 11; Munich: Kaiser, 1960) 11–17, here p. 11 (also in Eng. trans.: *Essays on Old Testament Hermeneutics* [Richmond, Va.: John Knox, 1963]).

14. Cf. Reventlow, *Problems,* 87–124.

debate over von Rad's _Theology,_ not least the notion of salvation history, was heated, due to the presumed discrepancy between the "salvation history" of the Old Testament and the scholarly critical picture of the (political, cultural, and religious) history of ancient Israel.[15] Thus, unlike other adherents of the modern critical and secular view of the history of Israel, _etsi deus non daretur,_ von Rad placed Yahweh, the God of Israel, central in the history of the people, especially wherever this history in its theological substance presents itself as "sacred history."

In view of von Rad's dictum of 1963 and his theologically understood history of Israel, we must ask, with some surprise: Why is von Rad so reluctant to see the concept of God as a unitary factor in the salvation history of the people of Israel? In order to get closer to the essence of this question, it may be useful to consider further his concept(s) of "history" in the Old Testament. This may even be significant for a proper understanding of his _Theology._

The "History of Israel" as depicted in the Old Testament appears to be the final form of a long and manifold tradition of history-telling, including deep historical and theological reflection; and in its late form, it reveals various layers from different times and diverse perspectives. Behind the final history of the people one may, among other things, recognize numerous locally-oriented stories of families and tribes as well as of various regions and local shrines. Over the course of time, many stories and individual traditions of diverse kinds were lifted from their original (and often cultic) contexts and were assembled in various literary compilations or composite traditions. This complex of literary forms and compositions also displayed a "history," a long and variegated history of traditions, including creative interpretations and reinterpretations of traditions. In its last stage, it gradually developed into a final, unified redaction that, in the end, included the canonization of some writings, resulting in what was to become the Hebrew Bible.[16]

---

15. See, among others, F. Hesse, _Abschied von der Heilsgeschichte_ (ThStud 108; Zurich: TVZ, 1971), and also the criticism of it by R. Schmitt, _Abschied von der Heilsgeschichte? Untersuchungen zum Verständnis der Geschichte im Alten Testament_ (Frankfurt am Main: Peter Lang, 1982); cf. further Hasel, _OT Theology,_ 57–75; Reventlow, _Problems,_ 59–87.

16. The complex question of _canon_ cannot be dealt with here, nor the particular "canonical approach" of B. S. Childs; but see the discussion of Childs in my "Vom

It is important to consider the whole of this history, with its different stages of various layers and viewpoints, not least for theological reasons. Von Rad, however, tended to favor what might be called the middle stage of the long tradition history, especially its specific historical components, as the best-suited or "operative" material for the presentation of an Old Testament Theology. In an important methodological introduction, he discussed what the subject matter (*Gegenstand*) of an Old Testament theology might be, focusing on the literary history of some main historical traditions (*Überlieferungen*), especially elements of these traditions with a Deuteronomistic flavor. From this nucleus he presented "a theology of the historical traditions."[17] Because of this approach, the main historical traditions essentially became the structuring components of the whole work, and von Rad treated them in the first volume of his *Theology*, which is its most distinctive part.

In the second volume, he presented individual prophetic traditions, based on the historical traditions, and a radical reinterpretation of them as well. Other significant parts of the Old Testament literature, however, were methodologically much harder for him to come to grips with—namely, the Psalms, the wisdom traditions, and the phenomenon of apocalyptic in the book of Daniel.[18] Not only had von Rad related his theological exposition to the formal structure of Israel's historical traditions, he had also materially made his treatment dependent on these traditions. He not only regarded the "history" mainly as salvation history, he also revived and used the old theological notion of 'promise–fulfillment' (*Verheissung–Erfüllung*). In fact, the promise–fulfillment pattern seems to have constituted the true dynamic structure of the "history of Israel." It is fair to claim, on the one hand, that in his *Theology* von Rad undertook a "historicization" of Old Testament theology, although from a wider perspective this historicization was somewhat limited. On the other hand, it is equally true that he also "theologized"

'Zusammendenken' zum Kanon: Aspekte der traditionsgeschichtlichen Endstadien des Alten Testaments," *Jahrbuch für Biblische Theologie* 3 (1988) 115–33.

17. See von Rad's *Theologie*, 1.117–42; *OT Theology*, 1.105–28, and also p. vii.

18. On the last item, see, among others, my "Old Testament Apocalyptic in Its Relation to Prophecy and Wisdom: The View of Gerhard von Rad Reconsidered," in *In the Last Days: Benedikt Otzen Festschrift* (ed. K. Jeppesen, K. Nielsen, and B. Rosendal; Aarhus: Aarhus University Press, 1994) 78–91.

Old Testament history. With his distinct combination of "history" and "theology," von Rad creatively fostered prolific new insights into the theology of Old Testament, and his *Old Testament Theology,* his momentous *chef-d'œuvre,* presented an essential, relatively coherent picture of some of the main theological idiosyncrasies of the Old Testament.

III

The proper context of von Rad's essay and dictum of 1963, therefore, is his *Old Testament Theology.* It may be asked, however, whether the dictum, composed a few years after the *Theology,* represented a step of self-correction by the author. Regarding the basic question of a probable unity and "center" of Old Testament theology, Hasel thinks that in the *Theology* von Rad has a "secret [*sic*] center from which [he] interprets the OT,"[19] namely, the Deuteronomistic theology of history, and in his essay of 1963 he both "indicates a considerable mellowing over against his earlier position" and "continues to maintain his secret center."[20] Further, referring explicitly to the dictum, Hasel claims: "In principle then G. von Rad does not deny the existence of a center; he inadvertently admits that the OT does have a center."[21] However, both of Hasel's claims are questionable.

First, as shown above, the Deuteronomistic theology of history did play a central role in von Rad's thinking and the structuring of his Old Testament Theology, but it can only lead to regrettable terminological confusion to call this a "center" or even a "secret center," a term that seems rather contrary to von Rad's methodological frankness. Second, and more substantially, von Rad's understanding of what a history of traditions, particularly the "continual actualization of the data of the saving history,"[22] really is about may necessarily carry a denial of a theological "center" in the sense of a single "point" or even "a system which allows the contents of the Old Testament to be developed in a really pertinent and organic way."[23] His view of the history of traditions and

---

19. Hasel, "The Problem of the Center," 74; here he also says: "G. von Rad has failed to justify this 'secret center' as *the* hermeneutical key to the whole OT."
20. Ibid., 74–75.
21. Ibid., 75 and n. 72.
22. Von Rad, *Theology,* 2.414.
23. Ibid., 2.411.

of the theological structure of "promise–fulfillment" were both significant to von Rad.[24] It may be said that his more-or-less pluralistic view was in fact consistent with his tradition-historical and literary-historical methodology. It should therefore be no surprise that, after having asserted in his *Theology* that it is "impossible to speak of a focal-point [*Mitte*] within the Old Testament which might have served as a constant standard for Israel,"[25] von Rad restates his rejection of the notion of a "center"[26] and gives further grounds for it in the essay of 1963. From the perspective of this essay, it also seems likely that S. Herrmann's claim that Deuteronomy should be regarded the "center" of the Old Testament[27] may to some degree be close to von Rad's *Theology*. Nevertheless, it is scarcely in line with its main cast and tendency. Finally, Hasel seems to overlook the fact that von Rad did not use the term *center* but preferred terms like "some characteristic, common, and continuing feature" and especially the term "typical," as in the phrase "the typical element in Israel's faith."[28]

In regard to von Rad's exegetical and tradition-historical procedures, it is fair to say in summary that von Rad shows a high degree of methodological coherence and theological consequence. In regard to the specific question of a theological "center" in the Old Testament, it is also fair to say that he may have proved that it hardly can be founded on tradition-historical grounds. However, what of the view of many scholars[29] that God is to be regarded as the theological "center"? This most basic theological question seems to be even more vexed and complicated than the question of "history" or tradition history. One may also ask whether von Rad's treatment of this question is as coherent as his treatment of the other one. Moreover, this question relates to the last part of his dictum.

---

24. Ibid., 2.425–28.

25. Ibid., 2.363.

26. Ibid., 2.411.

27. Herrmann ("Die konstruktive Restauration: Das Deuteronomium als Mitte biblischer Theologie," in *Probleme biblischer Theologie* [Gerhard von Rad Festschrift; ed. H. W. Wolff; Munich: Kaiser, 1971] 155–70; here 155–56) lists some points of connection in earlier books of von Rad, such as *Das Gottesvolk im Deuteronomium* (1929) and *Deuteronomium-studien* (1947); cf. also Smend, *Die Mitte*, 54 n. 231.

28. Von Rad, *Theology*, 2.414–15, 427–28.

29. Cf. Reventlow, *Problems*, 132–33.

In his essay of 1963 von Rad used quite a few question marks, and one wonders what argumentive value and function the interrogative form might have had. The questions may have indicated the author's uncertainty or hesitancy or, perhaps more likely, may have been rhetorical signs of his deep perplexity and quandary regarding the problems, or they may even indicate evasiveness. At any rate, von Rad asks in the dictum, "what kind of Yahweh is he?" Then he proceeds to a still more specific question: "Is he not a Yahweh who from time to time in his self-revelation is hiding himself more and more deeply from his people?" These questions, related as they are to the theological problem of a "center" in the Old Testament, might have been a mild form of denying such an idea, especially the suggestion that Yahweh should be that "center." The subject, however, seems to be more demanding and complex than this.

Within the framework of von Rad's exegetical and theological work, there is a distinct interest in the revelation of the God of Israel. His tradition-historical and literary-historical *Theology* is substantially occupied, not only with God's "salvation history," but also God's 'revelation history' (*Offenbarungsgeschichte*). God reveals himself to the fathers; God makes them promises; God elects and protects the people and makes a covenant (*berît*) with them; God is the sovereign guarantor for his promises and their fulfillment. All the way he meets his people as *Deus revelatus* in the realm of their history. Yahweh as the *Deus revelatus* is the God of the people's "salvation history" and represents the positive side of their sacred historical traditions.

On the other hand, Yahweh also was experienced by the people as a God of zealous wrath and judgment, especially in times of national crises and catastrophies. These experiences were essential parts of the multifarious message of the prophets, from the middle of the eighth century onward. In this respect, the rich and complex tradition of Isaiah's preaching is remarkable.

In a recent study on God's *opus alienum*[30] (partly with reference to von Rad's interpretation), Benedikt Otzen has shown that the expressions of Yahweh's 'strange deed' (Vg: *alienum opus*) and "alien work" in

---

30. B. Otzen, "Opūs Alienūm: Overvejelser over Jesaja 28," in *Verbūm Dei-verba ecclesiae: Festskrift til Erik Kyndal* (Aarhus: Aarhus Universitet, 1996) 1–11.

Isa 28:21[31] have a significant place in Isaiah's message of doom, since this passage and the similar one in 29:14 are connected with the fundamentally important Isa 6:9–10, where the prophet's call "to produce obduracy" is recounted.[32]

In fact, the problem of "obduracy" in Isaiah 6 represents an axis in von Rad's interpretation of Yahweh as the "hidden God." Using this text as his axis, he first treats some instances in the historical traditions and then refers to prophetic passages such as Isa 8:17, 30:8ff., and especially 29:9–14.[33] When he later returns to this problem, it is in his final discussion of the relationship between the Old and New Testaments.[34] Here, von Rad starts from "the New Testament saving event" in Christ, where there is "a deep *hiddenness on God's part*"; after this, he gives a brief survey of some central passages in the Old Testament material, beginning with Gen 12:3 and ending with Isa 45:15, that speak of Yahweh as 'the hidden God' (*Deus absconditus*), as mentioned above. However, regarding the question of God's hiddenness, there is a still wider and richer area of metaphorical theological reflection in the Old Testament, and even outside of it, as was fully demonstrated by L. Perlitt in his contribution to the Gerhard von Rad festschrift (1971).[35] First of all, Perlitt focused on the individual and (later) collective psalms of lament and on the prophetic traditions, especially on First and Second Isaiah and Third Isaiah.[36] In this connection, it is rather interesting that Perlitt also showed that references to Yahweh as *Deus absconditus* (not unexpectedly) are practically absent from the theology of the Deuteronomists. This

---

31. The translations are from the NRSV (1989).

32. Cf. Otzen, *Festschrift til Erik Kyndal,* 5–6; von Rad, *Theology,* 2.375.

33. Cf. von Rad, *Theology,* 2.151–55; here 152 n. 9; he also comments on F. Hesse, *Das Verstockungsproblem im Alten Testament* (BZAW 74; Berlin: Alfred Töpelmann, 1955) 40–79. As for his *Theology,* see first of all his treatment of the Saul tradition, 1.324–27.

34. Von Rad, *Theology,* 2.374–78.

35. L. Perlitt, "Die Verborgenheit Gottes," in *Probleme biblischer Theologie: Gerhard von Rad zum 70. Geburtstag* (ed. H. W. Wolff; Munich: Kaiser, 1971) 367–82; cf. also the recent book by Balentine, *The Hidden God,* as well as Crenshaw, "From Tradition to the Silence of God," in *Gerhard von Rad,* 161–65.

36. As for Trito-Isaiah, see also the dissertation by I. Fischer, *Wo ist Jahwe? Das Volksklagelied Jes 63,7–64,11 als Ausdruck des Ringens um eine gebrochene Beziehung* (SBB 19; Stuttgart: Katholisches Bibelwerk, 1989).

may also contribute to a better understanding of von Rad's essay and dictum of 1963.[37]

When assessing von Rad's view of Yahweh as a "hidden God" and his "strange deed" in the framework of his *Theology,* one could contend that he should have paid much more attention than he did[38] to these most significant *theologoumena* of ancient Israel. However, the actual state of affairs may be explained to some degree by the fact that the theological notion of Yahweh as *Deus absconditus* is not "typical" of the Deuteronomistic theology, as just mentioned. It may therefore not have been given the place and function in von Rad's *Theology* that it otherwise might have. Furthermore, when one considers the central and comparatively much greater role that Yahweh as *Deus revelatus* played in the "salvation history" of the historical and prophetic traditions, then it may to some extent be conceivable that the notion of Yahweh as *Deus absconditus* received a "place in the shadow" of the more positive perspective of the God of Israel. Finally, when one takes into consideration the above-mentioned reference to the New Testament and its saving event of Christ, then the last words of his 1963 essay become more understandable. There he says that Old Testament theology only has meaning through its relation to the New Testament; for if that is not the case, if one "analyses the Old Testament in isolation, then, no matter how devotedly the work is done, the more appropriate term is 'history of the religion of the Old Testament.' "[39] Therefore, it seems evident that for the unity of the Old Testament and, in particular, regarding the question of Yahweh as the "center" of the Old Testament, von Rad wished to have "open windows" to the New Testament and God's saving act in Christ on the cross.[40] Old Testament theology has to be part of a Biblical Theology; this is practically its *conditio sine qua non.*

---

37. Perlitt, "Die Verborgenheit Gottes," 379.

38. Cf. also von Rad, "Das Werk Jahwes," *Gesammelte Studien,* 2.236–44, where there is no focus on the "work" of the "hidden God."

39. Idem, *Theology,* 2.428–29.

40. See ibid., 2.374: "In Christ, God divested himself of his power and glory, indeed, he did his work among men *sub specie contraria,* veiled, and in weakness and shame. Ancient Israel also had to bear the mystery of God's withdrawal, and often spoke of the experiences and trials which this entailed. The whole history of the covenant is simply the history of God's continuous retreat." Cf. also Crenshaw, *Gerhard von Rad,* 164–65.

The *Theology* of von Rad is certainly central to his scholarly work, but it does not represent his last word on the issue. In his essay and dictum of 1963, he looked back at his *Theology* and the debate it had provoked; but in subsequent volumes his reflections went further. In his two later books, first in his study on *Wisdom in Israel*[41] and then in his very last book, on the theologically loaded narrative of Gen 22:1–19,[42] there are signs of a more comprehensive picture of the God of Israel that might have given some other evaluation of the question of the unity and "center" of Old Testament theology.[43] But that lies outside the scope of this essay.

---

41. Idem, *Weisheit in Israel* (Neukirchen-Vluyn: Neukirchener Verlag, 1970); English trans., *Wisdom in Israel* (Nashville: Abingdon, 1972).

42. Idem, *Das Opfer des Abraham: Mit Texten von Luther, Kierkegaard, Kolakowski und Bildern von Rembrandt* (Munich: Kaiser, 1971).

43. Cf. W. Pannenberg, "Glaube und Wirklichkeit im Denken Gerhard von Rads," in *Gerhard von Rad: Seine Bedeutung für die Theologie—Drei Reden* (ed. H. W. Wolff, R. Rendtorff, and W. Pannenberg; Munich: Kaiser, 1973) 37–54, 57–58. Cf. p. 50: "Die Spannung zwischen Israels Erfahrung einer Geschichte göttlicher Führungen und der Geschichtsfremdheit der Weisheit ist das offene Problem, das Gerhard von Rad nicht nur der alttestamentlichen Wissenschaft, sondern der Theologie überhaupt hinterlassen hat" ('The tension between Israel's experience of a history under divine leading and the indifference to history in Wisdom [literature] is the open problem, which Gerhard von Rad has left behind, not only with respect to Old Testament study but for theology overall '—trans. P. L. R.).

Patriarchal Models for Piety

LENNART BOSTRÖM

Örebo Theological Seminary

Introduction

In the impressive list of publications coming from Professor James L. Crenshaw's pen is a book entitled *A Whirlpool of Torment*.[1] In this book he discusses in a most stimulating and challenging way several Old Testament texts where God appears as "an oppressive presence." In this article I am interested in continuing the discussion concerning some of these texts. Job appears as a patriarchal figure, and in this paper I will try to relate him to two of the patriarchs: Abraham and Jacob. The biblical texts as well as later traditions show a marked interest in the theological and psychological aspects of the experiences of these patriarchal figures. The perspective of this article is that the stories about these patriarchal figures consciously are depicted so as to present these individuals as models for piety. The different, indeed contrasting, ideals of piety within Israelite religion mean that these portrayals are not concordant, and the texts express two ideals, one of submissiveness to God and the other of nonacceptance of divine rule.

Job and Abraham

From early times Job and Abraham have been linked to each other. This is only natural, because there are close similarities. Both are depicted as persons of early times.[2] The social life and circumstances as

---

1. J. L. Crenshaw, *A Whirlpool of Torment: Israelite Traditions of God as an Oppressive Presence* (OBT 12; Philadelphia: Fortress, 1984).

2. M. H. Pope, *Job: Introduction, Translation, and Notes* (AB 15; New York: Doubleday, 1965) xxxii–xxxiii. J. R. Baskin ("Rabbinic Interpretations of Job," *The Voice from the Whirlwind: Interpreting the Book of* Job [ed. L. G. Perdue and W. C. Gilpin; Nashville: Abingdon, 1992] 101–10) notes that much of the rabbinic discussion concerned whether

they appear in the texts are basically the same. The Septuagint even refers to Job as a descendant of Abraham.[3] According to the *Testament of Job*, Job was both "from the sons of Esau" and later married to Dinah, the daughter of Jacob and Leah, after his first wife had died during the ordeals they went through. With Dinah, Job had the second set of ten children. It is to them that the teachings of the book are directed.[4]

Job and Abraham share the fact that they became subjects of severe divine testing. Contrary to what seems to have been regarded as normal, their allegiance to God and their righteousness did not exempt them from misfortune. It was, rather, their righteousness that constituted the cause of their trials. In Genesis 22, where Abraham is tested in a gruesome manner, nothing is indicated about the reason for the test. However, Genesis 22 often has been interpreted along the same lines as the book of Job, as shown by this rabbinic story in *Sepher Yashar Wa-Yera*.

> Now there was a day when the sons of God came to present themselves before the Lord, and Satan came along among them. And the Lord said unto Satan, "From where have you come?" and Satan answered the Lord, and said, "From going to and fro on the earth and from walking up and down in it." . . . And the Lord said to Satan: "Have you considered my servant Abraham? For there is none like him in the earth, a perfect and an upright man before Me . . . and that fears God and eschews evil. As I live, were I to say unto him, Bring up Isaac, your son, before Me, he would not withhold him from Me, much less if I told him to bring up a burnt offering before me from his flocks and herds." And Satan answered the Lord, and said, "Speak now unto Abraham as You have said, and You will see whether he will not transgress and cast aside your words this day."[5]

Job was an Israelite. Job was generally regarded a pious non-Israelite but inferior to Abraham.

3. Job 42:17 (LXX).

4. *T. Job* 1:6. Dinah as Job's wife is also documented elsewhere in the Jewish tradition; see references in R. P. Spittler, "Testament of Job," in *The Old Testament Pseudepigrapha* (ed. J. H. Charlesworth; New York: Doubleday, 1983) 1.839 note m.

5. From B. Zuckerman, *Job the Silent: A Study in Historical Counterpoint* (Oxford: Oxford University Press, 1991) 28. See also *Jub.* 17:15–16, where the demonic figure Prince Mastema in the heavenly council asks God's permission to test Abraham's faithfulness by requesting him to offer his beloved Isaac as a burnt offering. "The motivation for the aqedah that Jubilees furnishes is the innuendo of Prince Mastema that Abraham's love for God and faithfulness to him are subordinate to his love for Isaac. The only way

The reader expects in the Genesis 22 story a prologue like the one in the book of Job. In Job, the test comes about because "the adversary," one of the sons of God, challenges God's positive view of certain people.[6] The only information supplied in Genesis 22 is that God for some unknown reason had decided to test Abraham.[7] It has been noted by scholars that the syntax emphasizes that it is God himself who puts Abraham to the test.[8] What is common to Genesis 22 and the book of Job is that both subjects are completely unaware of the cause of their problems. While the reader may wonder about the divine motives for the testings, neither Abraham nor Job has any knowledge at all about the reasons for the sudden change of fortunes in their lives. Nothing indicates any awareness that their bitter agonies are caused by some kind of divine test to determine whether they measure up to God's standards in terms of character, faith, or endurance.

The similarities between Job and Abraham are not limited to social circumstances, subsequent speculations about family ties, or possible psychological traits.[9] There are also interesting points of contact in terms of theological outlook and piety. Both are described as pious

---

God can disprove Mastema's impugning of Abraham is to order the Patriarch to offer up his son" (J. D. Levenson, *The Death and Resurrection of the Beloved Son: The Transformation of Child Sacrifice in Judaism and Christianity* [New Haven: Yale University Press, 1993] 177). This is self-evidently an adaptation to the prologue of Job to provide an answer to the question that "also bothered the rabbis of the midrash: what provoked this gruesome test, what could have been 'these things' on which the aqedah logically followed (Gen 22:1; see *Gen. Rab.* 55:4)?" (p. 178). Cf. *Tg. Ps.-J.* Gen 22:1, which supplies another explanatory introduction that is built on Isaac's quarreling with Ishmael concerning who has the right to become Abraham's heir.

6. This is not, of course, the only time the Old Testament supplies no material whatsoever that might help the reader understand the motives for divine activity; see, e.g., Exod 4:24–26.

7. D. Alexander ("Genesis 22 and the Covenant of Circumcision," *JSOT* 25 [1983] 17–22) suggests that there is a relationship between chapter 17 and chapter 22 that also may help us to understand why Abraham is tested. The conditional covenant in chapter 17 is here ratified through Abraham's obedient response to God's request. In this way Abraham shows that he is prepared to put God before his family.

8. G. von Rad, *Genesis: A Commentary* (2d rev. ed.; OTL; London: SCM, 1963) 233.

9. N. C. Habel (*The Book of Job: A Commentary* [OTL; London: SCM, 1985] 39–40) finds that the (pre)patriarchal setting is sustained throughout the book of Job and that it serves the purpose of making the audience conscious of the historical and theological gap between their world and that of the hero—Job.

people living righteous lives and standing in a unique relationship to God. They were God's friends and allies. In the texts, this relationship comes in focus even more clearly by virtue of the fact that they are depicted as living in times and circumstances when there was no institutional religious system of temple and priesthood that gave assurance of God's presence and blessing. The relationship between God and these righteous men was close and direct, but it did not result only in blessing and well-being. In Abraham's case, it may be regarded as implied; in Job's case, it is made clear to the reader that it was in fact these men's faith and relationship to God that led to the disasters that constituted ultimate testings from God. In a testing situation, roles may be reversed—just as God, their friend, suddenly appeared as an enemy. The tension of this two-sided experience of God and man's response to it is the focus of this paper.

The Ideal Man

The strong bond between God and the human individual is strongly emphasized in the texts about Job and Abraham.[10] For example, the section in Genesis immediately preceding chapter 22 concerns Abraham's covenant with Abimelech, who came to Abraham to arrange a covenant between the two. The reason was that Abimelech had noted that God was with Abraham in all that he did. In the Job prologue, it is God who directs the attention to Job, who appears to be something like God's favorite among men because of his outstanding morals. These portrayals envisage an ideal for piety and faith in Israelite culture. When Abraham and Job are referred to within the Old Testament as well as within Jewish and Christian traditions, it tends to be to hold them up as models for piety. Although the chronological setting precludes any ref-

---

10. See, however, P. R. Davies ("Abraham and Yahweh: A Case of Male Bonding," *BibRev* 11/4 [1995] 24–33, 44–45), who reads the Abraham stories in a completely different way, as a story of "male bonding" between Abraham and Yahweh. What Davies shows is that there may be other ways to read the stories about Abraham and that to the reader of today it is not entirely clear that Abraham represents an ideal of piety. There are certain connections between Davies's article and an earlier article by L. Bodoff. Bodoff ("God Tests Abraham, Abraham Tests God," *BibRev* 9/5 [1993] 54) also emphasizes the mutuality in the situation and argues that Abraham simultaneously tests God to see what kind of covenant and religion he, Abraham, was being asked to join.

erences to temple cult, it may be significant that sacrifices and obedience dominate the presentation, features that were prominent in later stages of Israelite religion.

Already in the first verse of the book, several designations are used to characterize Job. He was "blameless and upright, one who feared God, and turned away from evil." Exactly the same terminology is used twice in the prologue by God himself when he promotes Job in the discussions with the adversary. E. F. Davis notes that the particular form of the first term used (*tām* 'blameless') occurs only in connection with Job and Jacob in the entire Old Testament.[11] This may be significant and indicate a possible connection between the two. But, as noted by Brueggemann, the terminology also serves as a connecting point between the stories of Job and Abraham.[12] When the covenant is offered to Abraham in Gen 17:10–14, it is preceded by the charge that Abraham shall be 'blameless' (*tāmîm*), a trait that marks the portrayal of Abraham throughout the stories about him.[13]

The parallel terms to *tām* in the Job prologue ("upright, one who feared God, and turned away from evil") indicate that the noncultic use of the noun and adjective forms of the root *tmm* signify a person of high moral stature, of integrity.[14] Brueggemann argues for an interpretation of the term that is largely communal.[15] The person who is *tām* is one who acts or speaks in such a way that it enhances the well-being of others. E. F. Davis argues convincingly for a more transcendent aspect of the term, namely, that *tām* primarily is a theological virtue and only secondarily a social one.[16] This usage obtains in the Abraham stories as well

---

11. Gen 25:27. See E. F. Davis, "Job and Jacob: The Integrity of Faith," in *Reading between Texts: Intertextuality and the Hebrew Bible* (ed. D. N. Fewell; Louisville: Westminster/John Knox, 1992) 214.

12. W. Brueggemann, "A Neglected Sapiential Word Pair," *ZAW* 89 (1977) 241.

13. This form of the term is used only once elsewhere in Genesis, about Noah in Gen 6:9. See S. Spiegel ("Noah, Danel and Job," in *Louis Ginzberg Jubilee Volume* [New York: American Academy for Jewish Research, 1945] 1.305–7) for a connection between the two.

14. B. Kedar-Kopfstein ("*tmm*," *TWAT* 8.689; cf. 1.695–99) finds that the noun and the adjective forms of *tmm*, when used about people, denote 'Rechtschaffenheit' (honesty, uprightness) and that they primarily occur in wisdom texts and texts that are influenced by wisdom.

15. Brueggemann, "A Neglected Sapiential Word Pair," 239.

16. Davis, "Job and Jacob," 207.

as in connection with Job. The two are depicted as people who lived according to what was right in the eyes of both God and men. In the case of Job, the depiction of this piety goes to the extreme. His deep sense of responsibility as the patriarchal head of the household made him offer sacrifices for his grown sons and daughters *in case* they had sinned against God, more or less unknowingly, in their hearts. This remark serves the purpose of making clear that both the narrator and God were completely right in their appraisals of Job. In a less pronounced but similar way, Abraham is depicted as an ideal person in all his dealings with both men and God. Even in the narratives concerning the threat to his beautiful wife, the narrator seems anxious that Abraham receive no blame for the complications.

The Ideal of Submission and Silence

An important trait in the characterization of the ideal person in Israel seems to have been submission to divine rule. The person who obeys any divine command without objection is the model for piety. Here can be seen a parallel to the ideal of wisdom traditions, where the wise man was a person of self-control, especially in terms of speech. This is strongly emphasized in Egypt, where the ideal of the "silent" man is prominent, but there are also parallels in the book of Proverbs.[17]

It is characteristic that in the account where Abraham gets the call to leave his family and ancestral land, the next verse simply states: "So Abram went, as the LORD had told him." It is probably intentional that the command he gets decades later is phrased in a similar way,[18] but this time God's words contain no promises of land or offspring. Quite the contrary, this time Abraham is told to go the land of Moriah and sacrifice his beloved and long-awaited son as a burnt offering. This command must have been regarded as the abrogation of all of God's promises to Abraham about becoming the forefather of a great people. As the Genesis story is presented to us, Abraham has just lost Ishmael because of his wife's stinginess. Encouraged by God, he sent Hagar and her son away,

---

17. See N. Shupak, *Where Can Wisdom Be Found? The Sage's Language in the Bible and in Ancient Egyptian Literature* (OBO 130; Fribourg: University Press / Göttingen: Vandenhoeck & Ruprecht, 1993) 170–73, 342–43.

18. G. Wenham, *Genesis 16–50* (WBC; Waco, Tex.: Word, 1994) 104.

which meant that after this he had only Isaac. Now this same God tells him to sacrifice, with his own hands, Isaac, the son of promises. To the reader it is remarkable that there is no discussion or deliberation recorded in the text. Abraham just accepts the command. It is quite natural that subsequent Jewish literature tried to fill this gap. The following verse indicates no hesitance and can be interpreted as almost the contrary: Abraham rises early in the morning the next day and departs to carry out the command. The narrative style emphasizes the care with which Abraham carries out God's command; he does exactly what God has told him. This is underlined by the repetition of "the place of which God had told him" (v. 9) that echoes God's words (v. 3). The same term *hinnēnî* ('here am I'), expressing willingness and disposition, is used by Abraham at key points in the story in relation to God (v. 1), the angel of the Lord (v. 1), and Isaac (v. 7). The reference to Isaac as *yĕḥîdĕkā* ('your only son') in God's initial words (v. 2) is echoed in the words of the angel of the Lord (vv. 12, 16) in the end.

Crenshaw suggests that the particle *nāʾ* may have a more pronounced function in Gen 22:2, where it is used in an unusual way as part of a divine imperative. Crenshaw suggests that the verse be translated:

> Take, *I beg of you*, your only son, Isaac, whom you love, and go to the land of the Amorites. There you shall sacrifice him on one of the mountains that I declare to you.[19]

This translation indicates that God is aware that what he requests from Abraham is monstrous and this is why he is here pleading rather than commanding Abraham. This interpretation gains some support from the context. At this point, the restrained narrative style changes for a moment; it slows down and makes use of more words. The language used emphasizes the close relationship between Abraham and his son: Isaac is his only son, the son that he loves. The same phenomenon can be observed in v. 7, where repetition is used to emphasize the relationship between Isaac and his father: "And Isaac said to his father Abraham, 'My father!' And he said, 'Here am I, my son.'"[20] We noted above that the grammar of the text puts strong emphasis on God's active role in the

---

19. Crenshaw, *Whirlpool*, 14.
20. Ibid., 23.

drama. Here we see that the narrative style in subtle ways accentuates the horrific plight to which Abraham silently succumbs.

In the Job story, it is made clear in the dialogue in the prologue between God and the adversary that the issue at stake has to do with correct speech. The adversary is convinced that if only Job's fortunes were reversed he would abandon his piety. The ultimate sign of abandonment will be that he curses God, which is the complete reverse of the ideal of submission and silence. Job's concern over this sin has already been demonstrated in the story of his sacrifices for his children in case they might have cursed God "in their hearts." Both the adversary and Job's wife know that if Job curses God openly it will be the end of his life. The reader knows also that, if this happens, the adversary has won. The most pious man on earth will die as a sinner and the Lord will have lost his wager based on confidence in Job. Whether Job does curse God or how close he comes to cursing God in the following chapters can be debated, but, as the book stands, no such cursing occurs. Job and God are the "winners" in their respective dialogues. The adversary recedes into oblivion, and Job's friends can only be saved by Job's intercessory prayer.

What brings Abraham and Job (in the prologue) together is the monstrosity of the testing and their silent submission to it. Completely unaware of any specific reason for their suffering, they confront the loss of everything. This is a tragedy of the deepest kind for any person, but it is intensified by the fact that there is a theological dimension to it. To Job, and to his friends later in the dialogue, there is never any doubt that it is God who is the cause of Job's sorrows. In Abraham's case, it is God himself who asks Abraham to sacrifice his beloved son.[21] In both cases, the heroes face an inevitable crisis of faith. The God of promises and blessings becomes the God of oppressive presence. God, who was regarded as responsible for upholding the balance between life and destiny, between act and consequence, suddenly turns justice upside down.

---

21. Several scholars discuss the possibility that child sacrifice in an early period actually was practiced and that this story reflects the practice (see, e.g., Levenson, *Death and Resurrection*, 8–9) or possibly the abolishment of such practices (see, e.g., S. Spiegel, *The Last Trial: On the Legends and Lore of the Command to Abraham to Offer Isaac as a Sacrifice: The Akedah* [A Jewish Legacy Book; New York: Behrman, 1979] 8). It is possible that there were such practices in early Israel, as indicated also by other texts, but the test of Abraham is still monstrous, since God's promises to him were related to his son Isaac.

Anyone would wonder how that could be. What is emphasized in different ways in the texts is the submission and silence of the pious man. Abraham makes no objections, and neither does Job in the first two chapters of the book. Each man plays the role of the ideal pious man who undergoes human suffering without protest or questioning the goodness of God. What is dealt with, however, is not suffering per se but the theological and personal implications of suffering. The texts do not ask whether God has the right to deal with men contrary to what is generally regarded as justice, but they imply that God's sovereignty means that his actions cannot be restricted to a system of acts and corresponding consequences.[22]

I suggest that a "theology of testing" can be deduced from these texts. The test motif that occurs in so many narratives is here used in reference to God. This motif can be traced throughout the Old Testament. A recurring pattern in the Old Testament is that God blesses his people and then withdraws to see whether his chosen ones have the morale to live according to his will. It starts in the Garden of Eden, where a forbidden tree is put in the middle, and mankind is left to obey or disobey God's prohibition not to eat from it. This theme is repeated in numerous ways all through the Old Testament. As in many other stories, the ruler (here God) appears as a king surrounded by his subordinates. He decides to test certain individuals for future missions to learn the caliber of their allegiance. What is characteristic of testing situations is that traditional roles may have to be reversed to make the test real. In Genesis 22 and in the book of Job, God turns against the two most righteous people on earth. Often in a test it is necessary to push matters to the extreme in order to make the result unequivocal. This certainly applies to Abraham's and Job's cases.

R. Barthes makes an actantial analysis of another text in Genesis and notes that it is very rare that the "sender" in a story also is the "opponent." He suggests that the only type of narrative that presents this paradoxical form is a narrative relating an act of blackmail.[23] I suggest that this pattern applies even more to narratives about testing. At first God

---

22. See *Genesis Rabbah* 55. There is a stark contrast between Genesis 22 and Genesis 18, where Abraham confronts God's way of administrating justice.

23. R. Barthes, *Image, Music, Text* (London: Fontana, 1984) 138.

gives, but suddenly he takes away in order to test a person's integrity of faith, piety, or endurance. To this reversal, one can react in different ways: either in submission or revolt. Abraham in Genesis 22 and Job in the prologue exemplify the first alternative. In this kind of text, the theological problem of God's inconsistent behavior is pushed aside in order to focus on the human response and the ideal of submission that becomes the dominant feature.

Von Rad implies that the fact that the reader is informed in Gen 22:1 that the whole drama is a test invalidates the tension in the narrative. By this information the reader knows that God's demand is not intended to be taken seriously.[24] But the parallel with the book of Job shows that a test may be as real as anything else. Job not only was close to losing everything—he actually did. The test was certainly real. The information that the whole enterprise is a test changes, however, at least momentarily, the perspective of the reader away from God to the human subject and the outcome of the test. The question that comes into focus is this: "Will this person pass the test or not?" The theological problem—how God can do or demand such things—is still there, but the main tension in the story lies in the uncertainty about whether Abraham and Job will endure to the end.

We find a twofold viewpoint in both Genesis 22 and the book of Job. The reader has more knowledge than the characters in the story. This is especially clear in the book of Job. Even if much is enigmatic also for the reader, s/he has crucial information that the poor suffering Job and his wife do not. They just live their lives and suddenly experience total catastrophy. The ultimate testing meant total loss, not only of worldly goods and family, but also of life's security. In a world view built on a correspondence between piety and the fortunes of life, such an experience meant total instability. Where everything that happened was seen as coming from God, the theological dilemma was inevitable. Abraham's reaction in Genesis 22 and Job's (initial) reaction to the catastrophy is total submission to divine rule. "For some people, true worship means to walk alone in God-forsakenness, or worse yet, to discover the Lord as one's worst enemy."[25] In the hour of testing, God is

---

24. Von Rad, _Genesis_, 234.
25. Crenshaw, _Whirlpool_, 28.

not present to answer any questions or, even worse, he is present but appears to be the enemy of the pious man.[26]

It can probably be seen as symptomatic for the patriarchal pattern of many Old Testament stories that the wives of Abraham and Job have no prominent role in these texts, though disaster strikes them as hard as their husbands. *The Testament of Job* compensates for this omission and portrays Job's wife as faithfully supporting, until her own death, her husband during his twenty years of bodily suffering.[27] The tendency to give more attention to Job's wife can also be seen in the Septuagint.[28] In Genesis 22, however, Sarah plays no role at all, which stands in contrast to her prominent role in the preceding chapter, where it is her activity that leads to the expulsion of Hagar and Ishmael into the wilderness. In *Genesis Rabbah*, the account of Sarah's death in Gen 23:1 is linked to the preceding events. When Sarah heard what was happening to Isaac, she died, and Abraham went from Mount Moriah to mourn for her.[29]

Zuckerman suggests that it is not without significance that Job answers his wife in the plural: "Shall we receive good at the hand of God, and shall we not receive evil?"[30] This indicates that Job does not speak only for himself but for all humanity. This applies also to the depiction of Abraham and Job in these stories. Their submissive endurance is emphasized in order to set a model for pious people in all times. The history of

---

26. Crenshaw ("The Concept of God in Old Testament Wisdom," *In Search of Wisdom: Essays in Memory of John G. Gammie* [ed. L. G. Perdue, B. Scott, and W. J. Wiseman; Louisville: Westminster/John Knox, 1993] 12) observes: "Job's God, as presented in his speeches within the dialogue, is paradoxically both present and absent, an oppressive presence and a hiding friend."

27. *T. Job* 21–26 in Spittler ("Testament of Job," 848–51). P. W. van der Horst ("Images of Women in the Testament of Job," in *Studies on the Testament of Job* [ed. M. W. Knibb and P. W. van der Horst; Cambridge: Cambridge University Press, 1989] 93–116) notes that in biblical texts women occur in one per cent of the verses, but in the *Testament of Job* they occur in 107 of 388 verses!

28. See LXX Job 2:9.

29. *Gen. Rab.* 58:5. See also L. Ginzberg, *The Legends of the Jews* (7 vols.; Philadelphia: Jewish Publication Society, 1909–38) 1.286–87. If this legend is accepted, Isaac would be in his twenties or thirties at the time. (According to *Targum Pseudo-Jonathan*, Gen 22:3, Isaac was 37 years old!) In the story it is clear that he is at least not a baby, since he is able to carry the wood for the offering and he notices the absence of a sacrificial animal.

30. Zuckerman, *Job the Silent*.

interpretation shows that this was also the way these texts were received and expounded upon by future generations. The kind of piety promoted was that of acceptance and adaptation to the current state of affairs, which are seen as the result of God 's actions that men can never fully understand. This theme, as well as its problemization, can also be found in both Mesopotamian and Egyptian texts. For example:

> Indeed you do not know the plans of god,
> And should not weep for tomorrow;
> Settle in the arms of the god.[31]

The Ideal of Challenge and Nonacceptance

The sudden change in Job's attitude between the prologue and the dialogues has been a constant problem in the interpretation of the book of Job. At first Job adheres completely to the ideal of submissiveness and silence but then suddenly changes into cursing his existence and, in the debate with his traditional comforters, goes far toward challenging God's righteousness and goodness. To explain the difference diachronically or source-critically does not really solve the issue.[32] It is still a puzzle why any redactor or rewriter let the final shape of the book include such inconsistencies. It should be noted also in this respect that there is a clear parallel between the book of Job and the Abraham traditions. It is just as perplexing to the reader of the book of Genesis why Abraham silently agreed when asked to sacrifice his son, especially when taking into consideration other situations where Abraham did not hesitate to complain or debate with God. "The astonishing thing about this divine command is Abraham's readiness to accept such a word without the slightest whisper of objection. Where is the bold protest against injustice that characterized Abraham in the episode about the destruction of

---

31. From M. Lichtheim, *Ancient Egyptian Literature* (Los Angeles: University of California Press, 1976) 2.159. These lines occur twice in *The Instruction of Amenemope*: XXII 5–7 and XXIII 8–10.

32. See L. G. Perdue (*Wisdom and Creation: A Theology of Wisdom Literature* [Nashville: Abingdon, 1994] 123–29) for a presentation of the way the book evolved, literary forms used, and ANE parallels. See H. L. Ginsberg ("Job the Patient and Job the Impatient," *Congress Volume: Rome, 1968* [VTSup 17; Leiden: Brill, 1969] 88–111) for a thorough source-critical discussion of the material.

Sodom and Gomorrah?"[33] We may add: where is the boldness to complain about the unfulfillment of God's promises that characterized Abraham in Genesis 15?

I suggest that what we have in Job, beginning in chapter 3, is another model of piety and that the sudden change from the one to the other is intentional and designed to be abrupt. It is no longer the ideal of silence and submission to divine sovereignty that is in focus but another: the ideal of challenge and rejection of divine rule when it is incomprehensible. Job and Abraham are both also portrayed as models for this form of piety. Here appears another model of piety: the man of integrity stands up to question traditional interpretations of God and his activity in the world. This can be done directly in dialogue with God, as with Abraham, or more indirectly, as in Job's case.

It is natural that there is a different tone in the examples of direct communication with God. Zuckerman argues that the writer of the Job poem consciously and forcefully rejected the ideal of the prologue, where Job passively accepts anything as God's will. According to Zuckerman, the passive Job was not the ideal figure of piety but the ultimate fool.[34] Even if we do not follow Zuckerman all the way in seeing a total clash between ideals of piety, he points toward a reasonable understanding of the break between the two representations of Job. The patient and the impatient Job represent two contrasting ideals of piety that consciously have been juxtaposed. It is reasonable to assume that they were positioned together in order to challenge the more traditional ideal, that of submission under divine rule. This does not mean that these ideals are mutually exclusive; rather, they are complementary, as seen in the Abraham traditions. The conclusion of the drama and Job's responses to God's speeches may be interpreted as a victory for the more traditional ideal.[35] The fact that God himself pronounces that Job has spoken of him what is right must, however, be regarded as favoring the ideal of challenge and nonacceptance. If, as seems probable, the Job story was

---

33. Crenshaw, *Whirlpool*, 20.

34. Zuckerman, *Job the Silent*, 47.

35. See Crenshaw's comments (*Urgent Advice and Probing Questions: Collected Writings on Old Testament Wisdom* [Macon, Ga.: Mercer University Press, 1995] 454) on Zuckerman. See Davis ("Job and Jacob," 218), who is anxious that Job's responses are not interpreted as acts of surrender and humiliation.

well known, the effect of turning the roles around must have been most forceful. If Job was known as the patient and submissive person to the very end, and if his comforters, like his wife, were known to have challenged him to give up his integrity, it was ingenious to turn the roles around and now make the comforters defenders of traditional piety while Job represents a more controversial stance of piety. In any case, in the present shape of the book the tension between the two ideals is not abolished and was never intended to be.

The tradition of challenge and nonacceptance of divine rule is a theme that can be traced elsewhere in the Old Testament. To a large extent, the book of Job can be seen as a lament. It shares with lament psalms the questioning of God's way of upholding justice in the world.[36] There are also other texts that can be considered to have the same theme: Jeremiah's "confessions," David's fervent prayer to save his child, Moses' protest when God has decided to blot out the people in the wilderness, Amos's prayer that God repent from severe judgment, Habakkuk's complaints, Psalm 73, and so on.

An interesting connection can be made between Job and Jacob, who struggled with the angel of the Lord and in the end received God's blessing and a new name. As already mentioned, there is a linguistic connection in the fact that Jacob and Job are the only people in the Old Testament who are called *tām*. Jacob is an example of a person who struggled all his life to achieve more than his predetermined course. The reader may have objections to the means he used to achieve his goals, but the texts make it clear that Jacob, supported by the women around him, was strongly determined and successful in becoming something more than his brother. Barthes reads the Jabbok story as a narrative of blackmail, where God's blow on the hip was the distinguishing mark that Jacob received as a privilege from the battle.[37] I prefer to call the Jabbok story a narrative of testing, assuming that this enigmatic text as it now stands in some way refers to God's testing of Jacob for future missions. In Greimas's actantial grid, God was both the sender and the opponent to Jacob. He was the one who gave solemn promises to Jacob when he

---

36. See C. Westermann's discussion of the classification of the book of Job: *Der Aufbau des Buches Hiob* (2d ed.; BHT 23; Tübingen: Mohr, 1977) 12.

37. Barthes, *Image, Music, Text*, 133–35.

left the land and later told him to return, assuring him of his protection. At the ford of the Jabbok, the roles were suddenly reversed in a typical manner. There God detained Jacob close to the entrance into the land and just before the dreaded meeting with his brother. Jacob was expecting a fight with Esau but instead met God as an opponent. It seems reasonable to assume that the reason for the struggle, here described as physical in contrast to our other texts, was to see whether Jacob was worthy or, perhaps better, determined enough to receive the blessing and become the ancestor of the chosen people. Interpreted in this way, there is a relationship between this text, where Jacob struggles with God, and the texts about Abraham's and Job's struggles with an oppressive deity. Their struggle with God was of another kind but also eventually led to God's pronouncement of them as persons of integrity and faith.

Jacob's struggle with God led to a new destiny for him. In the first encounter with God, where God transferred to Jacob the promises to his fathers, Jacob responded by swearing a conditional pledge of allegiance to the God of his fathers. If the Lord would protect and lead him back to his father's house in peace, then the Lord would be his God, to whom he would give tithes. The Jabbok incident can be seen as the close of this episode. Jacob had tested God, and God had protected and blessed him. Now it is God who tests Jacob, and this test leads to a new experience of God. Jacob's words "I have seen God face to face, and yet my life is preserved" are similar to Job's words "I had heard of thee by the hearing of the ear, but now my eye sees thee. . . ."[38] Before the majesty of the elusive and inexplicable God, the man who has struggled with God bows down and accepts his limitations. Jacob's and Job's experiences led them to a deeper experience of God. In their struggles with the deity they are upheld as models for pious people of all ages who struggle with the questions of theodicy and human suffering.

---

38. Davis ("Job and Jacob," 218) suggests the translation "therefore I recant and reconsider about dust and ashes" for the second part of the verse to emphasize that what is referred to is a change of attitude on Job's part, not submission. Faced with the non-anthropocentric world view of the God-speeches, Job understands that he can do nothing but accept the world as it is. Davis says about Job: "With humility and dignity, he attests to his new understanding of the human condition, as befits one whom God has honored with a vision." Davis's interpretation of "dust and ashes" is that the expression refers to the human condition as contrasted with God's majesty.

Conclusion

We may now venture several conclusions, based on our discussion of different ideals of piety represented by stories about individual characters in patriarchal settings. We have suggested that the sudden change in the book of Job between the patient Job in the first two chapters and the impatient Job in the following debate to a large extent can be explained as the conscious juxtaposition of two different ideals of piety in Israelite religion: the ideal of silence and submission versus the ideal of challenge and nonacceptance of divine rule.

These two ideals conflict to a certain extent but need not be regarded as mutually exclusive. The very fact that these two ideals are exemplified in the life experiences of the same individuals—Job and Abraham—indicates that they are not contradictory. Job and Abraham are portrayed as models both for silent submission and nonsubmission in relation to God. Silence and submission seem to have been the traditional and more accepted ideal of piety that was challenged by the ideal of nonacceptance and revolt, which was more controversial.

There is an interesting difference between the two ideals. The texts that emphasize the ideal of silent submission tend to portray the person and the situation from "the outside." The suffering person is tested for the sake of others, to prove to God and to other people the quality of his faith and his allegiance to God. The reader feels like the unwilling spectator at a brutal tournament. He can only watch and hope for the victory of the hero and be encouraged by his example. The texts that describe the nonacceptance and revolt of pious people have their focus much more on "the inside" of the people involved. In this case, the reader is supposed to identify with the struggling person, which is what leads him to new insights and a deeper understanding of God and of his own existence.

Deus absconditus *and* Deus revelatus

Three Difficult Narratives in the Pentateuch

OTTO KAISER

Philipps University, Marburg an der Lahn

I

Our entire human experience militates against understanding God only as the beneficent, revealed God devoted to human beings in his salvific will. If indeed he is the Lord of all reality, then his nature also includes unpredictability, inaccessibility, and hiddenness, for everything that lives also suffers. Only an understanding that conceives his revealed nature together with this hidden quality preserves his comprehensive divinity. If we conceive him only as a loving and translucent God, we are then unavoidably seized by doubt in the face of innocent suffering; he appears either incapable of implementing his goodness on earth or disinterested in our welfare or suffering in the first place. One must either posit next to him an equally powerful countergod or must bid farewell to the God of the Bible in favor of the God of metaphysics. As long as we conceive God only as the origin, primal ground, and core of world and existence, he is not responsible for what happens in our concrete world. It is not he who is the Lord of our fate but the indissoluble nexus between causally determined natural occurrences and our own, in this case largely powerless, actions. If our faith is not to run aground on the

Author's note: This paper originated as a lecture given on March 15 and on June 4, 1996, at the invitation of the Catholic Theological Faculty of the Karl-Franzens University in Graz and the Protestant Theological Faculty of the University of Bern, respectively. It was translated into English by Doug Stott. I would also like to thank Martin Neher, Ingersheim, for his help in proofreading.

An earlier version of this paper was published in *Syrisches Christentum Weltweit* (W. Hage festschrift; ed. M. Tamcke et al.; Studien zur orientalischen Kirchengeschichte 1; Münster: LIT, 1995). I thank the representative of LIT Verlag for his kind permission to publish this altered version.

reef of concrete reality, there must be some mediation between the actions of the revealed God and those of the hidden God, between those of the *deus absconditus* and those of the *deus revelatus*. The traditional speculative solution to this problem by way of universal theodicy—that is, by way of some justification of God in the face of the evil of our world—transcends the limits of human reason. Being finite, human beings have no vantage point beyond the world of experience, certainly none from which they might, as it were, peek over God's shoulder. Accordingly, the mediation in question can be only practical rather than theoretical.

Rather than interrogating Holy Scripture at large in search of such guidance, let us focus today on the three admittedly most difficult texts in the Pentateuch: namely, Isaac's sacrifice or binding (Gen 22:1–19*), Jacob's struggle at the Jabbok (Gen 32:23–33), and Yahweh's nocturnal attack on Moses (Exod 4:24–26). In their present forms, all three derive from the postexilic period, and all three occupy prominent positions within the stories of the patriarchs and of Moses. In each story, after God has proved true to his promises or has called the person, pursuant to those promises, to be the instrument of his people's liberation, he then threatens to destroy the very meaning of the person's life. The stories are thus not concerned merely with the chosen persons' weal or woe; also at stake is the fulfillment of the promises made to them and thus the very existence of Israel itself. Our own, modern perception finds that the first issue is the most terrifying, the second the most fantastic, and the third the most obscure.

II

Contrary to widespread opinion, the first of the three biblical stories—that of Isaac's sacrifice in Gen 22:1–19*—contains hardly any genuinely older core of tradition;[1] in its present, concentrated conciseness, it is a masterfully composed theological narrative.[2] Its demand that Abraham present his only son as a burnt offering is concerned with test-

---

1. However, see for example, R. Kilian, "Isaaks Opferung: Zur Überlieferungsgeschichte von Gen 22," *Stuttgarter Bibelstudien* 44 (1970) 68–88.

2. See in this regard the more extensive examination in my "Isaaks Opferung: Eine biblische Besinnung über einen schwierigen Text," *Homiletisch-Liturgisches Korrespondenzblatt* n.s. 10 (1992–93) 428–41.

ing Abraham's fear of God, a fear whose unconditionality our own contemporary sensibility finds difficult to comprehend.[3] Although the story
is rounded off in the fashion characteristic of the so-called Elohist,[4] Yahweh's angel's second discourse (vv. 15–18, whether secondary or original)[5] represents an explicit connection with the theme of promise. It
commences in Gen 12:1–3 and provides the theological context for the
patriarchal narratives up to Exod 3:15 (compare 6:1–2). Hence, in its
final form, the story of Isaac's sacrifice contains a double message. As a
self-contained narrative, it addresses the theme of temptation and trial
with regard to the fear of God.[6] The God who makes the most extreme
demands puts Abraham to the test. If he passes it by granting God the
right to demand precisely that which gives his own life meaning and
content, God will return it to him. The element of terror attaching to
the concrete story recedes in this reduction to the structure of the action, and the intention of this story then differs hardly at all from the
narrative of Job's trials as found in Job 1:1–5, 13–22*; 42:11–17*.[7]

---

3. See in this regard also T. Veijola, "Das Opfer Abrahams: Paradigma des Glaubens
aus dem nachexilischen Zeitalter," *ZTK* 85 (1988) 129–64, esp. 138ff.; concerning the
religiohistorical background, see my "Isaaks Opferung," 434ff.; also idem, "Den Erst-
geborenen deiner Söhne sollst du mir geben: Erwägungen zum Kinderopfer im Alten
Testament," in *Denkender Glaube: Festschrift C. H. Ratschow* (ed. O. Kaiser; Berlin and
New York, 1976) 24–48 = idem, *Von der Gegenwartsbedeutung des Alten Testaments* (ed.
V. Fritz, K.-F. Pohlmann, and H.-C. Schmitt; Göttingen: Vandenhoeck & Ruprecht,
1984) 142–66; and further, idem, "Salammbo, Moloch und das Tophet: Erwägungen
zum Kinderopfer der Karthager," *Die Karawane* 19 (1978 1/2) 3–22, 130–33; concerning the problem of interpreting the Old Testament word *mōlek*, one should now certainly see J. Day, *Molech: A God of Human Sacrifice in the Old Testament* (UCOP 41;
Cambridge: Cambridge University Press, 1989).
    4. Concerning the problem of the Elohistic historical work, see my *Grundriss der
Einleitung in die kanonischen und deuterokanonischen Schriften des Alten Testaments I* (Gütersloh: Mohn, 1992) 70–77.
    5. Cf. also C. Westermann, *Genesis 12–36* (Minneapolis: Augsburg, 1985) 363.
    6. Concerning the role of the fear of God in the Elohistic narratives, including Gen
22:12, see J. Becker, *Gottesfurcht im Alten Testament* (AnBib 25; Rome: Pontifical Biblical
Institute, 1965) 193ff. Concerning the relationship between this story and the wisdom
tradition, see H.-C. Schmitt, "Die Erzählung von der Versuchung Abrahams in Gen
22,1–19* und das Problem einer Theologie der elohistischen Pentateuchtexte," *BN* 34
(1986) 82ff.
    7. See in this regard A. Alt, "Zur Vorgeschichte des Buches Hiob," *ZAW* 55 (1937)
265–68; L. Schmidt, *De Deo: Studien zur Literarkritik und Theologie des Buches Jona, des*

Reading the story as a continuation of the (again, Elohistic) narrative in Gen 21:8–21[8] initially confirms God's demonic features. Here he persuades Abraham to give in to Sarah, who is jealously watching over Isaac's rights, and to expel the son Hagar has borne him; Isaac is to become the progenitor of the chosen people (v. 12). But the same God who tells Abraham to expel Hagar and her son now also demands that he sacrifice his only remaining, beloved son Isaac. All of God's promises and instructions now appear to be the deceptive words of a demon who plies his gruesome game with the human desire for happiness. The narrator explicitly draws attention to the connection between the two stories by incorporating the departure formula ("So Abraham rose early in the morning") of 21:14aα into 22:3aα.[9] Because God demands it of him, the patriarch who sent away the half-legitimate son now prepares to depart with his only remaining, fully legitimate son as well. Against this background, the connection between the beginning of the narrative in v. 1a and the response Abraham gives in v. 7 to his son's perplexed question regarding the sacrificial animal acquires meaning. From the very beginning, the narrator leaves no doubt that God's nocturnal command to Abraham to sacrifice his only son to him is a temptation, a test of obedience. Hence, from the very outset, the demand itself is destined to be retracted. The God who abhors the offering for the ruler of the underworld, the king of terrors (Job 18:14, Lev 18:21, Deut 18:9–13), is not interested in having a youth sacrificed on his own altar. Neither then is Abraham's response to Isaac's question regarding the sacrificial animal to be understood as a considerate veiling of his gruesome intentions; it is the expression of his trust in God's reliability: "God himself will provide the lamb for a burnt offering, my son." Abraham's willing-

---

Gesprächs zwischen Abraham und Jahwe in Gen 18,22ff. und von Hi 1 (BZAW 143; Berlin: de Gruyter, 1976) 165–88; also my *Introduction to the Old Testament* (Minneapolis: Augsburg, 1975) 296–306; and idem, *Grundriss der Einleitung in die kanonischen und deuterokanonischen Schriften des Alten Testaments III* (Gütersloh: Mohn, 1994) 78–84; M. Witte, *Vom Leiden zur Lehre: Der dritte Redegang (Hiob 21–27) und die Redaktionsgeschichte des Hiobbuches* (BZAW 230; Berlin: Walter de Gruyter, 1994) 192.

8. Concerning the original position of 21:22ff. behind 20:17, see E. Blum, *Die Komposition der Vätergeschichte* (WMANT 57; Neukirchen-Vluyn: Neukirchener Verlag, 1984) 411–19.

9. See in this regard also I. Fischer, *Die Erzeltern Israels: Feministisch-theologische Studien zu Genesis 12–36* (BZAW 222; Berlin: de Gruyter, 1994) 311.

ness to offer his own son to God, the son who is the very meaning of his life, rests on his basic trust in God's intention of honoring his promise despite everything.

In the story of Isaac's sacrifice, the patriarch is thus portrayed as the prototype and model of the righteous believer[10] whose loyal obedience to God's instructions does not waver even amid the darkness of exile imposed by God. In the basic narrative, the mediation between the dark God on the one hand, whose demands threaten to destroy the very meaning of life, and the revealed God of the promise on the other, is provided by the notion of standing the test through obedience against the background of a fear of God that is simultaneously the highest trust in God. In the final form of the narrative, Abraham's obedience becomes the paradigm for Israel in its exilic suffering. If Israel keeps the revealed commandments of its God, it can trust that the promise originally given to the patriarch will indeed be kept.

III

Although the setting of Jacob's struggle at the Jabbok in Gen 32:23–33* is even more archaic, its imbalance and lack of plasticity betray its origin as a consciously constructed theological narrative. In the darkness of night, a 'man' (*'îš*) falls upon and wrestles until daybreak with precisely the person whom Yahweh had promised to bring safely back home after his flight (Gen 28:13–15) and to whom he had renewed this assurance of protection upon commanding him to return home (Gen 31:3). The patriarch fights so valiantly that this *man* is able to keep him at bay only by means of a wrestler's trick[11] and even then must ask Jacob to release him as day breaks, thereby betraying his own identity as a night spirit. Jacob, however, seizes the opportunity and demands a blessing in return, which he does indeed receive. Beforehand, however, the unearthly spirit gives him the name "Israel," because he has striven with God and with humans and has prevailed. The same Jacob who previously had deceived Esau and Laban of the promise or payment due him has now proven himself in nocturnal struggle with an unearthly

---

10. Documentation in my "Isaaks Opferung," 432-33.
11. H. Gunkel, *Genesis* (Macon, Ga.: Mercer University Press, 1997) ad loc.

spirit and in the process has acquired both a divine blessing and the honorific name Israel.

This redactional text, created specifically with its present location in
mind, nonetheless clearly betrays an older local legend as its basis, one
telling of the nocturnal attack of a river demon at the Jabbok.[12] This in
its own turn seems to have been prompted by the name itself, which
means essentially 'river of wrestling'.[13] The redactor did find the material problematic enough, however, that he refrained from actually identifying the *man* with Yahweh. Only the bestowal of the name Israel to
the patriarch along with its subsequent explanation ("for you have
striven with God and with humans")[14] enables the recipient of the story
to conclude that this night spirit is in fact a representative of God (v. 29)
and thus of Yahweh. The narrative reverently refrains from mentioning
his name, since it is only as his representative that the *man* can bestow
upon the patriarch—and thus also upon his descendants—the honorific

---

12. Scholars almost unanimously agree that its basic form is found in vv. 23aαb,
25b–26a, 27, 30b (+ 32a); cf. P. Weimar (who adds 32a), "Beobachtungen zur Analyse
von Gen 32,23–33," *BN* 49 (1989) 53–80, esp. 79; C. Levin, *Der Jahwist* (FRLANT
157; Göttingen: Vandenhoeck & Ruprecht, 1993) 250–54, esp. 251. Levin has correctly observed that v. 23aα picks up 32:14a anew and that the person responsible for
committing the story to writing (in his view, the Yahwist, to be understood in this case
as redactor) expanded the legend by the addition of vv. 28–30a. Peculiarly, however,
neither author is troubled by the fact that v. 23b reports the crossing of the ford in the
narrative. In eliminating v. 23aαb, both are forced to assign the additions in vv. 23*, 24,
and 25a to several different hands, though the reasons adduced do not seem particularly
persuasive. Things become simpler if one assumes that v. 23 was originally the continuation of v. 14a and that the expression "the same night" in v. 23aα has replaced an original *babbōqer*; v. 24 and v. 25a then come from the hand of the narrator himself as a
transition to the story he has inserted. At the end of the narrative, v. 31 was probably
added first, with its etiology for the paronomastically interpreted name Penuel (Peniel),
and then, with the insertion of v. 26b into vv. 32–33 or, if one does not ascribe v. 32a
to the narrator, then into vv. 32b and 33, the etiology for the taboo regarding the *nervus
ischiaticus* (?) was added.

13. See A. Dillmann, *Die Genesis* (5th ed.; KEHAT; Leipzig, 1886) 357; and then
J. W. Colenso, *The Pentateuch and the Book of Joshua Critically Examined* (London: Longman, Green, Longman, Roberts, & Green, 1863–70) 5/2.174, cited by Levin, *Der Jahwist*, 251.

14. Concerning the interpretation of the name, see H.-J. Zobel, "*yiśrāʾēl*," *TDOT*
6.399–400; or the concise information in H. D. Preuss, *Old Testament Theology* (2 vols.;
Louisville: Westminster/John Knox, 1995–96) 1.52–54.

name Israel and then bless both the patriarch and, in him, the people of Israel itself.[15]

The narrative has been accommodated to the piety of postexilic Judaism both through the prepositioning of the prayer in 32:10–13, as well as by the addendum in 32:31–33a, and yet both it and the following narrative of Yahweh's nocturnal attack on Moses stand like erratic blocks in the biblical landscape. Its incorporation can be explained only against the background of the increasing diastasis between God and world and the attendant growth of the belief in mediating figures who, though positioned below God, nonetheless yet stand above human beings. Thus the person responsible for incorporating this material into the Jacob narrative presented the *man* who falls upon Jacob at night as a representative of Yahweh on earth.[16]

Contemporary readers will benefit from a few remarks concerning the conceptual presuppositions underlying this narrative. The pre-Yahwist *Vorlage* apparently shared the ancient belief that a river is not merely a physical phenomenon but an entity animated by a divine or demonic being. One could not, for example, cross it without that being's consent or without at least frightening it away. To this end, one either brought offerings, employed *omina*, or tried to bridle it by means of apotropaic gestures.[17] We need only recall that after receiving an unfavorable omen, the Spartan king Cleomenes did not risk crossing the River Erasinus near Argos; instead, after sacrificing a bull at the nearby shore he set sail with his army and fell upon the city of Tiryns from the rear (Herodotus *Hist.* 6.76). No less impressive is Herodotus's report (*Hist.* 7.34–35) of Xerxes' hubris. After the first bridge (of ships) he has built across the Hellespont is destroyed by a storm, Xerxes has the sea

---

15. Cf. Levin, *Der Jahwist*, 250–51. The prayer inserted into 32:10–13 by a later hand confirms this conclusion. That this does not belong to the basic Yahwistic thread has been shown, for example, by Gunkel, *Genesis*, ad loc.; and, in continuation, also by Westermann, *Genesis 12–36*, 508. The same is suggested by the subsequently added etiology of the place name Penuel in 32:31–33a, in which Jacob himself explains the name: he has seen God face to face and yet has survived.

16. Cf. in this regard also Levin, *Der Jahwist*, 251.

17. See, for example, Ovid *Metam.* 9.1–96; and additional examples in T. H. Gaster, *Myth, Legend, and Custom in the Old Testament: A Comparative Study with Chapters from Sir James G. Frazer's Folklore in the Old Testament* (New York: Harper & Row, 1969) 205–12.

itself scourged with three hundred lashes, sinks a pair of fetters into it, and refuses to offer it any sacrifices.[18] A direct parallel to the biblical story is the myth of the struggle between the river-god Achelous and Heracles. Achelous challenges Heracles to a wrestling match for possession of Deianira. When Heracles subdues the god, it turns itself first into a serpent, then into a bull, and finally gives up the battle altogether, Heracles proving to be the stronger in every instance (Ovid *Metam.* 9.1–96). This fight, too, takes place at night. When the rays of the morning sun begin to shine upon the mountain top, the two combatants separate, and Achelous disappears beneath the waves.[19]

To identify with this story, the contemporary reader must imagine the patriarch's apprehension as he anticipates meeting the brother he once betrayed, and now, standing in the deep-cut river's ice-cold waters in the darkness of night, he sees on the other side the steep path leading upward. Viewed thus, Jacob's struggle at the Jabbok is the story of one's struggle with the primal fear of darkness and death, a struggle no human being is spared. Whoever passes this test by confronting the fear prompted by one's own mortality—that is, by accepting one's own finitude—overcomes that fear and goes away blessed with a liberating sense of personal stability. Confronted by the dangers of the night, the hitherto successful person is seized by a fear not entirely lacking an awareness of one's own guilt and its possible consequences. Victory can be won only by confronting the situation, acknowledging behind it the machinations of the obscure, angry God, and by not letting go until that God bestows his blessing. Stripped of its mythical covering, however, the struggle ultimately is not with some nocturnal waters but within human beings themselves, who must struggle with their own fears and

---

18. "Thou bitter water, our master thus punishes thee, because thou didst him wrong albeit he had done thee none. Yea, Xerxes the king will pass over thee, whether thou wilt or no; it is but just that no man offers thee sacrifice, for thou art a turbid and a briny river" (Herodotus, *Histories* [trans. A. D. Godley; LCL; Cambridge: Harvard University Press, 1922] 349).

19. J. B. Bauer ("Jakobs Kampf mit dem Dämon [Gen 32,23–33]," in *Die Väter Israels: Beiträge zur Theologie der Patriarchenüberlieferung im Alten Testament—Festschrift J. Scharbert* [ed. M. Görg; Stuttgart: Katholisches Bibelwerk, 1989] 17–22) adduces a parallel in the *Ephesiaca, or Anthia and Habrocomes,* from Xenophon Ephesius, in which a spirit of the dead carries out the assault, as well as analogous features in patristic literature.

anxieties. Deliverance is found only in the prayer to the God who, we must realize, afflicts us in our own fears.

The context makes it clear that prayer in fact does not protect a person from such an encounter with the dark God. In the final text, the demon representing Yahweh does indeed fall upon Jacob even though the latter had just prayed to Yahweh for deliverance from his brother and had reminded Yahweh of his promise and assurance of protection (v. 12). Let us also recall the addendum in v. 32. When Jacob passes by Penuel, he limps; whoever has encountered God will remain marked by him, even after having won the struggle with fear in prayer. Prayer itself thus mediates between the *deus absconditus* and the *deus revelatus*, between the God who delivers human beings over to their own fears and anxieties and the God who nonetheless promises his presence as the foundation of the basic trust from which they live (compare Gen 28:15, 31:3, and 32:10). The violent extortion in v. 27 in the basic narrative, "I will not let you go, unless you bless me," uttered in the shadow of the previous confession in v. 11a, "I am not worthy of the least of all the steadfast love and all the faithfulness that you have shown to your servant," ultimately comes to express the struggle for certainty regarding God's sustaining, sheltering presence.

IV

The third and final narrative we will examine, Exod 4:24–26, is a text of an apparent archaic savageness.[20] Before we examine it, however, we should consider that the God who tolerates no other gods beside himself, in truth, also allows no demons.[21] Accordingly, he is by nature not only the God of salvation but also the God of disaster (Isa 45:7). Unlike in Gen 32:23–33, in Exod 4:24–26 he behaves quite openly like a bloodthirsty vampire; the narrator does not introduce an angel or, as in Gen 32:25, an indefinite *someone* or *a man* as the assailant in Yahweh's stead.

---

20. The majority of section IV was translated by an editor.

21. See in this regard P. Volz, *Das Dämonische in Jahwe* (Tübingen: Mohr, 1924) 29ff.; also H. Duhm, *Die bösen Geister im Alten Testament* (Tübingen and Leipzig, 1904); for a broad view of ancient belief in malevolent spirits, see O. Böcher, *Dämonenfurcht und Dämonenabwehr: Ein Beitrag zur Vorgeschichte der Taufe* (BWANT 90; Stuttgart: Kohlhammer, 1970).

Viewed from the perspective of the history of traditions, the narrative does not stand on its own. It presupposes the directive of God to
Moses in 4:19 to return to Egypt to carry out the mission assigned to
him in Exodus 3. Clearly, 4:24–26 was written for this place in the text
and contains specific references to the context.[22] Christoph Levin even
speaks of this passage as a midrash. Regardless of whether this assessment
is correct, it remains to be proved that Moses entered his office without
himself having been circumcised.[23]

The passage reads,

> [24]And it came to pass on the way in a place where they spent the night
> that Yahweh met and sought to kill him. [25]Then Zipporah took a flint
> and cut off her son's foreskin and touched (it) to his feet and said: "Truly
> you are a bridegroom of blood to me." [26]Then he let him alone. At that
> time she said: "A bridegroom of blood as a result of circumcision."

One should not make this narrative more obscure than it is in and of itself.[24] It looks back past the later addition in vv. 21–23 to v. 20, which
reports that Moses departed toward Egypt with his wife and his son. It
follows, then, that he is the object of the divine attack in v. 24. Even so,
the question remains as to whose genitals (euphemistically called "feet")
Zipporah touched with her son's foreskin.[25] Those of the son himself
are out of the question, and no Israelite would be so presumptious and
disrespectful as to speak of the genitals of Yahweh. We may also leave
out the wife. The only option remaining is that Zipporah performed
this ritual on Moses. Furthermore, in view of the redactional character
of the text and its postexilic origin, it is useless to seek a ritual act based

---

22. Cf. B. P. Robinson, "Zipporah to the Rescue: A Contextual Study of Ex 4:24–
26," *VT* 36 (1986) 447–61, esp. 450–54.

23. Levin, *Der Jahwist*, 332. On the tertiary character of Exod 2:4, 7–10a see
p. 320. For a different opinion, see W. H. Schmidt (*Exodus, Sinai, und Mose* [Erträge der
Forschung 191; Darmstadt: Wissenschaftliche Buchgesellschaft, 1983] 121), who agrees
with H. Gressmann, H. Kosmala, H. Schmid, and others that the scene is at home in the
territory of the Midianites.

24. Cf. R. Blum and E. Blum, "Zippora und ihr *ḥtn dmym*," in *Die Hebräische Bibel
und ihre zweifache Nachgeschichte: Festschrift R. Rendtorff* (ed. R. Blum and E. Blum;
Neukirchen-Vluyn: Neukirchener Verlag, 1990) 41–54, esp. 42–43.

25. On the different possibilities, see W. H. Schmidt, *Exodus 1–6* (BKAT 2/1;
Neukirchen-Vluyn: Neukirchener Verlag, 1988) 220–26.

on a statue of Yahweh as the background because of the aniconic nature[26] of the official Yahweh cult and because the prohibition against
images had long been in effect.[27]

The inner logic of the narrative also presents difficulties. Apparently,
the manipulation of the genitals of the son causes Yahweh to leave Moses
alone. If one wishes to infer that God attacked Moses because he was
uncircumcised, it still remains unexplained why the son was circumcised
instead of the father. From the fact that he was circumcised, the opposite
would seem to follow: namely, that the uncircumcised condition of the
son or, if one prefers, "the unapproved family relationship" of Moses'
marriage to a non-Israelite provoked the wrath of Yahweh.[28]

The touching of the father's genitals with the foreskin of the son is
not, in my opinion, a West-Semitic rite, but there are ethnological parallels to consider. According to Paul Radin, a missionary named C. Streh-
low, who worked among the Australian Aranda (or Arunta) at the
beginning of the twentieth century, observed the circumcision rite
there. In the Aranda ceremony, the one performing a circumcision
pressed the foreskin of the boy against the stomach of his father and his
older brother. Supposedly, the pain the initiate suffered from the circumcision was softened by this act.[29] The question may be raised, however,
whether the explanation offered for this ritual is not a secondary ratio-
nalization, while the act originally symbolized taking the boy into the
community of relatives and men.

If we read the biblical episode from this perspective, its difficulty disappears. Apparently the blood rite brought about a new relationship between Zipporah and Moses. The phrase *ḥtn dmym*, with which she
signified this relationship, is usually translated 'bridegroom of blood', a

---

26. Cf. T. N. D. Mettinger, *No Graven Image? Israelite Aniconism in Its Near Eastern
Context*," (ConBOT 42; Stockholm: Almqvist & Wiksell, 1995) 135–97, esp. 191–97.

27. See also F.-L. Hossfeld, *Der Dekalog: Seine Späten Fassungen, die originale Kompo-
sition und seine Vorstufen* (OBO 45; Freiburg: Universitätsverlag / Göttingen: Vandenhoeck
& Ruprecht, 1982) 268–73; C. Dohmen, *Das Bilderverbot: Seine Entstehung und seine
Entwicklung im AT* (BBB 62; Frankfurt: Hain, 1987); W. H. Schmidt, H. Delkurt, and
A. Graupner, *Die Zehn Gebote im Rahmen alt. Ethik* (Erträge der Forschung 281; Darm-
stadt: Wissenschaftliche Buchgesellschaft, 1993) 59–77; and Otto Kaiser, *Der Gott des
Alten Testaments II* (Göttingen: Vandenhoeck & Ruprecht, 1998) §7.4–6.

28. So Blum and Blum, "Zippora und ihr *ḥtn dmym*," 45.

29. Paul Radin, *Primitive Religion: Its Nature and Origin* (New York: Dover, 1957) 87.

tradition that goes back to the LXX.[30] In Arabic the term *ḥitan* signifies 'circumcision' as well as 'father-in-law', 'son-in-law', and 'wedding'.[31] In the Old Testament as well, *ḥātān* can mean 'son-in-law' (see, for example, Isa 61:10, Jer 7:34, and Ps 19:6) and also those related through marriage (2 Kgs 8:27).[32] In all of these passages, one thing remains the same: the relationship is not biological but social. By contrast, however, Moses is said to have became a blood relative of Zipporah by the execution of rite. The classical translation 'bridegroom of blood' therefore is appropriate, though the translation 'marriage partner of blood'[33] might be clearer to us.

The assumption that the narrative is to be understood solely as an etiology for the formula 'bridegroom of blood'[34] appears to be unlikely, because in that case one would expect to read "it is said" instead of "she said."[35] Moreover, that assumption does not contribute to an understanding of the content of the narrative. The explanation offered by Julius Wellhausen was that the circumcision of the son was undertaken vicariously for that of the father (who actually would have undergone it at the latest before his marriage). In Wellhausen's scenario, the circumcision of the child is understood, then, as a milder equivalent for the circumcision of the man.[36] There is, however, a better way to understand the narrative than viewing the circumcision as a vicarious act. The view alluded to above, offered first by Ruth and Edward Blum, has much to commend it: the wrath of God was meant for the foreign wife and the uncircumcised son. Zipporah at once drew the necessary consequences and integrated herself and her son into the blood family of Israel by

---

30. Cf. E. Kutsch, "*ḥtn, ḥātān, ḥōtēn*," *TDOT* 5.276.

31. Cf. A. J. Wensinck, "Khitan, Circumcision," *Shorter Encyclopedia of Islam* (Leiden: Brill, 1953) 254a–255b.

32. Cf. Kutsch, "*ḥtn, ḥātān, ḥōtēn*," *TDOT* 5.270–77.

33. Ibid., esp. 5.277.

34. Cf. H. Schmid, "Mose, der Blutsbräutigen: Erwägungen zu Ex 4:24–26," *Judaica* 22 (1966) 113–18, esp. 114; Kutsch ("*ḥtn, ḥātān, ḥōtēn*," 5.276–77) agrees.

35. Blum and Blum ("Zippora und ihr *ḥtn dmym*, 50) point out that the narrative shows that the formula can be used otherwise.

36. Julius Wellhausen, *Prolegomena zur Geschichte Israels* (6th ed.; Berlin: Reimer, 1927) 338–39; cf. also idem, *Reste arabischen Heidentums* (Berlin: Reimer, [1887] 1963) 174–75.

means of the circumcision and touching. Her actions also led to the desired result, for Yahweh at once ceased his attack on Moses.

When one first seeks to grasp the whole course of the events, one will surmise that it is a fictive narrative. It does not assert that Moses fulfilled his own obligation[37] but that his wife and his son were integrated ritually into the blood community of Israel. The late narrator to whom we owe this episode probably possessed on the one hand the narrative of Jacob's battle at the Jabbok recorded in Gen 32:23–32 and on the other hand that of the divine Destroyer in Exod 12:23, who passed over the doors smeared with the blood of the Paschal lamb.[38] Admittedly, it is unusual that the narrator had Yahweh attack Moses and not his son, for according to Gen 17:14 any uncircumcised male was to be excluded from Israel.

When we look back on it, this history also speaks of the *Deus absconditus* as the *Deus iratus*, of the hidden God as the angry God. However, it follows immediately upon a narrative in which God's chosen one knew himself as Yahweh's messenger, sheltered in the protection of his Commander (Exod 3:12a). The reconciliation of the angry God followed by means of the execution of a rite of circumcision, by which the foreign wife secured membership for herself and her son in the blood community of Israel.

V

Our investigation has disclosed three types of mediation between the *deus revelatus*, as the revealed God who provides for the salvation and welfare of his people, and the *deus absconditus*, as the God who calls into question the entire meaning of life and spares not even the lives of his own chosen people. The progression of the narrative of Isaac's sacrifice, especially in its final, expanded form, shows that the *deus revelatus* conceals himself behind the *deus absconditus* in order to test the obedience of his chosen servant and then to reward him richly. This corresponds to the teaching that Ben Sira dispenses to his own pupil (Sir 2:1–6):

---

37. So Levin, *Der Jahwist*, 332.

38. These relationships have long been noticed; cf. Robinson, "Zipporah to the Rescue," 451–52.

My child, when you come to serve the Lord,
  prepare yourself for testing.
Set your heart right and be steadfast,
  and do not be impetuous in time of calamity.
Cling to him and do not depart,
  so that your last days may be prosperous.
Accept whatever befalls you,
  and in times of humiliation be patient.
For gold is tested in the fire,
  and those found acceptable, in the furnace of humiliation.

Trust in him, and he will help you;
  make your ways straight, and hope in him.

We hardly need to recall that this balance is not always settled in the way
the narrator and wisdom teacher imagine. Whoever finds in God a firm
foundation for life will indeed endure misfortune with considerably
more composure than someone who lives and hopes only from that
which this world offers. That person does not, however, have any guar-
antee that he or she will survive the sufferings and persecutions God im-
poses. Hence there is a need for certainty in the indestructibility of one's
relationship with God. The author of the Wisdom of Solomon has expressed this in words of consolation, encouraging those undergoing such
trials to remain loyal to their God; he has formulated this so expressively
that Christians, too, are drawn to them: "But the souls of the righteous
are in the hand of God, and no torment will ever touch them" (3:1).

The narrative of Jacob's struggle at the Jabbok teaches that one can
overcome the anxiety of death through struggle with God in prayer. If
by "prayer" we understand something more than merely a meditation
on finitude, we are presupposing that God is not just the neuter ground
of the world, but a person referring specifically to us.[39] This prompts a
further consideration that at the same time reinforces this presupposition. Even if we understand human beings, with their intellectual capacity for reason, within the boundaries of the pure natural sciences as an
autoepistemic system owing its origin to an immanent cosmic process,
we must nonetheless admit that the possibility of this autoepistemy, of

---

39. Regarding the necessity of speaking about God as a person, see F. Milden-
berger, *Biblische Dogmatik: Eine biblische Theologie in dogmatischer Perspektive II—Öko-
nomie als Theologie* (Stuttgart: Kohlhammer, 1992) 83–85.

self-understanding, is grounded in the presuppositions of human beings obtaining prior to the world itself.[40] Put biblically, this means that God himself is spirit and is the creator of the world antedating the world.

The narrative of Yahweh's nocturnal attack on Moses recalls the sanctified community into which the individual is accepted through a rite of sacramental inclusion. This rite, which includes the physical body, brings about a reconciliation with God transcending the intellect for those who through this rite interpret their own lives as members of the people of God.

For Christians, the initiatory rite of baptism has replaced circumcision, and the Eucharist the atoning sacrificial blood. In the purificatory bath of baptism, the baptized acknowledge the death of their sinful self-will and thus acknowledge their own finitude; in so doing, they become members of the people of God characterized by the hope in future life, life whose reality is secured by the Resurrected who appeared to the disciples, apostles, and brethren (1 Cor 15:1ff.).[41] Accepting their finitude frees them from the primal guilt rooted in hubris that prompts them to imagine they are their own god. Along the way, and in dark days, baptism reminds them that they have become members of a people of God enduring beyond time and the ages. In the Eucharist, however, they enter table fellowship with Christ pointing back to him who initiates and perfects faith and forward to the perfect communion with God. Consequently, this acceptance understands the life of Christians from the perspective of the ultimate communion with God that eradicates all sin and physically assures those who are subject to the tribulations of their own imperfections and to the godlessness of the world itself of their hope in eternal and blessed life.

Understood thus, these three narratives remind us that temptation and tribulation are part of faith and that behind all the suffering to which we, our fate, and our world are subject we must recognize the God who through this very suffering is instructing us in steadfastness and calling us to surrender ourselves in prayer to him as our God. *In these tribulations,*

---

40. See in this regard W. Hogrebe, *Prädikation und Genesis: Metaphysik als Fundamentalsheuristik im Ausgang von Schellings "Weltalter"* (Suhrkamp Taschenbuch Wissenschaft 772; Frankfurt am Main: Suhrkamp, 1989) 51ff.

41. See in this regard also my "Die Ersten und die Letzten Dinge," *Neue Zeitschrift für systematische Theologie* 36 (1994) 82ff., esp. 86ff.

however, God accompanies the Christian along the painful path of disfranchising the "self." It is precisely in this weakness that his strength acquires genuine power, and all attempts at theodicy represent final bastions of human and theological self-assertion along this path.[42] Within the parameters of our basic question this means that, just as every theodicy must fail, so also must every attempt at reconciling conceptually the *deus absconditus* with the *deus revelatus*. Mediation between the two leaves room for the kind of trust from which faith itself lives. It points to God's promise, in which faith can find its moorings; to prayer, in which he reveals himself as our God; and to the sacrament, as the sign that communion with him is reconciliation and that what we now hope will someday become full reality.

---

42. C. H. Ratschow, *Der angefochtene Glaube: Anfangs- und Grundprobleme der Dogmatik* (2d ed.; Gütersloh: Mohn, 1960) 291.

"You Cannot See My Face"
Seeking to Understand Divine Justice

LOU H. SILBERMAN

Vanderbilt University / University of Arizona

Reading the daily newspaper, listening to a radio news report, watching a television screen cannot but raise ever and again for anyone who shares in the religious traditions of Western culture the unsettling question of divine justice. Even those who, like Job's friends, know theoretically that an individual's suffering is a direct consequence of sin cannot but pause at the sight of the limp body of a child lying on the roadside somewhere in one of the many strife-torn lands of our world and wonder: "why?" How often has one heard a distraught person cry out in uncomprehending anguish: "why me?" "why us?" Poets and philosophers, theologians and plain folk wonder if it is possible to hold on to justice and to God, and how. Where and when does the question manifest itself? Where and when are answers sought for, and how are they found? The book of Job is a compelling struggle with the question.[1] Time and time again the prophetic texts of the Hebrew Scriptures wrestle with it. But whatever answers they proffer, they do not bring the query to an end. Human experience stumbles on it in many guises and in unexpected places.

On occasion a text that appears to us to have nothing to do with this problem suddenly becomes its focus. Such is the dialogue between Moses and the Lord in Exod 33:12–23. Moses asks first to know God's ways and then seeks the assurance that He will remain with the people

---

Author's note: For Jimmie Crenshaw, my student, colleague and friend.

1. See my "Questing for Justice:Reflections on Deuteronomy and Job," in *Founders Day Addresses, 1986* (Cincinnati: Hebrew Union College–Jewish Institute of Religion, 1986); and idem, "The Question of Job's Generation—*She'elat Doro Shel 'Iyob'*: Buber's Job," in *Judaic Perspectives on Ancient Israel* (Philadelphia: Fortress, 1987) 261–69.

on their journeys. Having received a favorable response, Moses asks: "Oh, let me see your face!" God replies: "I will make all my goodness pass before you, and I will proclaim before you the name Lord, and I will be gracious to whom I will be gracious and show compassion to whom I will show compassion." Then God continues: "you cannot see *pny* ('My face'), for man may not see Me and live." Finally, Moses is told to station himself in a cleft of the rock; the *kbwd* would pass by; Moses will be shielded and will be permitted to see *ʾḥry* ('My back') but not *pny* ('My face').

What is Moses asking to see? The divine *kbwd*. The RSV and NEB traditionally rendered it 'glory', while the NJPSV translates it 'Presence'.[2] It is here that the question with which we began quite unexpectedly appears in a series of interpretations of the passage found in various compilations of the *Yelammedenu* tradition.[3] I have taken *Exodus Rabbah* 2 (chaps. 12–40) as the basic text in this discussion because it is more extensive than either *Tanḥuma* (the common edition) or the *Tanḥuma* edition edited by Solomon Buber. In addition, I have used material found in *Yalquṭ Shimoni*. The discussion with which we are concerned begins:

> Another interpretation: [Ex. 33:18] He [Moses] said, "Oh, let me see Your *kbwd*. He was desirous of understanding [the nature of] the reward of the righteous and the well-being of the wicked.[4] Whence [is it known] that the reward of the righteous is designated *kbwd*? It is said (Prov. 3:35): "Wise men inherit *kbwd*." It is also said [Isa. 24:23]: "And the *kbwd* will be revealed to the elders." Whence [is it known] that the

---

2. To this, see KB 2.436: "etym. Macht, Autorität u. Ehre Gottes, anderseits oft mit Lichterscheinungen verbunden."

3. J. Mann, *The Bible as Read and Preached in the Old Synagogue* (Cincinnati, 1940). To this see J. Heinemann, "The Triennial Lectionary Cycle," *JJS* 19 (1968) 48: "[W]e must assume the *Yelammedenu* homilies . . . to be eclectic combinations of (parts) of earlier sermons preached in the Synagogue . . . [they] must be the work of earlier compilers who started from older, heterogeneous material."

4. In *Yalquṭ Shimoni Ki Tissa* (395) this is followed by a paraphrase of a citation from *b. Ber.* 7a: "*pny* (My face) will go before you and I will give you rest (Exod 37:14). Said R. Johanan in the name of R. Jose: Why is it written, 'My face will go before you and I will give you rest?' The Holy One blessed be, said to Moses, 'Wait with Me until My wrathful face shall have passed away, then I will give you rest.' From this one learns that one ought not try to placate a fellow at the time of anger." See below for more of the citation from this passage.

well-being of the wicked is designated *kbwd*? It says (Ps. 73:24): *w'ḥr kbwd tqḥny.*[5]

How is this concluding verse to be understood so as to indicate how *kbwd* refers to the well-being of the wicked? The NJPSV offers two translations, one in the text and one in the notes: 'and led me toward honor' or (noting that the meaning of the Hebrew is uncertain) 'and afterwards received me with glory'. The NEB translates similarly to NJPSV; RSV notes: 'to glory, or honor'. None of these suggests in any fashion how *kbwd* refers to the well-being of the wicked. What then is to be done? R. Samuel Strashun (19th century) in his novellae to *Exodus Rabbah* refers to Rashi's comment on the verse in which two interpretations are offered. The first, rejected by Rashi, provides the basis for understanding the verse as referring to the well-being of the wicked.

However, in order to understand the comment, one must first attend to the Psalm as a whole. Verses 2–12 deal with the well-being of the wicked. Indeed, v. 3 says: "I saw the wicked at ease." Rashi in his comment on v. 8 names Pharaoh, Sennacherib, and Nebuchadnezzar as the wicked, and v. 20 is understood to refer to Isa 37:35, the smiting of Assyria before the walls of Jerusalem. With all of this in mind, Rashi interprets Ps 73:24 in two ways. If the accent stress is on *kbwd*, then the phrase means: after Sennacherib has received all the *kbwd* (that is, the well-being that God has allotted to him), then God will perform amazing wonders for Israel and will destroy Sennacherib. In this case, *kbwd* is taken to refer to the well-being of the wicked. Rashi rejects this interpretation. The accent stress is on *'ḥr* so that the phrase means, similar to the translations cited above: 'You will bring me to honor; You will draw me after you to glory and honor'.[6] The Midrash, however, requires the first interpretation. It continues: "What was God's reply? He said: 'you cannot see *pny.*' This refers to the well-being of the wicked as it is said (Deut. 7:10) *wmšlm lšn'yw 'l-pnyw.*"

Again we are faced with the problem of understanding a verse (Deut 7:10) as the Midrash does. The NJPSV translates it: 'who instantly [the translation of *'l pnyw*] requites . . . those who hate Him . . .'. The NEB

---

5. *Exod. Rab.* 45. In *Tanḥuma* and *Tanḥuma* B this is the interpretation of v. 20, "You cannot see *pny.*" They do not offer an interpretation of *kbwd*.

6. The first interpretation is not found elsewhere.

translates: 'those who defy him and show their hatred to him he repays
. . .'. The RSV translates: 'and requites to their face those who hate
him'.[7] The means of understanding the verse is found in *ʾAbot de Rabbi
Nathan*. There, chapter 25 comments on Exod 33:23, which reads,
"And I will take away My hand, and thou shalt see My back [*ʾḥwry*] but
My face [*pny*] shall not be seen." It says: "*Face* refers to this world. *Back*
refers to the world to come." Thus the verse in Deuteronomy may be
understood: I will *reward* (a meaning of the verb *slm*) those who hate me
[*ʾl pny*] in this world. The phrase "My face shall not be seen" means that
what happens in this world (namely, divine indulgence of the wicked)
cannot be understood. This is the divine reply to Moses' request to see
the divine *pny = kbwd*. *ʾAbot de Rabbi Nathan* offers a second interpretation that parallels it. "*Face* refers to the suffering of the righteous in this
world and the tranquility of the wicked in this world. *Back* refers to the
rewarding of the righteous in the age to come and the punishment of
the wicked in Gehenna." However, it does not cite the verse from Deuteronomy to make its point; nor does it explicitly draw the conclusion
that the reason for this cannot be understood.

It is now possible to return to the Midrash to the clause in v. 23: "I
shall remove My hand and you shall see My back." The word "My
back" is interpreted to refer, as in *ʾAbot de Rabbi Nathan*, to the reward
of the righteous in the future. *Tanḥuma* (*Ki Tissa* 27) reads at this point:
"I will not explain to you the recompense in this world of those who
revere My name, but as for the world-to-come 'they have not heard,
not brought to ear, the eye has not seen, only You, O God' (Is. 64:3).
He will act on behalf of those who trust Him." This interpretation reflects the statement in *ʾAbot de Rabbi Nathan* that "face" refers to this
world, while "back" refers to the future.[8] R. David Luria (19th century) wrote something similar in his novellae to the passage in *Exodus*

---

7. Only the RSV preserves 'face', which is crucial to understanding the midrash's
use of the verse. Although the midrash cites the concluding word, *lhʾbydw* 'to destroy
him', it is not appropriate to the interpretation and must be ignored.

8. The reading in *Yalquṭ Shimoni* is *ʾny*—that is, 'I will explain'. *Tanḥuma* B reads
ʾyny 'I will not', but Buber emends it to *ʾny*. *Yalquṭ* also has a footnote indicating that the
"wicked" should be read in place of "fearers." These emendations fail to recognize the
interplay of ideas, or they represent discomfort with them. The phrase is lacking in *Exodus Rabbah*.

Rabbah: " 'You cannot see My face' refers to the well-being of the wicked in this world. Moses is told that he cannot understand it. Similarly, with regard to the suffering of the righteous in this world He says to him, I will show you the giving of reward to the righteous in the future but the reason for their suffering in this world He did not reveal."

Now the Midrash recalls v. 19: "I will cause all my goodness to pass before you," and the phrase "all My goodness" is interpreted to refer to the meting out of the reward and punishment. *Tanḥuma* enlarges on the interpretation, dividing the phrase into "My goodness" and "all My goodness" to indicate how both reward and punishment are included. Finally the remainder of the verse, "I will be gracious to whom I will be gracious," is interpreted. Moses is shown the treasuries in which the rewards of the righteous are stored, and at the end there is a large one. "For whom is it?" he asks. The reply is more radical than the declaration that the well-being of the wicked in this world is beyond human understanding: "For those who are deserving I have provided their reward; for those who have nothing, I will provide freely, giving them from this one. I will be gracious to whomever I wish to be gracious and I will be compassionate to whomever I wish to be compassionate."

Tanḥuma and *Yalquṭ Shimoni* add after "to whom I will be gracious," "it is not written 'who deserves to be shown favor (*nḥwn*)'[9] but *'ḥwn* 'to whom I will show favor.' " That is, they do not read a presumed *Niphal* singular participle but a *Qal* first-person singular imperfect. Buber explains that, in the reading in his text of *Tanḥuma*, *nkwn* means "one who is deserving of favor because of one's own good deeds, while the biblical text refers to such who stir up My compassion at that time even though they be not worthy." He continues, "Rashi attended carefully to this in his commentary *ad loc.*, 'I will be gracious to whom I will be gracious,' those to whom I wish to be gracious." Buber further notes that the text of *Exodus Rabbah* ought to be emended to conform to *Tanḥuma*.[10]

---

9. Buber's text reads *nḥwn*. He emended it to conform to the others.

10. The translation of the verse in the NJPSV: 'and the grace that I grant and show the compassion I will show', ignoring the relative *'ăšer* governed by the mark of the accusative, *'et*, translated 'to whom', suggests that modern Jewish translators, unlike some of their predecessors, are uncomfortable with a suggestion of divine arbitrariness in the text.

The passage from *b. Ber.* [7a] cited in *Yalquṭ Shimoni* in an abridged fashion[11] takes us back to the third generation of Tannaim (ca. 130–60 C.E.). It begins by quoting Exod 33:16.

"Is it not that You go with us so that I and Your people are distinguished?" R. Johanan in the name of R. Jose says that three things were asked of God by Moses and they were granted to him. The third of these was "show me Your ways." Moses said in the divine presence: Master of the Universe, why is it that some righteous persons prosper and others face adversity? Why is it that some wicked prosper and others face adversity? He replied: The righteous person who prospers is the child of a righteous person while the righteous who faces adversity is the child of a wicked parent. Similarly, the wicked who prospers is the child of a righteous person while the one who faces adversity is the child of a wicked person.

To this an objection is raised. "It is written (Ex. 34:7) 'Visiting the sin of the parents on the children'; and it is also written (Deut. 24:16) 'the children shall not be put to death for the parents.'" This is the reply: "there is no contradiction. One verse deals with those who follow after the parents; the other, those who do not. In the light of this it must be that God said to Moses that the righteous who prospers is a truly righteous person while the righteous who faces adversity is not, etc." R. Meir will have none of this. Moses was granted answers to two of his requests; to the third, to know the divine way, he was not. "Does it not say: 'I will be gracious to whom I will be gracious' even though that one is not deserving and 'I will be compassionate to whom I will be compassionate' even though unworthy."

Here in R. Meir's dissent is echoed Job's response to God's questions from the whirlwind.

Who is this who obscures counsel without knowledge?
Indeed, I spoke without understanding
Of things beyond me, which I did not know.[12]

Moses, this tradition tells us, though he may have spoken to the Divine face to face, never uncovered the mystery of the face that would have shown to him and thus to us the darkened way of the Divine in the

11. See above.
12. See the essays referred to in note 1.

world.[13] It was an understanding of divine justice that he sought, but it was not granted to him. What he learned was something other than he sought: the immensity of divine grace that lies beyond justice. Thus we remain, as Gordon Kaufman has told us, "In Face of Mystery."[14]

---

13. A *baraita* (*b. Yebam.* 49b) explains the contradiction between Moses' statement in Exod 33:20, " 'No man shall see my face and live,' and Isaiah's words 'I saw the Lord sitting on a throne.' All the prophets looked through a darkened windowpane. Moses, our teacher, looked through a clear windowpane. Rashi interpreted the words through a darkened windowpane to mean 'they [the prophets] thought they saw but did not.' Moses looked though a clear windowpane and knew that he had not seen Him to His face." I am indebted for this reference to Professor Yeshayahu Leibowitz's comment on the scriptural lesson *Beha'alotekha* (Num 8:1–12:16) published in the *Jerusalem Report,* June 2, 1994.

14. G. D. Kaufman, *In Face of Mystery: A Constructive Theology* (Cambridge: Harvard University Press, 1993).

Whose Agony? Whose Ecstasy?
The Politics of Deuteronomic Law

Douglas A. Knight

Vanderbilt University

On the face of it, the text of the Hebrew Bible does little to divulge the political and economic roots of its producers. This circumstance can have an especially significant effect on our estimation and understanding of the theological and ethical affirmations present in the biblical literature. For all the evident differences in the discussions by theologians and ethicists of the Hebrew Bible, certainly the dominant approach since Johann Philipp Gabler's programmatic lecture[1] in 1787 has been historical in nature. Scholars subsequent to him have generally tended to account for differences in perspectives about divinity and humanity in light of the history of the period, the stages or growth in the development of the traditions, or the competing views of various groups or individuals. In short, the theological interpretation of biblical materials is normally conducted with attention to the world in which the recounted events putatively transpired and in which the literature came

---

Author's note: This essay represents a translated and expanded version of "Herrens bud—elitens interesser? Lov, makt, og rettferdighet i Det gamle testamente," *Norsk teologisk Tidsskrift* 97 (1996) 235–45 (used with permission), which was based on a lecture delivered in Oslo, Bergen, and Stavanger, Norway, in November 1995.

1. *Oratio de justo discrimine theologiae biblicae et dogmaticae regundisque recte utriusque finibus* (Altdorf, 1787). Gabler's dominant concern was to separate biblical theology from dogmatic theology by distinguishing the former as a historical discipline and the latter as a didactic or interpretive enterprise. Such a depiction, for all of its influence on the subsequent two centuries of theological discussions, betrays an Enlightenment viewpoint that can hardly be sustained when one considers the interpretive nature of all historical work, on the one hand, and the historicality of every interpreter, on the other. In fact, it is precisely the political and ideological elements that are too often lacking from both sides of the equation.

into being. Considerable effort has, of course, gone into clarifying the character of life in those ancient times.

This interest in history, however, can give the impression of embracing the full range of human experience during biblical times. James Crenshaw was among the earliest of contemporary scholars to appreciate the religious diversity that existed among the people at large, whose point of view could often be at variance with the orthodoxy seemingly enshrined in the biblical literature.[2] To this important observation about the diverse religious perspectives and beliefs of the great masses of ancient Israelites should now be added the need to bring also the various dimensions of the people's political and economic life under the loupe. It is one thing to consider the monarchy, the priesthood, the grand building projects, and the wars; much of our usual history of Israel has tended to focus squarely on such subjects. But it is quite another matter to look for the subtleties of politics, the machinations and maneuverings by individuals and groups, the routine exploitation of the masses, the ideological undercurrents of the texts, and the special interests and driving forces behind the literature. For example, biblical statements about God's concern for the oppressed seem at times to reflect an undifferentiated if not even naïve view of the actual dynamics of oppression: how eagerly is change actually sought? There are profound moral injunctions about the need to alleviate the abysmal situation of the poor and the defenseless; but does not the very presence of such laws and admonitions indicate that victims of the system did in fact exist and were not being adequately aided, despite the moral rhetoric? Our own tendency as interpreters has been to elaborate on and interconnect such pronouncements without substantially subjecting them to political scrutiny. The hermeneutics of suspicion, which has become a crucial tool today for liberation theologians and ethicists of various types, tends to be applied to modern rather than ancient situations. But why should we not suspect the ideological leanings and political-economic motives behind biblical assertions as well?

Theological and ethical treatments of the Hebrew Bible do not routinely predicate their study explicitly on a political-economic reading of the texts. Such discussions rarely ask about the class status of the authors,

---

2. J. L. Crenshaw, *Prophetic Conflict: Its Effect upon Israelite Religion* (BZAW 124; Berlin: de Gruyter, 1971), especially 23–38.

their political agendas, the power moves, the social factors resulting in the recording and preservation of precisely the given statement rather than something else quite different. Political structures, to the extent that they are addressed, are in fact often projected into the divine sphere and thereby given ultimate and decisive legitimization; examples are the images of God as king, warrior, legislator, judge, and executioner. Could there be a more effective and convenient way of validating the actions of the human kings, warriors, lawmakers, judges, and punishers than to claim that they are acting on God's behalf? The pernicious forms that such presumption takes in our own world should alert us to the possibility of comparable conceit in the biblical literature, and not only by those vilified there but especially by the powerful and privileged who are not criticized.

To inquire into the political and economic moorings of the text, both its parts and the whole, involves putting the question pointedly: Whose text is it? For whom and why was it important to fashion the stories, laws, proverbs, songs, prophetic sayings, and more into their present forms? Who stood to gain? Who had the power to see to the survival of the text? Of course, answering these questions depends on how one understands gain or benefit, and on one level one might argue that the whole people of Israel, together with their successors, benefited from having a national literary heritage and a religious and moral system. But only in an attenuated sense can the whole people be regarded as the producers of the text, so the question perforce must focus more directly on those immediately responsible for the text's production and conservation. We can assume, I believe, several factors operative for these individuals and groups: (1) They were literate or could cause literate persons in the society to compile and write the materials that eventually came to constitute our present text. (2) The producers of the text were knowledgeable of a wide range of the people's traditions and experiences, or they were immensely imaginative in creating a literature of such broad scope. (3) The producers had some standing in the community that enabled them to get these literary materials accepted by the community or at least to ensure preservation of the literature in the face of any initial nonacceptance or even outright opposition. (4) And finally, the social locations of those immediately responsible for the production of the biblical literature corresponded to their intentions for writing; in other words, their compositions were designed to attain certain goals economic and political in nature, and such ideological characteristics of the text may still be recoverable, at least in part. I do not mean to suggest that these were the only purposes for producing the text—only that the longstanding focus in our discipline on the religious and moral aspects of the text has diverted our attention from some of the real practicalities that were at play during the period of composition and preservation. To the extent that the Hebrew Bible consists of "partisan collections and revisions,"[3] the partiality of its collectors and revisers is just as likely to touch on their vested social interests as on their religious beliefs and ideas.

The political, economic, and social values encoded in the Hebrew Bible are more difficult to decipher than are the religious beliefs, which should not surprise us, since the same situation is likely to pertain in any context, including the modern period. For example, the Deuteronomistic interpretation of the exile as a punishment for centuries of apostasy and injustice is quite transparent in the structure and language of the Deuteronomistic History, whereas it is less obvious whether a group or individual standing behind this historical writing was seeking with it to gain control over the exilic or postexilic community and to benefit thereby from the political and economic power that would result. Such a political agenda in the text is not readily apparent. Except for crass displays of power, such as military actions, most political moves are concealed in order to be effective, with few in the wider public aware of them until the lot improves for certain persons and degenerates for others. The political impulses will be found in the interstices of the text, in the unstated consequences of actions, in the excessively or repeatedly avowed assertions, in the efforts to control behavior and thought. Thus the so-called "plain meaning" of the text may in fact be concealing quite the opposite political and economic import or ideology. To understand the agony and the ecstasy of faith within the Hebrew Bible requires that a hermeneutic of suspicion be consistently applied to the text itself, for in all likelihood individuals and classes reveled and suffered in large part as a result of their differing circumstances, about which the biblical literature on its face gives insufficient information.

---

3. M. Smith, *Palestinian Parties and Politics That Shaped the Old Testament* (London: SCM, 1971) 11.

Ancient Israel as an Agrarian Society

Before attempting a political-economic reading of some of the biblical laws, we must have an idea of the kind of society that apparently existed in ancient Israel, an imprecise term used commonly to designate the peoples living in the Palestinian region from the Iron Age through the Persian and even the Hellenistic periods.[4] The agrarian state[5] is known to us from many areas and periods throughout the world, from large empires such as the Roman, Byzantine, Ottoman, and Chinese empires to more limited nation-states, such as ancient Israel and Judah. Substantial variation exists among the political structures identified with this model, but they share several characteristics in common, elements evident in Israel from the onset of the kingship and forward. Typical is a pronounced social inequality in power, privileges, and honor, and the centralized state itself functions as the source of this inequality. Kings view the state as their own property to use as they will, and any archives they leave behind tell mainly about them, their wars, and their building projects—and almost nothing about the lives of the common people except insofar as they intersect with the interests of the monarchic government. However, in addition to the royal house there is also a ruling or governing class, a small minority normally less (often much less) than 2% of the whole population, who exercise political and economic power at the national level: high state officials, chief military officers, large landowners, wealthy merchants, priestly leaders, and others to whom the king grants land, offices, or special rights.

The balance of power between these two groups—the king and the royal government on the one hand and the ruling class on the other—can be unstable: each will often attempt to dominate the other and thereby gain the upper hand in controlling the country and its economy. But more importantly, they generally collaborate to hold the populace in

---

4. See the distinctions highlighted by P. R. Davies, *In Search of "Ancient Israel": A Study in Biblical Origins* (JSOTSup 148; Sheffield: JSOT Press, 1992).

5. A detailed description of agrarian societies is provided by macrosociologist G. Lenski, *Power and Privilege: A Theory of Social Stratification* (Chapel Hill: University of North Carolina Press, 1966, 1984). See also M. Mann, *The Sources of Social Power*, vol. 1: *A History of Power from the Beginning to* A.D. *1760* (Cambridge: Cambridge University Press, 1986).

check, both the peasants in the countryside and the artisans and laborers in the cities, in order to extract from them as much of their economic surplus as possible. The result is that typically less than 2% of the total population will receive in excess of 50% of the national income.[6] In addition, there is essentially no class in agrarian states comparable to the independent middle class in modern industrial states. Instead, a small group of specialists enjoys some status and privilege in comparison to the exploited masses: bureaucrats, functionaries, retainers, merchants, and priests. This group, usually only 5–10% of the total population, is dependent on the elite for its income and position, and the elite group uses it to manage the affairs of the government, collect taxes and rents, and generally make life comfortable for the royal house and the governing class. Ultimate power resides securely in that top 1–2%, and all others are largely at their mercy—especially the peasants and crafts-workers who make up the bottom 90% and who can barely survive in the subsistence economy. Additional characteristics of the agrarian society include technological advances, wars and internal conflicts, urban domination of the country, diversity of specialized professions, trade and commerce conducted by a merchant class, and a religious institution intermeshed with the centralized state and often afflicted with internal strife.

On the whole and on the basis of our current knowledge, ancient Israel seems to fit quite well this model of the agrarian society, as long as one makes the necessary adjustments to the pattern in light of the various situations and regions during the monarchic and colonial periods. The first two centuries of the Iron Age, prior to the founding of the monarchy, should be regarded as a variant of the pattern, an agricultural society scattered in small villages over the countryside and lacking a political and economic center. Lenski has suggested that the people living on the land during this period appear to conform well to the sociological model of a frontier society.[7] While this characterization may seem

---

6. As disproportionate as such figures appear, the situation is actually not much different from the prevailing distribution of wealth in the United States in the 1990s, where the total net worth of the top 1% of the population represents more than 40% of the total private wealth.

7. Lenski's proposal is found in his review (*RelSRev* 6 [1980] 275–78) of N. Gottwald, *The Tribes of Yahweh: A Sociology of the Religion of Liberated Israel, 1250–1050 B.C.E.* (Maryknoll, N.Y.: Orbis, 1979). Among others, Israel Finkelstein has argued that, when

too modern, it is certainly correct that international political interests in the highlands were diminished during the Early Iron Age, that the petty kings of the city-states in the lowlands presumably had little interest in areas outside their limited realms, that families could subsist on crops and herding in these marginal regions, that a type of ideology not based on political or economic centralization could develop in such a situation and could acquire quasi-religious dimensions, and that the population could gradually consolidate itself and eventually become ruled along the conventional lines of hierarchy and centralized power. All of these elements are typical characteristics of a frontier society.

However the social model may need to be refined or replaced, viewing ancient Israel as an agrarian society, with the inequalities fundamental to it, has clear implications for our perspectives on the Hebrew Bible. At the most immediate level, it helps us to locate socially those who wrote and preserved the text.[8] While some minimal literacy may have been rather widespread among the Israelites, only a small number would have been fully literate: archivists in the king's court, certain priests, perhaps some merchants, and the like. In terms of the categories mentioned above, these people belonged largely to the privileged group directly under the king and the governing elite, and the ruling groups called the piper's tune. Thus, unless they wrote surreptitiously or deceptively, their texts must have satisfied the interests of the rich and powerful, for whose pleasure they served. At the same time, and here the picture becomes complex, the text as it was being developed had to resonate in some

---

viewed over the long term of the previous two millennia, there is strong archaeological evidence for a cyclic process of sedentarization and nomadization of indigenous groups in this region in light of fluctuating social, political, and economic circumstances; thus the development of the frontier in Iron I, while distinctive in certain respects, is also parallel to the settlement of the region in the Chalcolithic and Early Bronze I period and again in the Middle Bronze II–III period. See Finkelstein, "The Great Transformation: The 'Conquest' of the Highlands Frontiers and the Rise of the Territorial States," in *The Archaeology of Society in the Holy Land* (ed. T. E. Levy; New York: Facts on File, 1995) 349–62. See also R. B. Coote and K. W. Whitelam, *The Emergence of Early Israel in Historical Perspective* (SWBA 5; Sheffield: Almond, 1987), especially 27–80.

8. S. Niditch, *Ancient Israelite Literature: Oral World and Written Word* (LAI; Louisville: Westminster John Knox, 1996); and P. R. Davies, *Scribes and Schools: The Canonization of the Hebrew Scriptures* (LAI; Louisville: Westminster John Knox, 1998).

manner with the sentiments of the masses if it was to be acceptable to them. Of course it is conceivable that the producers and preservers of the text had little or no interest in having the masses approve of the literature that eventually came to be included in the Hebrew Bible. But to the extent that such literature was to serve the purposes of the powerful in extracting surpluses from the general populace, it had to have some appeal for the latter group. It would thus appear that the biblical text represents a mixture of values, both power oriented and populist. To separate the one from the other is basic to ideological criticism and political exegesis.

Law and Power

Where do laws fit into this picture? Do the biblical laws derive from the masses, from the king or governing class, or from privileged groups such as the priests or scribes? A substantial number of laws articulate principles of justice for the oppressed, and one's first impression could be that human rights and high moral values underlie these ordinances. Can this be the case?

As a first step, it is important to distinguish between two entities that should not be equated or confused: *Israelite* laws on the one hand and *biblical* laws on the other. Israelite laws belong to the actual legal systems operating in the Israelite society, either at the level of the centralized state or within the more immediate communities of the people. They are the laws that actually existed in order to affect behavior in that society according to enforceable controls and to help the judicial system decide a case involving crimes and conflicts between parties. Biblical laws, in contrast, are literature. They probably include some of the Israelite laws—that is, the "living" laws—but any number of laws (quite plausibly the vast majority) existing in that society during some part of its long history or within the diverse regions and villages of the country were not incorporated in the Hebrew Bible. For this reason, neither the term *code* nor the term *collection* applies appropriately to the biblical laws: neither were they issued by the king or some other legislative body to serve as the legal basis for the society, nor were they assembled by means of gathering into one place the disparate laws of the culture. Rather, the biblical laws came into existence through literary activity, and they should be viewed as literature—with, in principle, neither more nor less connection to "real life" in Israel than may be true for other parts of the Hebrew Bible.

What factors influenced the inclusion of certain laws, the exclusion of others, and the composition of the whole into its present form? While the latter part of the question would require a lengthy discussion, we can at least make some progress here on the first two. For the answers should not come as a complete surprise to us if we are at all realistic both about typical legislative activity in modern societies and about the political and economic aspects of literary production: Precisely those laws and traditions were included that in some way corresponded to the strategies and self-interests of those who drafted and compiled them. This principle underlies the modern field of legal theory known as Critical Legal Studies—that all law is politics. While many of the biblical laws articulate exemplary moral principles, indeed some of the most humane norms known to us, we should nonetheless also be prepared to suspect the motives behind their compilation. For the groups in ancient Israel who would have had the training, the opportunity, the funding, and the means for preserving such legal literature must certainly have belonged to the scribal class or the priests. In both cases, according to the model of the agrarian state, these groups owed their status and privileges to the central state and the governing elite, even if they might have been able to identify to an extent with the vulnerability of the masses. The composition of laws into literature would thus have served the ends of those who possessed or sought power.[9]

With the demise of first the Northern Kingdom in 722 B.C.E. and then the Southern monarchy in 587 B.C.E. and the subsequent establishment of a colonial government in the Judean province, power relations underwent a shift that changed the face of society and religion. Whereas previously there had been a fragile balance of power between the king and the governing class, now in the Babylonian and Persian periods power relations became realigned as diverse religious and political factions competed for the upper hand and as various individuals, probably

---

9. Power relations in ancient Israel are discussed in my "Political Rights and Powers in Monarchic Israel," *Semeia* 66 (*Ethics and Politics in the Hebrew Bible*; 1994) 93–117.

many of the descendants of the old wealthy elite, sought to regain the property and prestige enjoyed by the upper class prior to the Babylonian and Persian reorganization of the country.[10] To legitimate such a shift it was necessary to transform force into authority and might into right.[11] Or to use the metaphor of the great Italian sociologist Vilfredo Pareto, "the lions" of the old order became "the foxes" of the new.[12] This new kind of elite in the postexilic period was driven as much by self-interest and partisanship as was the governing class during the monarchic period, but the new elite, like the fox, had to operate with more cunning than had previously been necessary, when power and force were centralized in the monarchy, not the least because acceptable relations had to be negotiated with the imperial government. Members or associates of the new priestly establishment, presumably backed by the new elite, found it advantageous to compose or edit Israel's legal traditions in a manner that would promote the interests of their new supporters. But inasmuch as law exists ostensibly to further social order and justice, it would have seemed opportune for the legal literature to give the appearance of affirming the old communitarian principles of justice, even though at the same time the laws were formulated in a way that would favor the special interests of the new elite as well as those of the occupants of the institutionalized positions of the priests. The social values of the many thus became manipulated to the benefit of the few.

---

10. An early discussion of postexilic factions is present in Smith, *Palestinian Parties*, and several more recent studies of the ideology of texts from this period have taken up the question of power maneuvers by the elite in connection with the people's return to the land. See, for example, N. K. Gottwald, "Social Class and Ideology in Isaiah 40–55: An Eagletonian Reading," *Semeia* 59 (*Ideological Criticism of Biblical Texts*; 1992) 43–57; and R. P. Carroll, "The Myth of the Empty Land," *Semeia* 59 (1992) 79–93. Further discussion of local elites within the Persian Empire is available in P. Briant, *Histoire de l'empire perse de Cyrus à Alexandre* (Paris: Fayard, 1996) 53–59 and passim; in English translation, *From Cyrus to Alexander: A History of the Persian Empire* (Winona Lake, Ind.: Eisenbrauns, forthcoming); J. L. Berquist, *Judaism in Persia's Shadow: A Social and Historical Approach* (Minneapolis: Fortress, 1995) 131ff.; and L. L. Grabbe, *Judaism from Cyrus to Hadrian*, vol. 1: *The Persian and Greek Periods* (Minneapolis: Fortress, 1992) 103–19 and passim.

11. Lenski, *Power and Privilege*, 52.

12. V. Pareto, *The Mind and Society*, vol. 4: *The General Form of Society* (New York: Harcourt, Brace, 1935; trans. of *Trattato di sociologia generale*, 1916) §2178.

Leadership

Three types of examples will be taken from the book of Deuteronomy to demonstrate this hermeneutic of suspicion, questioning the
intentions behind the laws in their present form by examining the political and economic benefit accruing to the laws' compilers and other
powerful groups following a major political change. Traditional biblical
scholarship has for some time now argued that the laws of Deuteronomy 12–26 were recorded during the seventh century B.C.E. by descendants of Northern Israel, now living in the South, who compiled
them in order to preserve the Northern heritage and perhaps also to ex-
ert a reforming influence on Southern society. In my view, the stimulus
for writing these laws is better explained as a power move, either by certain groups following the Assyrian decline and the nationalistic rebirth
of Judean autonomy under Josiah, or (and this is more likely) by a new
elite seeking political and economic advantage in the exilic or postexilic
period.[13]

(1) The Deuteronomic laws dealing, first, with *secular leadership* demonstrate the authority structure desired by the laws' compilers and the
new elite. It is reasonable to assume that the masses during the monarchy would have had little reason to develop social norms or laws about
centralized leadership, except in a more negative sense: how to show
sufficient respect and compliance to national leaders to keep at a minimum their interference in the lives and livelihood of the peasants. In
contrast, the Deuteronomic laws in their present form legitimize a centralized and hierarchical political structure. Moses is lionized as God's
law-giver and mediator, thus as the people's unquestioned head whom
one opposes at great peril. The monarchy is explicitly authorized in the
well-known "law of the king" in Deut 17:14–20, and the limitations
included there may well reflect popular sentiment: that the king should
not acquire too many horses, should not send the people to Egypt for
his own benefit, should not marry many wives, should not collect great

---

13. See my "Deuteronomy and the Deuteronomists," in *Old Testament Interpretation: Past, Present, and Future—Essays in Honor of Gene M. Tucker* (ed. J. L. Mays, D. L.
Petersen, and K. H. Richards; Nashville: Abingdon, 1995) 61–79.

quantities of gold and silver. It should be noted, however, that such restraints, which hardly carry constitutional weight, serve the interests not only of the masses but also of the nonroyal elites. As previously indicated, it is imperative in the structure of the agrarian state that the king's power not become absolute but that the governing class share the power and prestige in the political and economic spheres. This "law of the king" represents, in my view, a prime example of how the new elite, after Judah's social and political upheaval, could rewrite popular values into a generalized system of justice that might gain maximum public support even though the special interests of the elite were thereby surreptitiously favored.

The same could be said of the system of judicial appeals, which in effect seeks to shift absolute authority to the central courts. Deut 17:8–13 ordains the proper process for cases involving conflicting types of violence or other controversies that have been appealed because the local judges found them too difficult to resolve: The parties are to approach the central priests and the state's judges who sit in "the place that YHWH your God will choose"—that is, Jerusalem—and who will adjudicate the matter. The text concludes: "and all the people shall hear and be afraid and shall never again act rebelliously" (17:13). Everyone in the country, in other words, is subordinated to the supreme courts in the capital city. The legendary tale of Solomon in 1 Kgs 3:16–28 reinforces the centralization of justice: Inasmuch as Solomon was wise enough to settle the complicated conflict between two women, each of whom claimed that the living child was hers, so should all Israel stand in awe of Solomon because he possesses God's wisdom (3:28)—and implicitly: the Israelites are to submit to all succeeding kings and state judges.

Deuteronomic law presents, in a word, a structure of order and authority that is cephalous and centripetal in character, hierarchically and centrally organized. A theology of obedience reinforces this structure. As William Moran perceived decades ago, when "love" is "commanded" in Deuteronomy, it is no emotional sentiment or pious attitude that is held in view but rather an allegiance translatable into patterns of behavior, just as a Near Eastern sovereign commanded loyalty of subjects and vassals in the empire. Somewhat similarly, Niels Peter Lemche has recently argued that a patron/client system existed on a widespread basis in Israel and is reflected in the word *ḥesed*, the covenant loyalty that could be required of clients, or by God of worshipers.[14] In both conceptions, obedience to those in authority is expected, which in Deuteronomy is projected as a divinely ordained response and is reinforced with blessings and curses (Deuteronomy 27–28). Those in economic or political power would have found such a system eminently convenient and profitable.

(2) The Deuteronomic laws dealing with priests, Levites, and the cult achieved a similar end, although with notable differences.[15] While it seems unlikely that the general populace of Israel and Judah would have voluntarily sought out a centralized, hierarchical political and economic system, they certainly developed religious practices and beliefs of their own. Both the archaeological record and the biblical traditions indicate a remarkable religious pluralism throughout the monarchic period and beyond. Popular piety responded to multiple influences and the efficacy of specific acts that appeared to protect life, bring rain, or increase fertility. Is it credible to suppose that the people would have voluntarily abandoned their pious practices and moved all cultic activity to the Temple in Jerusalem? Inaugurating a decisive shift, Deuteronomy presents laws that sought to stamp out the local cults and their priests by ordering the centralization of all cultic activity in "the place that YHWH your God will choose" (for example, 12:5), again undoubtedly Jerusalem. To the extent that this policy was successful, it represented an inordinate focalization of control and power in the hands of the Jerusalem priesthood. If attempted during Josiah's reign as described in 1 Kings 22–23, centralization also suited ideally the political and fiscal reforms of the new government. Beyond this effort to eradicate competing cultic sites, the laws targeted the pluralism of religious belief as well, condemning everything

---

14. W. L. Moran, "The Ancient Near Eastern Background of the Love of God in Deuteronomy," *CBQ* 25 (1963) 77–87; N. P. Lemche, "Kings and Clients: On Loyalty between the Ruler and the Ruled in Ancient 'Israel,' " *Semeia* 66 (*Ethics and Politics in the Hebrew Bible*; 1994) 119–32.

15. See the sociohistorical description of the Israelite priesthood in J. Blenkinsopp, *Sage, Priest, Prophet: Religious and Intellectual Leadership in Ancient Israel* (LAI; Louisville: Westminster John Knox, 1995); and L. L. Grabbe, *Priests, Prophets, Diviners, Sages: A Socio-Historical Study of Religious Specialists in Ancient Israel* (Valley Forge, Penn.: Trinity, 1995).

other than Yahwistic religion as apostasy, stipulating unequivocally what causes defilement (Deut 14:3–21; 23:11–12[10–11]), and even excluding certain types of persons from participation in the cult (23:2–4[1–3]). In all, the laws as compiled tapped the wellspring of popular piety—but also took advantage of it for the benefit of the Jerusalemite priesthood as well as others at the center of power. Actually, however, it may be that we can also perceive in these cultic regulations some division between the priests on the one hand and the new elites on the other. The priests and Levites are due certain perquisites, tithes (14:22–29; 26:12–13), and sacrifices (18:1–8), described in 18:3 with the legal phrase *mišpaṭ hakkōhănîm*, the priests' rightful claim to a portion of the sacrifices brought by the people. Such a provision argues strongly in favor of identifying the priests or others close to them as the compilers of the laws. They as an institution stood especially to gain.

Justice

(3) We will conclude our examples with the laws that would seem most to disprove my thesis concerning the dominant political and economic interests reflected in the Deuteronomic laws. The *laws of release* belong among the most memorable and potentially most reforming of the biblical traditions in social ethics. The forgiveness of debts and the manumission of slaves every seven years represent nothing less than radical moves toward the redistribution of wealth within the society, which the laws in Leviticus 25 extend even further by prescribing the return of families to inherited land that they were forced through financial exigency to sell. The Deuteronomic collection contains further miscellaneous injunctions to help the needy: leaving the harvest gleanings for the widows, orphans, and strangers (Deut 24:19–22); contributing a tithe every third year for Levites, widows, orphans, and strangers (14:28–29); not charging interest on loans to fellow Israelites (23:20–21[19–20]); dealing considerately with certain items given in pledge for loans (24:6, 10–13, 17b); and paying poor laborers their wages daily (24:14–15). To my mind, such provisions would not have been volunteered by profiteers. Rather, they point to a communitarian context in which a genuine concern for the plight of the vulnerable, especially in the face of a widening gap between the haves and the have-nots, was translated into some provisions for relief, however slight. We can also assume that the very

presence of a law would normally imply a real problem or conflict at that point in Israelite society: that Israelites *were* charging interest on loans to other Israelites, that poor laborers could *not* count on receiving their wages daily, that indebtedness and slavery *could* easily become a permanent condition for an individual. The prophets themselves confirm the abysmal economic situation in which many people lived.

But why are such protections and reforms included in the Deuteronomic collection? We can perhaps find a clue in the fact that there is pitifully little evidence in pre- or postexilic Israel for the global release of debts, slaves, or inherited lands. Furthermore, these laws of protection have no teeth, no provisions for enforcement and no remedies for violations—only moral appeals with the promise of divine blessing or punishment. Is it too cynical of us to wonder whether the Deuteronomic compilers and the new elite of the period after the exile might in fact have incorporated these so-called "humanitarian laws" deliberately and with calculated intent—namely, to deceive the masses into thinking that the new order after the Babylonian conquest was going to be based on the kind of justice and morality the poor and disempowered longed for? If the populace could be brought to support the new order, institutions such as the priesthood could be legitimized, and power and wealth could move into the hands of the new elite. The cunning of foxes is not to be underestimated.

Conclusion

I conclude with six brief thesis statements.

1. Law is not simply what the legislators enact or the courts decide. All law has a political edge.
2. The laws recorded in the Hebrew Bible are more literature than they are laws. As literary texts they were produced by persons or groups, probably in conjunction with significant social and political transition points, and they provided an ideal opportunity for groups and institutions to secure popular backing by appealing in clever and calculated ways to the needs and traditions of the general populace.
3. Much effort has already been spent on the theology and ethics of Deuteronomic and other laws, and it is now important for us to inquire also into the political and economic import of these laws.

To this end, the leading questions are: Whose laws are these? Who stands to gain from them? It lies in the very character of political texts not to be forthcoming on these points.

4. Popular values are reflected in certain laws, such as some of those contained in the Deuteronomic collection. But it should come as no surprise to us that these values were appropriated and reused to quite different ends by the compilers—in other words, that the popular values are now reflected in a mirror that has been considerably clouded by special interests.

5. By the same token, of course, we must be cautious not to assume that the pre-Deuteronomic laws and social norms, the popular values, were themselves free of political and economic self-interests. Oppressive and exploitative structures can exist on all levels of society, and the tiny, isolated village eking out an existence in the Israelite hinterland was no haven of equality or of the fair distribution of power and resources.

6. This political and ideological reading of the biblical laws can, however, be instructive to us. Negatively, it helps us to perceive the unfair and unfortunate effects of self-interest. Positively, it enables us to identify those moral values that derive from contexts in which they were genuinely intended to assist persons in need, values that can still be affirmed today in the effort to establish a just world.

Achan's Sin: Warfare and Holiness

R. E. CLEMENTS
Cambridge, England

From the perspective of a revelation of the dark and terrifying face of the deity, few biblical stories match in stark horror that of the execution of Achan and his family as a result of Achan's having offended the rules of warfare governing devoted things (*ḥerem*).

> Then Joshua and all Israel with him took Achan son of Zerah, with the silver, the mantle, and the bar of gold, with his sons and daughters, with his oxen, donkeys, and sheep, and his tent and all that he had; and they brought then up to the Valley of Achor. Joshua said, "Why did you bring trouble on us? The LORD is bringing trouble on you today." And all Israel stoned him to death; they burned them with fire, cast stones on them, and raised over him a great heap of stones that remains to this day. Then the LORD turned from his burning anger. Therefore that place to this day is called the Valley of Achor. (Josh 7:24–26)

There are clearly many biblical tales involving far more cruel atrocities and many that involve a far higher death toll of innocent victims than the story of the unrecorded number of family members who died along with Achan. In fact the execution of innocent sons and daughters along with an individual culprit, in contravention of the ruling prescribed in the Deuteronomic law of Deut 24:16, cannot be regarded as more than an incidental feature of the story. Yet for all the parallels involving the killing of innocent persons and the execution of persons for religious offenses, the execution relating to Achan possesses a note of distinctive terror. The involvement of innocent members of a household in the infliction of punishment in ancient Israel reflects widespread assumptions about the quasi-infectious understanding of holiness and about kingroup solidarity that existed in varying degrees in ancient Israelite society throughout the biblical period. Although it raises questions about the applicability of legislative procedures in which proper awareness of individual responsibility was overridden, it is not primarily on this account that the story retains the capacity to shock and alarm.

More directly, the unwary reader is likely to find the story intensely disturbing because it clearly has didactic intent. The story is constructed so as to inculcate a lesson that the reader must heed. Nevertheless, what it teaches projects a portrait of a deity who is cruel, petty, and vengeful. The demand for religious loyalty and obedience is absolute and tolerates no infringements of any kind. At the same time this obedience is not much concerned with loyalty to the community but hinges on a quasi-magical understanding of the nature of sin and guilt. By his action Achan sinned directly against God, and the account goes even further by insisting that what was hidden from the eyes of fellow human beings could not be hidden from God. In short, the story provides a paradigmatic instance of the sage's insistence that

> the eyes of the LORD are in every place,
>   keeping watch on the evil and the good. (Prov 15:3)

So the understanding of sin implicit in Achan's tragic story conveys a rather confusing ethical message and rests on assumptions that are at variance with a number of important legal prescriptions found elsewhere in the Old Testament. What is carried out by the community in the name of God is what is expressly forbidden to be done in other, more conventional, judicial processes. Nor can the reader overlook the point that a major feature of the development of ancient Israel's legal system, as of similar systems elsewhere, was the complex process of ascertaining satisfactory proof of guilt. Quite evidently, a major purpose of the Achan story is to be found in its illustration of the claim that God himself may unerringly and incontrovertibly provide this proof with only minimal human assistance (Josh 7:16–18).

The Nature of Achan's Sin

The narrative of Josh 7:1–26 has evidently been skillfully crafted to teach a significant number of fundamental beliefs about the nature of God and of human sin. Implicit among these is that, even though a particular offense may fall outside the normal judicial and moral concerns of society, it may, nonetheless, bring great harm to the community. Achan stands accused of a uniquely heinous action, and his guilt is readily shown up by God and later openly confirmed by his confession. The necessary punishment is then inflicted by the community without compunction or mercy. Apart from Achan's admission that the initial temptation to sin was sparked by covetousness (v. 21) and thereby infringed on the tenth commandment (Deut 5:21), the nature and seriousness of his offense are held to lie beyond the boundaries of everyday moral choices. In a unique way it is against God that he has sinned, and all Israel is forced to suffer until his guilt is purged.

The recognition that a sin had been committed is held to have become evident because of the withdrawal of the divine power to give miraculous victories to Joshua's military force. However, instead of taking immediate direct action against the infringement of the requirements of holiness, as in the case of Korah (Num 16:20–35) or even Uzzah (2 Sam 6:7), in which case only Achan and his family need have died, the community was called upon to act on God's behalf. Had God acted promptly and directly in identifying and punishing the real culprit, the thirty-six Israelite soldiers (Josh 7:5) would have been spared. Instead God appears unwilling, or possibly unable, to act directly but reveals an intense depth of anger indirectly, thereby compelling the larger community to act for God. The point might appear to be a rather marginal one, were it not for the fact that it concerns an issue that reappears prominently and repeatedly in several biblical affirmations concerning the nature of retribution for human wrongdoing. Sometimes it appears that retribution occurs as an expression of a self-adjusting process of the natural world; at other times God is held to act directly to punish the sinner; while at other times still, as here, the community is called upon to take action on God's behalf. However, the problems experienced by the community make it clear to them that it is in their own interest to act.

Achan's sin is presented as an offense that was uniquely against God, and it was on this account that the divine anger was initially vented against Israel in general. When examined carefully, the story is surprisingly replete with information concerning the nature of Achan's sin, since he confesses the details with complete frankness.

> And Achan answered Joshua, "It is true; I am the one who sinned against the LORD God of Israel. This is what I did: when I saw among the spoil a beautiful mantle of Shinar, and two hundred shekels of silver, and a bar of gold weighing fifty shekels, then I coveted them and took them." (Josh 7:20–21)

The overt context, which is given to elucidate the nature of this offense, is that of the rules governing the disposal of spoil after a military victory given by God. Such a victory is assumed to be a "gift" from God, and the soldiers involved in its conduct should not thereby profit from it. The profits of the battle belong to God (Josh 6:19). In the wider Deuteronomic context, the danger posed by the alien cultic associations of the spoils of war are regarded as posing a threat to Israel's obedience to the divine law (Deut 20:16–18). In military campaigns conducted against the towns of the land given to Israel, the community is commanded to kill all prisoners of any age or gender and to destroy completely the material spoils. Only against more distant nations may a less stringent policy than this genocide and wholesale destruction be implemented (Deut 20:10–15). From the rather miscellaneous items of information recorded in narrative sources of the Old Testament that are likely to reflect the actual practices of Israel in the conduct of war, it becomes apparent that no clear uniformity of practice regarding the disposal of spoils was enforced. In fact the very concept of the so-called "holy war" as an ongoing feature of early Israelite society must be regarded with a great deal of caution.

A central feature of the story of Achan's sin is its attention to the threat posed to the community of Israel by the spoils of war, with their foreign, and hence potentially idolatrous, associations. The story is, in effect, a kind of exemplary illustration of the principle laid down in Deut 20:16–18. Until Achan had been singled out and his sin identified and punished, the entire nation was liable to suffer the consequences of the divine anger. It is this point that echoes throughout the narrative episode. So the story seeks to highlight the circumstances in which divine support for those in covenant with God may be withdrawn. It shows reasons why that support may not be forthcoming when needed and why those who ventured into battle in God's name could be abandoned to ignominious defeat.

The story of Achan is a story about warfare and the maintenance of holiness; yet these activities do little more than provide the background and occasion for the display of divine wrath that is revealed. More central to the story is its anxiety to demonstrate that sins carried out in secret may nevertheless have very strong public consequences. Since these sins will be known to God, they may be difficult to discover by human agency, and a form of sacred lot may be necessary to establish guilt. The message is clearly that God will know! Guilt could then be satisfactorily confirmed to comply with legal constraints by the culprit's confession— a feature that is given prominent expression in the narrative (vv. 19–21). The didactic intention behind the story must assuredly lie primarily in its insistence that secret sins against God will be known to the all-seeing deity and will not escape punishment. Achan is assumed to have "stolen" from God. It is a paradigmatic illustration of the priestly admonition: "Be sure your sin will find you out" (Num 32:23). It is regrettably on this account as well as on account of its smooth literary texture and compactness that homiletical use is frequently made of it with scant regard for the complexities of the nature of the offense that is punished so severely.

The severity of the punishment that is inflicted accords fully with the severity demanded in other parts of the Deuteronomic legislation for the punishment of those who incite defection from sole allegiance to the LORD God of Israel (see Deut 13:15–18). In detail, the specific injunction concerning the total destruction of an apostate town and all its spoil highlights clearly where Achan was held to have offended: "Do not let anything devoted to destruction stick to your hand, so that the LORD may turn from his fierce anger and show you compassion, and in his compassion multiply you, as he swore to your ancestors" (Deut 13:17).

Part of the background to the story is undoubtedly its concern with the nature of community and the way in which the disloyal activities of individuals within it may prejudice its ability to prosper and win battles. The conduct of warfare, with its inevitable risk of incurring bloodguilt, and the threat to cultic holiness by the capture and retention of alien cult objects were clearly recognized to provide just such occasions of danger and threat. It must be noted, however, that it is the story's interest in warfare that places it within the framework of a very distinctive strand of theology that belongs to the Deuteronomic movement. Whereas the wealth represented by the two hundred shekels of silver and the bar of gold that caught Achan's roving eye (Josh 7:21) associate his actions with the dangers of covetousness, the mantle of Shinar with its foreign associations hints strongly at the danger of idolatry and alien cult. Covetousness merely provides a reason for Achan's failure to comply with a far more compelling demand.

Warfare and Its Spoils

If the prime purpose of the story is to reveal the complex nature of sin and its potential consequences for human society, it achieves this purpose by highlighting the danger posed by private and secret sins. In particular, Achan has withheld from God property that rightly belonged to the sanctuary and has hidden objects that had associations with foreign culture. That it draws upon a particular religious aspect concerning conduct in warfare is not in itself an occasion for great surprise. On close examination, however, it becomes apparent that the treatment and disposal of the spoils of war is little more than a thin cover for the author's deeper concern with the nature of sin, the danger of the guilt it incurs, and the need for the community to eradicate it. From the details given of the culprit's identification and eventual confession, the story is evidently most concerned with the threat posed to the maintenance of the purity of Israel's cultic holiness by alien, forbidden objects. Whether they possess the explicit form of idols is regarded as immaterial in view of the scale of the danger.

We must conclude that the aim of the story is partly apologetic in that it offers a reasoned explanation for an experienced military defeat, and it is partly admonitory and intimidating in warning of liability to the most severe penalties on the part of those who disobeyed the covenant demands of the LORD God in the matter of forbidden objects. The introduction of an implicit condemnation of covetousness appears marginal rather than central. The narrative's apologetic character, offering explanation for military defeat, serves to show why a further overwhelming victory on the scale claimed for the capture of Jericho was not repeated at Ai and so, by inference, it upholds the claim that such divinely wrought triumphs, given miraculously, are possible when the conditions are right, but only then. Its admonitory aim serves to reinforce the necessity for the community to act severely against people harboring illicit objects associated with apostate neighbors and enemies, contrary to the strict requirements of God's covenant.

The range of practices and ideas relating to the conduct of war are widely evidenced in the Old Testament and have received considerable attention in an extensive range of studies (von Rad 1991; Jones 1989; Niditch 1993; Lind 1980). It is in no small measure the existence of these practices, their theological implications in what has frequently been termed the idea of "holy war," and their implicit demand to explore some of the ethical implications of warfare that call for close attention to the uniqueness of the story of Achan's sin. In spite of attempts to comprehend its essential form and character in terms of the belief that all Israel's battles were fought under a mantle of sacred power and authority, the story fits only very imperfectly within the known history of these constraints. In reality, Deuteronomy and the Deuteronomistic History express a wide range of variation in the details concerning Israel's conduct of warfare.

In this corpus of writings it becomes apparent that there is no comprehensive and consistent polity of holy war, even though various battles and the subject of warfare appear prominently both in historical narrative and prescriptive regulations. The stories of Joshua 1–9, Deuteronomy 1–11, and certain passages of the legal corpus of Deuteronomy 12–26 imply a different understanding of warfare from that which pervades the stories of military exploits in the book of Judges. This understanding is still more remote from the picture presented in 1 and 2 Samuel and 1 and 2 Kings. Achan's downfall belongs within a highly distinctive treatment of the subject connected with the conquest of the land promised to Israel's ancestors. It is closely related to the demand for exclusive allegiance to Yahweh as God posed by the vestiges of the religion practiced by the former inhabitants of Israel's promised land. The theology of Israel's wars of conquest belongs closely to the violent anti-Canaanite, anti-idolatry stratum of Deuteronomic thinking.

In its immediate literary context, the story of Achan has evidently been constructed to serve as a complement to the narrative of Josh 5:13–6:21, which recounts the conquest of Jericho. It forms an essential follow-up to the report of this great conquest, the theology of which is further reflected in the Deuteronomic claims to victory over the Transjordanian kings Sihon and Og (Deut 2:16–3:7). In these stories Israel's conquest of territory is claimed to have been a divinely given miracle. In order to receive these miracles, Israel was first and foremost called upon to show courage and unflinching loyalty to its covenant with God. God then gave the victory directly through divine intervention, leaving Israel the recipient of victory in battle. The specific goal of these battles was consistently taking possession of the promised land.

Holiness and Human Responsibility

In spite of J. S. Kaminsky's concern to focus the story of Achan prominently on the issue of corporate responsibility within Israel (Kaminsky 1995), this cannot have been the feature uppermost to the story's purpose. To some extent the story assumes that a rather opposite viewpoint prevailed, since it is concerned to show that, where certain types of cultic offense were concerned, even the normal constraints of legal rectitude needed to be overridden. Infringements of the demands of holiness imposed dangers that called for punishments more severe than those normal in judicial procedures. Moreover, the Deuteronomic legislation makes it plain that use of priestly (cultic) intervention to settle legal problems, as is implicit in Achan's sin's being discovered, was more normally regarded as a matter of last resort (Deut 17:8–13). The execution of Achan's family illustrates that, where there was a threat to Israel's covenant status through the harboring of objects forbidden by the deity, then even the restraining provisions of the law that protected the children of a criminal from arbitrary punishment could not be applied (Deut 24:16). A terrible infection had been brought into Israel and had to be removed. Even domestic animals who had been in contact with the illicit objects had to be totally destroyed by fire so as to remove completely the danger of further spread of the infection of the sin.

The story of Achan is about holiness and its preservation rather than about warfare and its aftermath. The death of the culprit and his family presupposes the application to warfare of rules of holiness appropriate to a very taboo-ridden view of cultic purity. In the light of these observations, it must be accepted that, even though the Deuteronomic legislation does contain a number of provisions concerning Israel's conduct of war, this story belongs to a quite narrow and specific stratum of this legislation. It is more about cult than about warfare! This theology of warfare focused on the expectation of divine miracles to bring victories, as is claimed for the battle of Jericho. Its theme is set out by Moses at the beginning of Deuteronomy: "The LORD your God, who goes before you, is the one who will fight for you, just as he did for you in Egypt before your very eyes . . ." (Deut 1:30; cf. 2:25, 3:22).

Overall, the message of the speeches ascribed to Moses in Deut 2:26, 3:22, 9:1–3, 11:22–25 is clear. The previous occupants of the land pose no real threat to the incoming Israelites: "Do not fear them, for it is the LORD your God who fights for you" (Deut 3:22). "Know then today that the LORD your God is the one who crosses over before you as a devouring fire; he will defeat them and subdue them before you, so that you may dispossess and destroy them quickly, as the LORD has promised you" (Deut 9:3).

It is here that we have a clear doctrine affirming that Israel's wars to gain possession of the land were to be won by the direct action of God, requiring from Israel only that it should show obedience, courage, and faith. Unwavering loyalty and purity of religious allegiance were the primary requirements for success, with no mention made of military strategy, tactics, or equipment. Rhetoric predominates in the exhortations. Certainly the assurances are hortatory in character, but what they promise exceeds what could be expected as typical of holy war ideology in which the Deuteronomic regulations (for example, Deuteronomy 21) take it for granted that human military action would be required. Over the question of the disposal of the spoils of war, older Deuteronomic regulations stand explicitly at variance with the harsher procedures demanded in the genocidal demands for the removal of the previous inhabitants.

In the Joshua story it becomes a point of importance that the defeat at Jericho required the destruction of all the erstwhile inhabitants of Jericho, together with "oxen, sheep, and donkeys" (Josh 6:21). This requirement contrasts with the note set in Deut 3:7 to the effect that, after the defeat of Og, the captured livestock was preserved alive. Since the prospect of spoils after a battle was widely accepted as a reward for the victors, even in Israel it becomes evident that the question of destroying all such booty and of devoting the more precious objects to God was regarded as a matter of unusual restraint. It is on this account that it occupies a prominent role in the story of Jericho's capture (Josh 6:19).

We are not therefore presented in Deuteronomy, or the Deuteronomistic History taken as a whole, with a fully coherent and uniform doctrine of war or with any wholly consistent doctrine concerning the extent of human cooperation and action required to achieve the divine purpose. So far as the conquest and settlement of the land are concerned, a stricter demand than was customary for warfare is claimed to have been imposed, consistent with the need for upholding Israel's exclusive cultic purity. It is on this front that Achan is condemned. For the conquest of the land, poetic exhortations to courage in the face of overwhelming dangers are intimately related to the demand for genocidal rigor in exterminating the previous inhabitants and an expectation of direct interventions by God to give victory.

Outside of the books of Deuteronomy and Joshua, however, there is a parallel to the miracle of the fall of Jericho to be found in the story of how Jerusalem was delivered from the besieging army of the Assyrian king Sennacherib in 701 B.C.E. After Hezekiah's position appeared altogether hopeless, we are told (2 Kgs 19:35 // Isa 37:36) that an angel of the Lord went forth and slew 185,000 of the besieging soldiers, forcing Sennacherib to retreat and return home.

B. C. Ollenburger (1987: 102) notes similarities between this narrative and the narrative in which Jericho was overthrown by miraculous and sudden divine action. S. Niditch (1993: 144–49) would consider emphasis on divinely given miracles (including Joshua's) as the key to victory in battle to be a theological motif evidencing a shift toward nonparticipation in military action. Yet this positive and optimistic interpretation of the situation appears to be more than is truly warranted. Communities of all ages appear to have found a belief that victories may be God-given signs or proof of divine approval rather than a turning toward more peaceful ways of settling conflicts. The parallel extends even to the appearance of a heavenly warrior-angel, since Joshua is said to have been privileged before the battle to have been visited by the commander of the army of the Lord (Josh 5:13–15). The important point, however, is that the victory is given by a direct act of divine intervention that obviates any concomitant human fighting. It is true that one is a battle of conquest and the other a battle of defense, but this is not highlighted as significant except that it is the Lord's city, Jerusalem, and the kingship of David's dynasty that are defended.

The Literary and Historical Context of Achan's Sin

The significant conclusion that must be drawn from the form and structure of the story of Achan's downfall is that it has been specifically formulated with the purpose of drawing attention to a number of issues relating to the conquest and occupation of the land. These issues were the result of reflections made long after the events they related to had actually occurred and reflect markedly more contemporary concerns regarding the land and Israel's ability to retain possession of it. From a literary and historical perspective, it is impossible to escape the conclusion that it was related closely to the aftermath of the early sixth century B.C.E. when Judah collapsed before Babylonian imperialist incursions in the Levant. The land promised to Israel's ancestors had effectively been lost.

The author's interest in Achan's breach of a holiness taboo relating to the booty of war appears to have been developed from what was originally a more marginal feature of Deuteronomic theology. After the catastrophe of 587 B.C.E., this feature appears to have been elevated into an attempt to purge the survivors in the land of all those persons who were regarded as unduly tolerant or careless in regard to the eradication of surviving vestiges of the ancient religion of the Canaanites. Who the parties were who formed the unfortunate target and victims of such a purge we can no longer discover. Overall the most rigorous stratum of this anti-idolatry, anti-Canaanite polemic that we find in the Deuteronomist literature appears to belong to the post-587 attempt (see Nielsen 1995: 4–13) to reformulate the older Deuteronomic legislation into a program of reconstruction. It sought, by a rigorous purge of a less zealously-minded community, to work for a renewed Israel after the disasters of the early sixth century B.C.E. had brought an end to the last remnants of the old state of Israel. However, so fervent and rigorous a doctrine, calling for the extermination of whole populations of whatever age or gender, appears as a heightening of a Deuteronomic emphasis, rather than representing a wholly novel doctrine.

If this exilic period provides the setting in which the stories of Joshua 1–9 reached their conclusive form, along with the Deuteronomic calls for genocide, then we do at least have some basis for understanding the apologetic aspects of the Achan story. The vigorous accusation that Achan had disobeyed God over the matter of holy rules and the forfeiting of plundered objects belonging to God must have related to some potential problem that the story's author considered merited such sharp condemnation. In particular the charge that he had been covetous in retaining for himself valuable spoils taken from the enemy indicates that the secret retention by wealthy Judahite citizens of forbidden treasures, most of which would have carried strong cultic associations, may at this time have been thought responsible for Israel's defeat by the Babylonian forces. Judah, like Achan, had been negligent in implementing God's demands concerning total allegiance to the covenant.

In searching for reasons for Jerusalem's capture and the destruction of the Temple on Mount Zion, it appears that a wide variety of "explanations" were sought, several of which now appear strange and unconvincing. Most forcefully argued in the Deuteronomistic gallery of reasoned explanations is the enormity of King Manasseh's sins (2 Kgs 21:10–16, 23:26), but they do not stand alone. King Hezekiah's foolhardy showing of his treasures to emissaries from Babylon is adduced as a reason for future setbacks for the Davidic dynasty (2 Kgs 20:12–19). The king's pride of possession (2 Kgs 20:13) conveys some similarities with Achan's covetousness, perhaps suggesting that Achan was looked upon as a prototypical precursor of this Judahite king. In a related vein of guarded praise masking broader national condemnation, the assurance to Josiah attributed to Huldah after the king's major reforms of the Jerusalem cultus offers no more than a temporary postponement of the inevitable day of judgment (2 Kgs 23:18–20). So when, after the disaster of 587 B.C.E., a new purge against all associated aspects of idolatry was instituted in a belated attempt to carry to its limits the ideals of cultic uniformity and exclusivity that had increasingly dominated the reforming zeal of the Deuteronomic movement, it is credible that many citizens resisted. Such noncompliant and self-serving rebels are portrayed by the picture of the hapless Achan. Like Achan, they would have countered attempts to remove all forbidden cult objects by hiding in the earth their traditional household treasures, including their household gods. The story of Achan's death is intended to serve as a warning to all such persons!

Overall it is arguable that the frenetic passion of the Deuteronomic-Deuteronomistic calls for the removal of all vestiges of the religious practices of the land's previous occupants emerged as a response to the guilty despair of reforming circles in Judah. Certainly it provides some sort of ideological context for the violence and vindictive intensity of the accusation that Achan's sin had been revealed by God and was duly punished. The strange and unconvincing doctrine that when Israel's conquest of the land was first carried out miracles were expected and did indeed take place reads oddly among the more realistic portrayals of the vicissitudes of human warfare that the Old Testament more generally presents. It is not the miracles of God-given victories that nourish the Old Testament's longing for peace, but the terrifying descriptions given by such prophets as Jeremiah and Ezekiel of the pain of war, the miseries of widowhood, and the degradation of once fertile lands into a wilderness.

It must certainly be recognized that the Deuteronomic calls for a religiously based form of genocide, with all of its unabashed cruelty and inhumanity, remains one of the most shocking and dangerous features of the entire literature of the Old Testament (see Van Winkle 1989). Such teaching remains indefensible and repugnant to the present day and must surely warn solemnly against the potentially harmful consequences of thoughtless, if well-intended, religious teaching based on uninformed and uncritical reading of such biblical narratives as the one concerning Achan.

Achan might have endeared himself and his family's name to all future generations had he nobly and self-sacrificially protested in the name of a merciful God against the wholesale slaughter of the inhabitants of Jericho and the taboo-ridden waste of the silver, gold, and clothing that were to be forfeited to the sanctuary of the LORD God of Israel. He would then have become a martyr figure like some more modern-day protester against the horrors of the holocaust and of ethnic cleansing and of the many misguided ways in which religion has been turned into an agency of cruelty, intolerance, and destruction. Instead he merely coveted valuable property for himself and, in doing so (so it was claimed) infringed on the rule that objects belonging to God alone cannot be freed for human use. He represents the many generations of temple-plunderers, grave-robbers, and iconoclasts who have tarnished human behavior in times of war and social change. He was believed to have "stolen" from God so, and thus he and his family were forced to pay the ultimate penalty.

It is difficult to find within the story of Achan's sin any residual merit or moral lesson. Yet, like several other biblical stories that hinge on complex and confused ideological doctrines, it is skillfully crafted, and its anecdotal clarity and forcefulness provide a constant temptation for the exegete to seek to wrest from its painful savagery some lesson of more lasting worth than the circumstances of its origin properly support. That

some form of monument was associated with the story in the form of a
great heap of stones and the naming of its location as the Valley of Achor
(Trouble) may nevertheless serve as a helpful reminder of the potential
dangers of religion. The fact that faith can promote hatred, intolerance,
and a guilt-ridden savagery, as well as love, joy, and peace remains a necessary warning to every serious-minded exegete of the Old Testament.
That Professor Crenshaw has so ably and enthusiastically counseled the
importance of wisdom and discrimination in the exegete's task makes it
not inappropriate that we should remember Achan. In researching the
past we may, like Achan's zealous accusers, uncover truths that we do
not expect to find. It then falls to the interpreter to handle such truth
with tolerance and discernment, so that further tragedies may be averted.

Bibliography

Jones, G. H.
.1989   The Concept of Holy War. Pp. 299–321 in *The World of Ancient Israel*,
         ed. R. E. Clements. Cambridge: Cambridge University Press.
Kaminsky, J. S.
1995   Pp. 67–95 in *Corporate Responsibility in the Hebrew Bible*. JSOTSup
         196. Sheffield: Sheffield Academic Press.
Lind, M. C.
1980   *The Theology of Warfare in Ancient Israel*. Scottsdale, Penn.: Herald.
Niditch, S.
1993   *War in the Hebrew Bible: A Study in the Ethics of Violence*. New York:
         Oxford University Press.
Nielsen, E.
1995   *Deuteronomium*. HAT 1/6. Tübingen: Mohr.
Ollenburger, B. C.
1987   *Zion, The City of the Great King: A Theological Symbol of the Jerusalem
         Cult*. JSOTSup 41. Sheffield: Sheffield Academic Press.
Rad, G. von
1991   *Holy War in Ancient Israel*. Reprinted, Grand Rapids, Mich.: Eerdmans.
Van Winkle, D.
1989   Canaanite Genocide and Amalekite Genocide and the God of Love.
         Winifred E. Weter Faculty Award Lecture. Seattle Pacific University.

The Problematic God of Samuel

MARTI J. STEUSSY
Christian Theological Seminary, Indianapolis

Introduction

"Does God pervert justice? Or does the Almighty pervert the right?"
(Job 8:3). Bildad posed the question to Job. My first-year seminary students raised it with respect to Saul. When I asked a recent class to write, then answer, three questions about the books of Samuel, twenty-six of twenty-eight queried the justice of Saul's fate. Twenty-three of the twenty-six then assured me that Saul deserved what happened to him.

Deep in their hearts they knew otherwise. If Saul's fate were so obviously merited, they would not have questioned it to begin with. But they assumed—as did Job's friends—the justice of God. God rejected and persecuted Saul; therefore Saul must have been bad. "Does God pervert justice?" First-year seminarians were afraid to look too closely.

Biblical scholars, especially those doing final-form literary study of the Samuel books, have been somewhat less timid. Gunn's influential monograph on *The Fate of King Saul* concludes, "Yahweh manipulates Saul mercilessly, and he does so for what, on most people's terms, must count as less than honourable motives. He is insulted, feels jealous, is anxious to justify himself. . . . [W]e might say that here we see the dark side of God" (Gunn 1980: 129). Eslinger's study of 1 Samuel 1–12 proposes that the people request a king in "reaction to Yahweh's hostilities towards Israel" and that God's response to the request "characterizes him as a powerful, domineering God . . . who will not admit his mistakes" and hopes to find in Saul a pliable "dupe" (Eslinger 1985: 60, 307, 312).[1]

---

1. Both Gunn (1980: 130–31) and Eslinger (1985: 428) refer to Job in their concluding remarks. Fokkelman (1986 and 1993), Miscall (1987), and Polzin (1989) also offer final-form literary readings that in varying degrees question the justice of Saul's fate. Humphreys (1985: 23–66) also shows deep sympathy for Saul, but his work takes more account of postulated editorial levels.

When it comes to God's character in the Samuel books, moreover, the "Saul problem" is only the tip of an iceberg. What of the Israelites who lose their lives with Saul at Gilboa (1 Samuel 31) or Uzzah's death (2 Samuel 6) or the illness and death of Bathsheba's child (2 Samuel 12) or the human sacrifice in Gibeon (2 Samuel 21) or the strange incident of the census and plague that lead to the sacrifice of oxen on Araunah's threshing floor (2 Samuel 24)? Just what kind of God do we meet in the books of Samuel?

Rather than follow the usual procedure of focusing on human characters in the Samuel books and secondarily sketching the implications for our understanding of God, I propose in this essay to look directly at the characterization of God. We will inevitably be drawn into a discussion of human players but only insofar as their merits and shortcomings impinge on the primary question of God's character.

Let me underscore several points about this approach at the outset. First, we will work with what the books of Samuel give us, without invoking assumptions about God derived from other parts of the canon. Second, we will work with the final form of 1 and 2 Samuel, which were originally a single book, rather than trying to separate out the layers and chunks of which the present Hebrew text is probably composed.

Third, and most important, the reader should remember that this study asks not who God is for theology and faith but the much more circumscribed question of how God appears as a literary character in the books of Samuel. At the close of the essay I will make a few suggestions about relating this literary picture to our larger concepts of God, but until then let us keep questions about who God "really is" separate from our inquiry into God as a character in this particular stretch of biblical text.

The Samuel books and the characters therein have a great deal to say about God. How shall we organize this mass of information? Rather than proceeding sequentially through 1 and 2 Samuel, I propose to cluster character clues by type, looking first at the most reliable clues and letting them set the tone for interpretation of more ambiguous types of information.

Robert Alter's landmark book *The Art of Biblical Narrative* offers a convenient summary of the means by which biblical narrators reveal character—here arranged in descending order of certainty (Alter 1981: 116–17).

1. Statements by the narrator
2. Character's thoughts
3. Character's speech to others
4. Other characters' comments
5. Character's appearance
6. Character's actions

Alter considers actions and appearance relatively unreliable character clues because of the interpretive gap between such bare data and a character's feelings and motives. Speech (by other characters and by the one under study) provides more direct claims, but these claims may be based on incomplete or inaccurate information, or characters may be deliberately lying. Our most straightfoward insights into character therefore come, according to Alter, from a character's thoughts and from direct narratorial evaluations of him or her.

Alter's scheme will need some adjustment for our exploration of God's character in the books of Samuel. The Samuel narrator tells us nothing about God's appearance and never makes an explicit character evaluation of God, so we can eliminate clue types 1 and 5 entirely. The narrator does allow us a few glimpses into God's feelings and motives, and we will give these top priority in our characterization.

Alter's next two categories involve speech. The Samuel books report a great deal of speech both by and about God. However, we shall discover a significant amount of misinformation and misdirection in both categories (speech by God and speech about God). Rather than follow Alter's prioritization of speech, I will adopt the principle that "God is as God does" and take God's actions (as known to us through narratorial report) as the second most reliable level of information about God. Having looked at God's "walk," we will then be ready to assess God's "talk." Last, we will examine a few of the many, and sometimes memorable, statements made about God by characters in Samuel, asking among other things whether priestly and prophetic speech exhibits the reliable knowledge of God so often attributed to it.

This leaves us with the following revised list of character clues for God in Samuel:

1. God's inner life (explicitly reported feelings and motivations)
2. God's walk (actions as reported by the narrator)

3. God's talk (narratorially and prophetically reported divine speech)
4. God-talk (by prophets, priests, kings, and ordinary persons)

God's Inner Life

Table 1 lists for us the handful of insights that the books of Samuel offer into God's feelings and motives. Chapter and verse numbers refer to the New Revised Standard Version (which I quote unless otherwise indicated). I have attempted to capture the essence of the biblical phrasing in each entry. The Hebrew terminology of 1 Sam 2:25 has more emotional color than the NRSV's translation: God is pleased to or desires (rather than simply "wills") to kill Eli's sons. In the following verse God's role is less active than the NRSV's 'favor' suggests—the Hebrew says something like 'Samuel walked in size and goodness both with God and with people' (2:26, my translation).

Table 1. God's Inner Life in the Books of Samuel

1 Samuel	
2:25	desires to kill Eli's sons
2:26	Samuel walks well with God
15:35	God sorry to have made Saul king
2 Samuel	
6:7	*anger* kindled, God strikes Uzzah (who dies)
11:27	David's act bad in God's sight
12:24–25	loves Solomon, sends message by Nathan
17:14	defeats Ahithophel's counsel in order to ruin Absalom
24:1	*anger* kindled, incites David
24:16	relents "concerning the evil"

Table 1 depicts a passionate, labile God, whose feelings and motives are more often negative than positive. In only two cases are God's purposes revealed, and in both the purpose is destruction: of Eli's sons in 1 Sam 2:25 and of Absalom in 2 Sam 17:14. God accomplishes this destruction by blocking good advice. Ironically, the advice in the first case is to show greater respect for God; in the second case the person targeted for destruction is fulfilling a divine decree (God's declaration of punishment on David's house in 2 Sam 12:10–12). In both cases, not only the advisees, but also the advice-givers (Eli and Ahithophel, whose counsel "was as if one consulted the oracle of God," 2 Sam 16:23) are brought to ruin.

In 1 Sam 15:35 and 2 Sam 11:27, God is displeased by the behavior of someone whom God has hitherto supported. God is also sorry about past behavior in 2 Sam 24:16 ('relented' translates the same Hebrew verb as 'sorry' in 1 Sam 15:35), but here the behavior is God's own.

In two "kindling" passages (2 Sam 6:7 and 24:1) the initial grammatical subject is not God but God's "anger." It is hard to tell whether the narrator thinks of this as an emotion that God has or as a mode of God's presence in ordinary reality (comparable to God's "word" or "glory" elsewhere in the Bible). God's anger in 2 Sam 6:7 seems triggered by Uzzah's touching of the ark, but the Hebrew text of the explanation is very obscure (so obscure that the NRSV's translators draw on the parallel verse from Chronicles)—something along the lines of, 'God struck him there for the error'. The anger seems much like what is warned against in Exod 19:21–25: a flash of energy triggered by contact rather than a considered act of divine decision.[2] In 2 Samuel 24 the cause of God's anger remains unexplained. Both times, the kindling of God's anger results in death—seventy thousand deaths in the second instance.

The narrator tells us of positive divine feeling toward only two people: Samuel in 1 Sam 2:26 and Solomon in 2 Sam 12:24–25. In Samuel's case, favor apparently results in Samuel's replacing Eli. God's briefly-mentioned affection for Solomon receives no further development in the books of Samuel but comes to a bloody and vengeful denouement with Solomon's accession in 1 Kings 1–2.

Our information about God's inner life—the most secure evidence for God's character—suggests that readers who see this narrative's God as a wrathful one are correct. We have yet to see, however, how this corresponds with other aspects of God's characterization in the Samuel books.

---

2. The nonrational aspect of "bursting forth" is clearer in Exodus, where the very fact of God's warning suggests that God does not *will* to 'break out' (same Hebrew word as 'burst forth' in 2 Sam 6:8).

God's Walk

Table 2 lists God's actions as reported by the narrator of 1 and 2 Samuel. Possible intermediary agents such as God's anger, word, hand, spirit, dread, or a "deep sleep from the LORD" (1 Sam 26:12) are underlined.

Table 2. God's "Walk" in the Books of Samuel

1 Samuel	
1:5–6	closes Hannah's womb
1:19	remembers Hannah (she gets pregnant)
2:21	takes note of Hannah (she has more children)
2:25	Eli's sons don't listen, for God desires to kill them
3:1	God's *word* rare
3:19	with Samuel, lets none of his words fall to the ground
3:21	continues to appear, reveals self to Samuel by *word*
5:6	*hand* heavy on Ashdod, terror and tumors
5:9	*hand* against Gath, panic and tumors
5:11–12	*hand* heavy on Ekron, panic and tumors
6:19	kills seventy (or 50,070) at Beth-shemesh
7:9–10	answers Samuel, thunders and confuses Philistines
7:13	*hand* against Philistines all Samuel's days
10:9–10	gives Saul another heart, *spirit* puts Saul in prophetic frenzy
10:26	touches warrior hearts to follow Saul
11:6	*spirit* kindles Saul's anger
11:7	*dread* falls upon people
12:18	sends thunder and rain at Samuel's request
14:15	there is very great panic (Hebrew: 'panic of God')
14:23	gives Israel victory
14:37	does not answer Saul
16:13	*spirit* comes mightily on David
16:14	*spirit* departs from Saul, *evil spirit* torments him
16:23	*evil spirit* is on Saul, departs when David plays
18:10	*evil spirit* on Saul while David plays (Saul raves, throws spear)
18:14	David succeeds because God is with him
19:9	*evil spirit* while David plays (Saul throws spear)
19:21	*spirit* sends Saul's messengers into prophetic frenzy
19:23	*spirit* sends Saul into prophetic frenzy

Table 2. God's "Walk" in the Books of Samuel

23:14	does not give David into Saul's hand
25:38	strikes Nabal (who dies)
26:12	*deep sleep* on Saul's camp
28:6	does not answer Saul
2 Samuel	
5:10	David grows greater and greater because God with him
6:7	*anger* kindled, God strikes Uzzah (who dies)
6:11	blesses Obed-edom and house
7:1	gives king (David) rest from enemies
8:6	gives David victory wherever he goes
8:14	gives David victory wherever he goes
12:1	David's act bad in God's sight, sends Nathan to David
12:15	strikes Bathsheba's first baby
12:24–25	loves Solomon, sends message by Nathan
17:14	defeats Ahithophel's counsel in order to ruin Absalom
21:14	heeds supplications for land
22:1	delivers David from all enemies and Saul
23:10	brings about great victory
23:12	brings about great victory
24:1	*anger* kindled, God incites David to take census
24:15–16	sends pestilence (seventy thousand die), relents "concerning the evil"
24:25	answers supplication (plague averted)

Table 2 does not include occasions on which something simply happens in God's presence (for instance, 1 Sam 2:21, "Samuel grew up in the presence of the LORD"). It does include verses in which the narrator specifically tells us that God did *not* do something (for instance, 1 Sam 23:14, in which God does not give David into Saul's hand), since this helps us characterize God's "walk." An attentive reader may notice that some "actions" center on speech, such as 1 Sam 3:21's revelation to Samuel by word. I include these here because primary stress seems to lie not on what is said—which in most cases is not even reported (in 1 Sam 7:9–10 it may be a thunderstorm rather than words)—but on the fact of saying (or not saying). Some passages about God's inner life reappear here because they are associated with action.

Casual readers sometimes suppose that God's first act in the books of Samuel is to provide a child to the longing Hannah. Not so. The Samuel books' first assertion about God's action is the statement in 1:5, repeated in 1:6, that the "LORD had closed her [Hannah's] womb."[3] Hannah's name means 'favor' or 'grace', and her husband's means 'God has acquired' or 'God has created'—using the same verb as Eve's exclamation, "I have *produced* a man with the help of the LORD" (Gen 4:1, emphasis added)—but Hannah and Elkanah have been prevented by their God from having children.

Eager to find a loving, life-giving God, we move quickly forward to the clear statements of 1:19 and 2:21 that God does support Hannah's bearing, first of Samuel and then of three other sons and two daughters. But what are we to make of the fact that the problem here "solved" by God was of God's own making and that what intervened between God's closing and God's opening was a woman's vow to give her child to God?

The question might be taken as cynical were the dynamic not repeated. Take, for instance, God's protection of David. In 1 Sam 19:21 and 23 God protects David by having a spirit throw Saul's messengers and Saul himself into a prophetic frenzy. In 23:14 the narrator assures us that God did not give David into Saul's hand. But Saul persecutes David precisely because God has withdrawn the spirit from Saul, afflicted Saul with an evil spirit (16:14 and 23) and transferred support to David. (Note the tight association between God's sending of the evil spirit and Saul's spear-throwing in 1 Sam 18:10 and 19:9.) The persecution from which God delivers David—albeit not without David's fleeing to the wilderness and eventually to the Philistine court—has been instigated and encouraged by God. (For more detail on this, see Gunn 1980: 116–23.)

In 2 Samuel God again "solves" problems of God's own making. Love for Solomon, which prompts God to send Nathan in 2 Sam 12:25, looks suspiciously like compensation for the previous child's death, which Nathan announced in 12:14. God saves David by defeating Ahithophel's counsel (2 Sam 17:14), but the defeated rebellion itself had

---

3. Polzin raises the possibility that these verses give us Elkanah's and Peninnah's understanding of the situation in addition to or even rather than the narrator's independent assessment of it (Polzin 1989: 20–21). I think he may be right, especially in 2:6, that the narratorial voice conveys Peninnah's reasoning, but I also see no indication that the narrator disagrees with the assessment; 2:5 may even be the narrator's confirmation.

played out God's threats in 2 Sam 12:10–11. In 2 Sam 21:14, God responds to supplication after a period of famine for which God seems to accept responsibility in 21:1 (this is, however, divine speech rather than a narratorial report). This time, between the harm and the correction lie multiple human sacrifices.

The story of plague and offering in 2 Samuel 24 ends with a similarly worded divine response to supplication, but this time responsibility for the problem is clearly stated: "the LORD sent a pestilence on Israel from that morning until the appointed time; and seventy thousand of the people died" (24:15). However, this is still not the full story: the plague punishes a census that itself was ordered by God, for reasons as unexplained as the outburst against Uzzah. This time the final response to supplication is preceded by David's purchase of a threshing floor and presentation of burnt offerings. In the meantime, seventy thousand people have died. However positive the spin usually given to these actions, we may fairly question whether this particular withdrawal of divine affliction should be credited to God as blessing.

In light of this pattern of harm-then-amelioration, the order of actions in Hannah's psalm may be significant: "the LORD kills and brings to life . . . he brings low, he also exalts" (1 Sam 2:6–7).

Table 2 also tells us something about God's *modes* of action in the books of Samuel. Setting aside for a moment the question of God's ends, let us look simply at the means by which God accomplishes them. A quick scan of the table reveals a proponderance of deleterious actions against individuals (for instance, closing Hannah's womb, working to slay Eli's sons, tormenting Saul with an evil spirit, and striking Uzzah) and against groups (for instance, the plagues in Philistia, the slaughter in Beth-shemesh, and various battle victories).[4] In all, about three-fifths of God's reported actions are accomplished by destructive mechanisms. The ark, God's "hand," God's "anger," and (in a majority of its appearances) God's "spirit" are especially associated with destructive action. Only in 1 Sam 16:13 does the spirit seem clearly positive. Elsewhere, it

---

4. Passages showing negative action against individuals include 1 Sam 1:5–6; 2:25; 14:37; 16:14, 23; 18:10; 19:9, 21, 23; 25:38; 26:12; 28:6; and 2 Sam 6:7; 12:15; 17:14; 24:1. Actions by battle or other processes of mass destruction occur in 1 Sam 5:6, 9, 11–12; 6:19; 7:9–10, 13; 14:15, 23; and 2 Sam 7:1; 8:6, 14; 22:1; 23:10, 12; and 24:15–16.

usually serves to impede progress by throwing persons into prophetic frenzy or whatever other sort of madness prompts Saul's spear-throwing.

Positive actions comprise less than a fifth of the total in table 2.[5] The remaining actions, such as God's thunder and rain in 1 Sam 12:18, do not fall into clear categories of positive and negative—although since the thunder and rain come on the day of the wheat harvest (12:17), I may be too generous in deeming them neutral.[6] As we have already seen, a goodly number of "positive" actions (at least half of the instances) involve the undoing or countering of some prior negative action.

In short, the God shown us by the narratorial assertions of 1 and 2 Samuel engages in smiting and terror far more often than healing or encouragement. However, most readers do not evaluate the *means* of God's actions so much as the *impacts* of those actions on favored characters in the story. Thus, for instance, we applaud God's routing of the Philistines in 1 Samuel 7 and 14 because we are rooting for the Israelites.

God comes off somewhat better in impact-oriented analysis: of the 53 passages listed in table 2, 17 report actions clearly favorable to Israel.[7] Only 3 (the Beth-shemesh slaughter of 1 Sam 6:19 and the inciting and plague of 2 Sam 24:1 and 15–16) are clearly negative.

In the majority of the passages in table 2, the impact on Israel is more difficult to evaluate because God acts vis-à-vis particular individuals. Most of us have been taught, more or less subtly, to assume that when God sends an evil spirit upon Saul or gives David victory wherever he goes, God does this for the benefit of Israel. But how warranted is this conclusion?

One way of pursuing the question would be to probe the consequences of God's involvement in individual instances. For instance, when God prevents Eli's sons from heeding their father's warning (1 Sam 2:25), is the outcome more beneficial for Israel than if the sons had listened and changed their ways? Or, assuming that David is indeed a better king for Israel than Saul, could not Saul and his successors have

---

5. "Positive-mechanism" actions by God would include 1 Sam 1:19; 2:21; 16:13; 18:14; 2 Sam 5:10; 6:11; 12:24–25; 21:14; and 24:25.

6. What are we to make of the fact that the Beth-shemesh slaughter also comes while the people are harvesting wheat (1 Sam 6:13)?

7. These include God's actions against the Philistines in 1 Samuel 5, 7, 10, 11, and 14; and 2 Samuel 7, 8, and 23, as well as the heeding of supplication in 21:14 and 24:25.

perished without the massive national defeat reported in 1 Samuel 31? Might Absalom, supported by Ahithophel's counsel, have made a better king than David or Solomon?

Rather than indulging in piecemeal speculation, however, let us note that most instances of "individual meddling" on God's part involve Saul's downfall and David's success. Arguably, even the stubbornness of Eli's sons and God's support for Samuel move toward this end. Does this broad pro-David trajectory work to Israel's benefit?

Some memorable lines in the Samuel books affirm this: "David then perceived that the LORD . . . had exalted his kingdom for the sake of his people Israel" (2 Sam 5:12). "David administered justice and equity to all his people" (2 Sam 8:15). Or consider David's "last words."

> One who rules over people justly,
>   ruling in the fear of God,
> is like the light of morning,
>   like the sun rising on a cloudless morning,
> gleaming from the rain on the grassy land. (2 Sam 23:3–4)

At a minimum, God's support for David provides military security for the people—although this support could also have been provided through Saul, as we know from the Nahash incident. Military security is nothing to be sneezed at. We also hear (for instance, in 1 Sam 30:26–31; 2 Sam 8:9–12, 12:30) of wealth from other peoples taken as tribute or booty. Some of the projects to which such wealth would be dedicated might conceivably have benefited David's people (an example might be the strengthening of the capital reported in 2 Sam 5:9).

But as the Bathsheba/Uriah story of 2 Samuel 11–12 makes unmistakably clear, David is not simply a benefit to his people. Although leadership in battle is part of the king's primary job description (1 Sam 8:20), David stays home and "takes" while "all Israel" besieges Rabbah. David then murders Uriah for not cooperating in a cover-up. David's punishment is that the sword will never depart from his house (2 Sam 12:10)—but that sword is not confined to his house. It devours twenty thousand men in the battle between Absalom's forces and David's, "and the forest claimed more victims than the sword" (2 Sam 18:7–8).

Absalom's rebellion also reveals Israelite dissatisfaction with David's justice (2 Sam 15:1–6). The stirring of another rebellion in 20:1–2 shows that this discontent was no passing whim.

Is David's success a benefit for Israel? Even within the books of Samuel, we see reason to question this equation. If we allow ourselves to glance ahead into Kings, the people's dependence on David's house leads to division and, ultimately, loss of the land. Over against these problematic consequences of David's rule, favorable statements from David and his courtiers and the isolated narratorial statement about just rule in 2 Sam 8:15 become less convincing.

To this point, we have discovered a God of strong likes and dislikes, more adept at thunder and smiting than at healing. Within the boundaries of Israel, God's feelings and actions tend to concern individual leaders rather than the people at large, but God's interventions for and against these leaders have substantial consequences for the people. God's fascination with David is by no means an unmixed blessing for them.

God's Talk in the Books of Samuel

Table 3 lists passages in which the books of Samuel report God's speech. In some cases, closely related utterances are listed together, such as God's calls to Samuel in 1 Sam 3:4, 6, 8, and 10. The passages fall into several categories, distinguished from one another in the "source" column. In the simplest and most common category the narrator quotes divine speech directly; for example, 1 Sam 3:4: "Then the LORD called, 'Samuel! Samuel!'" In such cases I list God as source. Elsewhere the narrator tells us about God's speaking or refusal to speak, without directly quoting. For these passages, (some of which also appear in table 2), I show the narrator as source.

Table 3. God's Talk in the Books of Samuel

Location	Source	Addressee	Content
1 Samuel			
2:27–36	man of God	Eli	oracle against Eli's house
3:1	narrator	—	word rare
3:4–14	God	Samuel	calls Samuel, declares doom on Eli's house
3:21	narrator	Samuel	God reveals self by word to Samuel
7:9	narrator	Samuel	God answers Samuel
8:7–9	God	Samuel	tells Samuel to listen to people and warn them
8:22	God	Samuel	tells Samuel to listen to people and make them a king

Table 3. God's Talk in the Books of Samuel

Location	Source	Addressee	Content
9:15–17	God	Samuel	predicts Saul's coming and identifies him to Samuel
10:18	Samuel	people	rehearsal of history
10:20–21	lots	people	selection of king
10:22	God	people	Saul is with the baggage
14:37	narrator	—	God doesn't answer Saul
14:41–42	lots	Saul	identifies oath-breaker
15:2–3	Samuel	Saul	instructions about attacking Amalekites
15:10–11	God	Samuel	regrets making Saul king
16:1–3	God	Samuel	instructions for Samuel's Bethlehem trip
16:7	God	Samuel	rejects Eliab
16:12	God	Samuel	tells Samuel to anoint David
23:2–4	God	David	information about Keilah
23:11–12	God	David	information about Keilah
28:6	narrator	—	God doesn't answer Saul
30:8	God	David	instructions on following Amalekites
2 Samuel			
2:1	God	David	instructions on going to Hebron
5:19	God	David	instructions on fighting Philistines
5:23–25	God	David	instructions on fighting Philistines
7:5–16	God	Nathan	dynastic oracle
12:7–12	Nathan	David	punishment oracle
12:24–25	narrator	—	sends a message by Nathan about Solomon
21:1	God	David	bloodguilt on Saul's house
24:1	God	David	commands census
24:11–12	God	Gad	offers choice of punishments
24:16	God		plague angel commands angel to hold
24:18–19	Gad	David	instructions for altar

Table 3 also includes speeches made on God's behalf by prophets. Rather than regarding everything a prophet says as accurate information about God, I list in this table only clearly marked oracles (for instance, oracles beginning "thus says the LORD"). My reasons for this selectivity will become apparent when we examine other prophetic speech later in this paper. I also include Gad's orders to David (2 Sam 24:18), which are *not* marked by any particular formula. In the next verse, however, the narrator refers to "Gad's instructions" as what "the LORD had commanded," apparently confirming that the instructions were divine in origin.

Prophetically conveyed divine speeches carry the prophet's name in the "source" column. The word "lots" in this column indicates a presumably divine response reported as an outcome of lot-casting rather than as a divine statement.

One might question whether even oracular speeches by prophets should be considered divine speech, especially in view of the fact that the narrator presents the key dynastic promise to David (2 Sam 7:5–16) by allowing us to eavesdrop on God's dictation of the message to Nathan (thus "God" in table 3's source column). The tactic implies that merely hearing Nathan's delivery to David might leave us in doubt. Yet in cases where we have means to verify prophetic oracles, they hold good. God's words to Samuel in 1 Sam 3:11–14 agree with the man of God's oracle in 1 Sam 2:27–36 and even apparently refer back to it as "all that I have spoken concerning his [Eli's] house" (3:12). Similarly Samuel's instructions to Saul in 15:2–3 are referred to by God as "my commands" in 15:11 (assuming that these are indeed the commands in question). The judgment oracle pronounced by Nathan follows a notice that "the LORD sent Nathan to David," and its particulars are fulfilled later in the story. Thus it seems reasonable to understand prophetic oracles in the books of Samuel as, in the narrative's terms, direct quotations of God's speech.

Ancient Near Eastern leaders expected their deities to provide counsel, either directly through oracular word or less directly through a variety of omens and lots interpreted by priests. Almost all of God's talk in the books of Samuel has such practical significance. This is most obvious, for the modern reader, in chapters such as 1 Samuel 23 or 2 Samuel 5, where God gives David direct military counsel in response to direct military questions. However, practical matters are also at stake in passages such as 1 Samuel 2 or 2 Samuel 16, in which God affirms or repudiates a particular leader (or his descendants), and in a passage such as 2 Samuel 21, where information about the divine cause of a famine suggests a way to counter it. With the importance of God's practical guidance in mind, let us consider God's readiness to speak to four key leaders: Eli, Samuel, Saul, and David.

God's only recorded speech to Eli is one of repudiation and doom (1 Samuel 2). Thereafter we hear that "the word of the LORD was rare in those days; visions were not widespread" (1 Sam 3:1). The final oracle repudiating Eli's family comes to Samuel, not to Eli himself.

To Samuel, however, "the LORD continued to appear at Shiloh, for the LORD revealed himself to Samuel at Shiloh by the word of the LORD" (3:21). This summary report is confirmed by many instances in which God speaks to Samuel or Samuel speaks for God. The nature of God's "answer" to Samuel in 1 Sam 7:9 is unclear; the response may be verbal or it may lie in thunder and rout (7:10) as it does in 1 Sam 12:18 ("Samuel called upon the LORD, and the LORD sent thunder and rain that day"). Our uncertainty about the mode of answering does not reduce the importance of the fact that when Samuel calls, God does answer.

Saul, like Eli, receives very little oracular assistance from God. Even before Saul's falling-out with Samuel in 1 Samuel 13, the king's experiences with God involve frenzied possession rather than rational communication. Saul aborts his first recorded official attempt at inquiry mid-process (1 Sam 14:18). God then refuses to advise Saul on whether to pursue the Philistines (14:36–37). Saul next challenges God to reveal by the Urim and Thummim (sacred lots, which may also have been used in the previous inquiry) the person who has broken the terms of Saul's oath. The lots identify the correct person, suggesting that God has indeed spoken, but the outcome is phrased entirely in passive language: "were indicated," "was taken." This allows the narrator to avoid saying that God answered Saul, while still letting God give Saul some very bad news.

Table 3 shows us that God speaks words to Saul only once—the battle instructions, conveyed by Samuel in 1 Sam 15:2–3, which lead to Saul's final rejection. Long chapters pass in which God's only message to Saul is torment by an evil spirit. At the end of Saul's life we encounter two more explicit statements of God's refusal to answer, from the narrator in 28:6 and Saul himself in 28:15. Is Saul, too, among the prophets? Not in any sense that is helpful to him.

God evinces no such reluctance to answer David, who receives more reported oracles from God (I include here the messages delivered to or by prophets) than any other character, including Samuel himself. The inquiries reported in 1 Samuel 23 and 30 and 2 Samuel 2 and 5:19

probably involve the Urim and Thummim: they begin when Abiathar arrives in David's camp with the ephod and involve a characteristic form of two yes/no questions. However, the narrator emphasizes God's clear communication with David by reporting the answers as dialogue ("the LORD said to David").

Even David's adultery and murder (2 Samuel 11) do not close off his communication with God, for afterward we see not only the positive message of 2 Sam 12:25 but a positive response to the prayer for confounding of Ahithophel's counsel (2 Sam 15:31 and 17:14). The books of Samuel conclude with fresh assertions of God's willingness to respond to supplication (2 Sam 21:14, 24:25). David's "last words" are even referred to as an "oracle," as if David were a prophet (2 Sam 23:1).

Are the withholding of divine communication from Eli and Saul and its generous provision to Samuel and David based on the relative worthiness of these different recipients? We do not have space here for an exhaustive analysis of the issues, but table 4 sets out some of the basic considerations. For more extensive discussion, I refer the reader to Gunn (1980 and 1988) and to my own book (1999).

Table 4. Comparison of Key Leaders in the Books of Samuel

	Eli	*Samuel*	*Saul*	*David*
Status with God	rejected, descendants also rejected	supported, descendants' fate not noted	rejected, descendants also rejected	supported, descendants also supported
sins with a high hand?	No	No	? (see discussion)	Yes
Sons sin with a high hand?	Yes	Yes	No	Yes
Rebukes sons?	Yes	No	(no need)	No
Yields position graciously?	Yes	No	No	Yes

Table 4 reveals no consistent relationship between various aspects of merit and God's treatment of these leaders and their descendants. In 1 Samuel 2 and 3 God attributes Eli's rejection primarily to his sons' behavior. The only charge leveled against Eli himself is this: "I announce to him that I am condemning his family once and for all, because of this crime: though he knew his sons were blaspheming God, he did not reprove them" (3:13, NAB).[8] However, Eli *did* reprove his sons (1 Sam 2:22–25). If the issue is not whether he *attempted* to stop them but whether he succeeded (as implied by the NRSV's 'restrain'), we must consider the stated reason for the sons' refusal to listen: "it was the will of the LORD to kill them" (2:25).

Samuel also had two corrupt sons (1 Sam 8:3). No attempt at correction on his part is recorded. Israel's elders cite the corruption among their reasons for wanting a king (8:5), but Samuel makes no response to that part of their argument (Fokkelman 1993: 338). Yet Samuel suffers no punishment, nor do we even hear that God takes action against the sons (who are apparently still around in 12:2).

One might then contend that Eli's sons blasphemed (1 Sam 3:13), while Samuel's merely took bribes and perverted justice (8:3). If this is the reason for the difference in divine response, it reveals a God who is far more touchy about personal insults than about subversion of legal systems, again raising the question of whether Israel's welfare is the driving concern in God's actions. However, the explanation is circular because it rates blasphemy a more serious offense on the basis of punishment received, then defends the difference in punishment on the grounds that blasphemy is the more serious offense. The logic reduces to "this is fair because it's what God did"—precisely Bildad's point.

Eli accepts being disowned with a graciousness ("it is the LORD; let him do what seems good to him," 1 Sam 3:18) matched only by David's yielding response to Absalom's rebellion and Shimei's curses ("let him alone, and let him curse; for the LORD has bidden him," 2 Sam 16:11).

Samuel, by contrast, shows a distinct reluctance to step aside when his moment comes (see especially Eslinger 1985: 251–82; and Polzin 1989: 80–88). He himself has 'judged' (Hebrew *špṭ*) Israel and also appointed his sons as 'judges' (same Hebrew verb, 1 Sam 7:14–15). But

---

8. In the Hebrew text the sons "blasphemed for themselves" rather than "blasphemed God." However, rabbinic tradition supported by the Greek text identifies "for themselves" as a euphemism replacing an original "God" because the phrase "blaspheming God" was too offensive to let stand (McCarter 1980: 96). The word translated 'reprove' is a rare one; the NJPSV translates it 'rebuke', and the NJB reads 'corrected'.

because of Samuel's age and his sons' corruption, Israel's elders ask for "a king to govern [*špṭ*] us" (8:5). The Hebrew wording reveals what the NRSV's translation obscures: the king will be taking over the job (governing: *špṭ*) formerly performed by Samuel and his sons. This king will be Samuel's replacement.

And what is Samuel's concern? That Israel thereby rejects its God? No, it is *God* who introduces that issue into the conversation (Gunn 1980: 59). God's response suggests that Samuel's concern is Israel's rejection of Samuel, to which God replies comfortingly (!), "they have not rejected you, but they have rejected me" (8:7). God then tells the prophet—thrice!—to "listen to the voice" of the people and anoint them a king (1 Sam 8:7, 9 and 22). Instead, Samuel tells them to go home. But God does not curse or disown Samuel.

If Samuel will not go find a king, God will (in the next chapter) send the king to Samuel (Polzin 1989: 90). However, Samuel cannot quite give up power. Even after anointing the new king, Samuel continues to try to run the show (1 Sam 10:8, 17–25; 11:14; 12:23). What are the consequences of this for the next leader, Saul?

Saul's sin in his first falling-out with Samuel (1 Samuel 13) is—as my students sensed and as Gunn details at length (1980: 33–40)—far from clear. Does Saul sin by presuming to offer sacrifice? When David makes burnt offerings (2 Sam 6:17 and 24:25), we hear no complaints about violation of prophetic privilege. Or is the problem Saul's failure to wait for Samuel? "He [Saul] waited seven days, *the time appointed by Samuel*; but *Samuel* did not come," the narrator tells us (1 Sam 13:8, emphasis added). Yet Samuel insists that the failure is Saul's, not his own.

Saul's violation of divine command in 1 Samuel 15 seems somewhat clearer, although even here he may simply be interpreting the command differently from Samuel (Gunn 1980: 41–56). David is never burdened with such restrictions on the handling of booty: he takes even Amalekite booty freely (1 Sam 30:20) and uses it to advance his own cause (30:26).

Once David appears on the scene, Saul's story is a downward spiral of jealousy and madness, but the madness follows rather than precedes Saul's torment under the evil spirit from God. To blame Saul for his jealousy of David is somewhat like blaming Eli's sons for not heeding their father's advice.

Samuel is no more gracious than Saul in standing aside for his successor, but only Saul is disowned. Samuel places his corrupt sons in
office but is never chastised for their behavior. Saul's son Jonathan, by
contrast, is perhaps the most unambiguously virtuous character in the
books of Samuel (certainly more so than David), but father and son alike
are disowned by God.

David, like Eli and Samuel, has problematic children. Unlike Eli and
Samuel, he is also personally guilty of sin. Like Eli, he yields graciously
to divine edicts (we will look at the instances a little later). Both houses
(David's and Eli's) are placed under curse of a sword (1 Sam 2:33, 2 Sam
12:10). But Eli and his entire line are removed from office, and God's
word is "rare." David remains in office. God pledges to keep his descendants there in perpetuity and continues to communicate with David and
his family.

There seems no consistent pattern to God's variable willingness to
speak to the four major leaders in Samuel except, perhaps, that God is
more patient with Samuel than with his predecessor Eli and more patient with David than with his predecessor Saul. Perhaps God learns
from Eli that one cannot expect a leader's sons to follow his footsteps;
perhaps God learns from Saul that kings need a freer hand than Samuel
and God have allowed.

After our lengthy discussion of issues surrounding God's willingness
to speak to various persons in the books of Samuel, we return to table 3
to ask about the most common topics of God's speech. In five passages,
God reviews divine assistance for David and/or Israel (1 Samuel 2, 8, and
10; 2 Samuel 7 and 12). In six passages God responds to David's que-
ries—mostly about battle, sometimes with promises of deliverance
(1 Samuel 23, twice, and 30; 2 Samuel 2 and 5). In eight passages God
chooses someone or promises to do so (1 Samuel 2, 9, 10, 16; 2 Samuel
7, 12). Ten passages center on rejection, identification of a guilty party,
or punishment (1 Samuel 2, 3, 15, 16; 2 Samuel 12, 21, 24).

These topics suggest a God conscious of having rendered past favors
and—in David's and Samuel's cases—continuing to give assistance. But
God punishes and rejects more often than God elects. Rejection
speeches outweigh election ones in length as well as number. "Choosing" statements are, except for 2 Samuel 7, very brief. However, there
are three long rejection/punishment speeches: 1 Sam 2:27–36, 3:11–14;

2 Sam 12:7–12. This bit of narrative design contributes to our impression of God as a threatening, punishing deity.

God's speeches in Samuel also raise questions about divine integrity. Early in 1 Samuel, a "man of God" tells Eli on God's behalf, " 'I promised that your family and the family of your ancestor should go in and out before me forever,' but now the LORD declares: 'Far be it from me . . .' " (1 Sam 2:30). Lest we miss the point, we hear again in the next chapter, "I will fulfill against Eli all that I have spoken concerning his house" (3:12). "All that I have spoken" does not refer to the promise "forever." Instead, says God, "I am about to punish his house forever . . . the iniquity of Eli's house shall not be expiated by sacrifice or offering forever" (3:13–14).[9]

The sobering impact of this sequence is to alert us, before any king has been named, that God is quite capable of turning a promise "forever" into punishment forever—perhaps misrepresenting the case in the process ("he did not reprove them"). Gunn proposes—I think correctly—a similar dynamic for Saul's condemnation: an angry God pronounces rejection without too close an examination of the case (Gunn 1980: 123–26).

These transactions cast a sobering shadow over God's later pledge to establish the Davidic throne "forever" (2 Sam 7:13 and 16). God even refers in that oracle to withdrawing steadfast love "from Saul, whom I put away from before you" (7:15). There is something quite unnerving about a promise never to withdraw "steadfast love" that in its very enunciation mentions that God has a track record of withdrawing such loyalty.

---

9. Eslinger cites some of these same passages in an excursus, "For Ever or For a While?" in which he argues that "only when there is an unusual context in which indefinite term is specifically at issue" should the Hebrew expression in question be translated 'forever' (Eslinger 1994: 46–48, with reference to Tsevat 1980: 106–7). I would agree that in some cases something like 'for as long as the issue is relevant' might be a better translation than 'for eternity' (with respect, for instance, to Samuel sitting before God 'forever' in 1 Samuel 22), but citing the promise to Eli's ancestor as evidence that the term does not mean 'forever' begs the question of whether God broke the promise. Nor does attachment of an "if" to certain promises mean that they are not "forever"—the "if" simply limits the conditions under which the "forever" applies. The question regarding 2 Samuel 7 is not whether ʿad-ʿôlām means 'forever' but whether the conditions upon it have been adequately declared.

God indulges in misdirection again at the opening of 1 Samuel 16. Samuel protests that he cannot go to Bethlehem because "if Saul hears of it, he will kill me." God responds, "Take a heifer with you, and say, 'I have come to sacrifice to the LORD.'" One might argue that if the sacrifice was indeed carried out (presumably it was, although the text does not tell us this), then this is not technically a lie. On the other hand, it is hardly the truth. Why did Samuel go to Bethlehem? Not to make a sacrifice, but to anoint a king (as the elders of Bethlehem apparently suspect in 16:5). However understandable the ruse of the sacrifice, it remains a ruse—a divinely endorsed one.

Later in the same chapter, Samuel assumes at first sight that Jesse's eldest son, Eliab, is the king-to-be. God replies, "Do not look on his appearance or on the height of his stature, because I have rejected him; for the LORD does not see as mortals see; they look on the outward appearance, but the LORD looks on the heart" (1 Sam 16:7). This eminently quotable bit of rhetoric intimates volumes while actually saying nothing more than that Samuel should not be impressed by Eliab's size and looks. It does not even tell us for certain that Samuel had been impressed by Eliab's size and looks, although that might have been the reason for his erroneous assessment of the candidate. However, Eliab is only a bit player in Samuel, hardly important enough to elicit such a pregnant theological comment. Readers conclude that the remark must really apply to someone else, and a candidate is not far away: Saul, who is tall (10:23), handsome (9:2) and, like Eliab, rejected (16:1). "Saul was chosen by the people," my students write in their reaction papers, "but David was chosen by God." Now that the people and Samuel have seen what a disaster monarchy is when humans choose a king for his looks, the time has come for a proper, divinely chosen king—or so God insinuates.

However, Saul was not chosen by the people or Samuel. Saul was chosen by God. This is crystal clear in the anointing story (1 Samuel 9), where God identifies Saul to a truculent Samuel: "Here is the man of whom I spoke to you. He it is who shall rule over my people" (9:17). It is confirmed again through selection by lot (10:20–22). God's own words in 15:11 and the narrator's remark in 15:35 acknowledge divine responsibility for making Saul king. But in 1 Samuel 16, God seems eager to disclaim that act.

After this divine speech about looking upon the heart rather than appearances, it is highly ironic that God's "rise and anoint him; for this is the one" (16:12) follows a description of David's good looks. The impression—if not the reality—of this sequencing is that God has once again recognized a royal candidate by his looks.

God's speeches allow us to probe a bit further into the argument that God's favor for David can be identified with favor for David's people. In 1 Sam 9:15 God declares Saul to be the one who will "save my people from the hand of the Philistines; for . . . their outcry has come to me." This God sounds much like the one who delivered the people from Egypt. However, there is a disjunction between God's words and the situation that unfolds: Saul defeats Ammonites and Amalekites but, aside from the summary notice in 1 Sam 14:47, all narrated victories against the Philistines come through Jonathan or David, and Saul's story ends in a terrible defeat of Israel by the Philistines.

In the promise to David, God also speaks of concern for the people: "I will appoint a place for my people Israel and will plant them, so that they may live in their own place, and be disturbed no more; and evildoers shall afflict them no more" (2 Sam 7:10). Yet in 2 Samuel's very next oracle God proclaims, "I gave you your master's house, and your master's wives into your bosom. . . . I will take your wives before your eyes, and give them to your neighbor" (2 Sam 12:8 and 11). As Robert Polzin points out, these statements suggest that in the past and future *God* has played and will play the "rich man's" role, taking from a second party to give to a third (1993: 122–26). But the "lambs" taken and given by God are human beings. What impact has God's "justice" on their lives? The glimpses we get in the books of Samuel are not encouraging (2 Sam 3:15–16; 6:16, 20–23; 15:16; 16:22; 20:3).

We have already discussed the ramifications of God's justice for Israel in rebellions and plagues. We now add the famine of 2 Samuel 21. God does not explicitly take responsibility for this famine, but the divine response in 21:1 certainly does not repudiate the supposition that God has sent the famine, and it clearly indicates that the Israelites are suffering once again because of the action of an anointed one.

Our survey of God's talk in the books of Samuel largely reinforces the impressions gained from narratorial information about God's inner life and God's walk: God is more inclined to anger than love. Divine

means are largely negative. God favors David both in action and in willingness to communicate, but the results are not all favorable for David's
people. Furthermore, God's turning against Eli and Saul raises questions
about the long-term reliability of divine favor. Questions about God's
integrity are reinforced when God's own words confirm a tendency to
twist truth and break promises.

God-Talk from Human Characters

Table 5 (p. 150) lists the statements made to and about God by
prophets and priests in the books of Samuel, including first-person oracles from God (shown also in table 3), many of which we have already
discussed. Eli's comments pertaining to God are all brief and, as far as
we know, accurate. They depict a God who can bless as well as punish
but a God with whom it is pointless to argue (3:18)—especially when
that God has been personally offended (2:25). Gad's remarks in
2 Samuel 24 are similarly brief and to the point; the narrator endorses
them as faithful reports of God's remarks, even though they do not contain oracular formulas.

Philistia's priests show a surprising cognizance of Israel's God, although they view the "salvation history" from Pharaoh's point of view
(6:6). They suspect that the harm that has struck them comes from Israel's God and that golden offerings may appease him, but they know
that with this God one must never presume ("perhaps," 6:5). Their instructions result in safe transport of the ark (contrast the disasters at
Beth-shemesh and with Uzzah in 1 Sam 6:19 and 2 Sam 6:6–7).

The prophet Samuel has a great deal to say about God. In 1 Sam 7:3
he tells the Israelites, who have "lamented after the LORD" for twenty
years (! 7:2), to put away their foreign gods. He says that if they worship
their God alone, God will deliver them. But as Eslinger points out, he
fails to acknowledge that they had turned from God only after God had
delivered them to defeat (1 Samuel 4) and created great slaughter among
them (6:19; Eslinger 1985: 235).

When deliverance comes again, Samuel pointedly attributes it to
God (7:12). But his mood turns sour when the people ask for a king. His
speech against kingship does not mention God until the final line: "And
in that day you will cry out . . . but the LORD will not answer you"
(1 Sam 8:18). He knows that God has chosen Saul (10:1, 7, 24) yet,

Table 5. God-Talk from Prophets and Priests in the Books of Samuel
(verbatim oracles italicized)

1 Samuel	
Eli	
1:17	God grant Hannah's petition
2:20	blessing on Elkanah and his wife with children
2:25	who intercedes for sin against God?
3:8–9	identifies caller (inner life) and instructs Samuel about response
3:18	let God do what seems good to him (response to curse)
man of God	
2:27–36	*oracle against Eli's house*
Philistine priests	
6:3–9	how to return ark
Samuel	
7:3	serve God only and you will be delivered
7:12	God has helped us
8:18	you will cry and God will not answer
9:27–10:7	God has anointed Saul; signs including spirit upon Saul and God with Saul
10:18–19	*deliverance history* and accusation of rejection
10:24	see king God chose
12:5–17	God as witness, deliverance history, warning about king
12:22	God will not cast away unless people do wickedly
13:13	Saul has disobeyed, will be disowned, God has sought another
15:1–3	*Go smite Amalek*
15:16–29	discussion of Amalekite spoil; *quote of instructions*
16:8–10	God rejects Jesse's older sons
28:16–19	Samuel's ghost reviews rejection of Saul, predicts defeat
2 Samuel	
Nathan	
7:3	build temple because God is with you
12:7–12	*condemnation oracle*
12:13–14	God has put away sin but child will die
Gad	
24:13	choice of punishments
24:18–19	build an altar

rightly or wrongly, cannot believe that God really desires this state of affairs. At Mizpah, Samuel appends his own sermon on rejection (10:19) to God's self-identification as the one who delivers from Egypt (10:18). In his "farewell speech" Samuel invokes God as witness between himself and the people (12:3 and 6–7), emphasizing the people's past transgressions, warning against future ones, and calling a thunderstorm upon the wheat harvest. He cannot quite bring himself to speak of blessing. The best he can say is God will "not cast away his people" (12:22) but, by the closing line of the speech, he has returned to the language of "you shall be swept away" (12:25).

All of Samuel's God-talk from this point onward concerns rejection and punishment (even the divine instructions about Amalekite spoil in 15:2–3 concern retribution). To Saul, Samuel asserts, "the Glory of Israel will not recant or change his mind; for he is not a mortal, that he should change his mind" (15:29). Yet the whole sequence began with God's declaring 'I regret' (*nḥm*, 15:11—same word as 'change his mind' in 15:29). It ends with narratorial confirmation that 'the LORD was sorry' (*nḥm* again, 15:35). This shows us that in general God can and does *nḥm*. What we do not know is whether God might *nḥm* in response to a joint prayer from Saul and Samuel (15:24–25). Through his brooding vision of a God driven by vengeance, Samuel keeps us from finding out.

This peculiar dynamic, in which the prophet's rejection becomes a self-fulfilling prophecy that prevents the seeking of forgiveness from God, leads us back to a narratorial comment about Samuel at the outset of his career: "the LORD was with him and let none of his words fall to the ground" (3:19).[10] To what extent does Samuel simply reflect God's feelings and decisions? To what extent are Samuel's ill feelings controlling the interaction between Israel (including Saul) and God (Brueggemann 1990: 117)? To what extent is the problematic God of the books of Samuel a mirror of the problematic prophet Samuel?[11]

---

10. The Hebrew text could possibly be construed to say, 'was with him and he [Samuel] let none of his [God's] words fall to the ground', but I agree with the NRSV translator that the natural flow of the sentence makes God the one who does not let words fall.

11. In Samuel's defense, I observe that Nazirite service was ordinarily entered voluntarily and temporarily (Num 6:1–21), but Samuel had been committed to it for life

Samuel speaks of God's choices on only two occasions after this. In 1 Samuel 16 he responds favorably (and wrongly, according to God) to David's eldest brother, then enunciates God's rejection of all of the older brothers. (The narrator does not report any words from Samuel about the positive choice of David in 16:13.) Many chapters later, Samuel returns from the grave to tell Saul a final time that Saul is rejected and another has been chosen (1 Samuel 28).

David's prophet Nathan has far less to say to his king than Samuel did to Saul (perhaps to David's benefit). Nathan's initial response to David's temple proposal (2 Sam 7:3) contrasts sharply with God's response as reported in the following verses. Resulting uncertainty about the prophet's reliability shadows Solomon's succession (in which Nathan plays a crucial role, 1 Kings 1).

The NRSV renders Nathan's final response in the confrontation after Uriah's murder 'the LORD has put away your sin' (2 Sam 12:13). Readers usually understand this as 'you are forgiven' and are puzzled to hear that David's child must nonetheless die. But Nathan's response, in Hebrew, employs a causative verb form that might be translated 'transferred', yielding an interpretation like that of the NEB: "the LORD has laid on another the consequence of your sin." Apparently when God gets angry, the punishment must go somewhere. David uses the same verb later when he prays in the aftermath of the census, 'transfer the guilt of your servant' (2 Sam 24:10, my translation). Seventy thousand then die by plague.

We turn now from the God-talk of religious professionals to that of other human persons in the books of Samuel. Since there is a great deal of such talk and its content is less decisive than the other types of statements we have studied, I will not list the passages in table form (I will, however, register all of them in notes).

Saul has even more to say about God than Samuel does, and his words have a surprisingly positive tone.[12] His first God-statement expresses praise and blessing (1 Sam 11:13). In 1 Samuel 13 and 14, however, he

---

before his birth (1 Sam 1:11). Add to this the character of his first prophetic experience (1 Sam 3:10–14) and we may find it understandable that he sees little flexibility in God.

12. Saul speaks of God in 1 Sam 11:13; 13:12; 14:24, 34; 14:37, 39, 41, 44; 15:13, 24–25, 30; 17:37; 18:17; 19:6; 23:7, 21; 24:17–21; 28:10, 15.

seems anxious to know and influence God's plans, prompting Polzin to accuse Saul of entering "the Philistine territory of sorcery and divination" (Polzin 1989: 139). In these chapters Saul utters three different curses that condemn his son Jonathan (once unknowingly, once hypothetically, once deliberately; 14:24, 39, and 44). By contrast, Jonathan's own words protect divine freedom (for instance, "it may be that the LORD will act for us," 14:6).[13]

At the end of 1 Samuel 14, the army counters Saul's oaths with its own: "Far from it! As the LORD lives, not one hair of his [Jonathan's] head shall fall to the ground" (14:45). These criss-crossing oaths raise a question about the efficacy of vows and curses. Is Saul's failure to keep his vows a hidden cause of his own downfall? Do the vows indeed work themselves out in Jonathan's fate? Or are all of the pronouncements "mere words," revealing human intent but of no import for God's action?

In 1 Samuel 15, where Saul apparently misunderstands God's command rather than blatantly disregarding it (Gunn 1980: 41–56), Saul's God-talk shows a progressive loss of confidence. He blesses Samuel and assures him that God's commands have been carried out, then wavers about whether the commands have been fulfilled, and finally speaks (like the people in 1 Sam 12:19) of the deity as "your [Samuel's] God" (15:13, 24–25, and 30).

Saul's subsequent God-talk appears more positive. Perhaps the debacle with Jonathan or the experience of being cast off has taught him to be wary of invoking God for death. He wishes God's presence with David (1 Sam 17:37), swears not to put David to death (19:6), blesses David and wishes him well (23:21 and 24:17–21) and assures the medium that she will not be punished (28:10). To be sure, his talk of David's fighting God's battles in 18:17 has a cynical tone (since he hopes David will be killed in those battles), and his belief that God has given David into his hand is misguided (23:7). It is hard to tell whether Saul in 28:15 has finally come to grips with God's rejection, or whether he calls up Samuel in the desperate hope that God may yet turn and be merciful.

---

13. Jonathan speaks of God in 1 Sam 14:6, 8–10, 12; 19:5; 20:12–16, 20–23, 42.

Saul's successor, David, has an enormous number of things to say about God in a variety of modes.[14] Like Saul, he frequently invokes God in oaths, curses, and blessings. If failure to follow through on such pronouncements merits disownment, David deserves it several times over. His vow not to cut off Saul's descendants (1 Sam 24:22) is violated at least in spirit when he hands them over to the Gibeonites for impaling in 2 Samuel 21. Only when constrained by Rizpah's public vigil (21:11–14) does David allow burial of the victims, although earlier he had blessed the people of Jabesh-gilead for retrieving the remains of Saul and Jonathan (2:5–6). David's treatment of Saul's descendants in 2 Samuel 21 lends a cynical ring to his question about finding a survivor to whom he can show God's kindness (2 Sam 9:3, which seems to presuppose 2 Samuel 21).

In 1 Sam 25:22 David swears not to leave any of Nabal's men alive, then in 25:32–34 and 39 credits God (and Abigail) with stopping him from carrying through. He declares in 26:16 that Abner deserves to die but anxiously denies responsibility for the man's eventual death (2 Sam 3:28 and 39). David swears that Amasa will replace Joab as army commander (2 Sam 19:13), although he knows how Joab deals with rivals (2 Samuel 3, 20:7–13). He swears that Shimei will not die (19:23), but if we look ahead to 1 Kgs 2:8–10 and 36–46 we find David commanding a violent death for the man. His refusal to drink at the risk of men's lives (2 Sam 23:17) calls up troublesome memories (Gunn 1988: 303 and 298).

While the frequency of David's oaths and his shaky record in following through might give the impression that David takes God lightly, his other comments about God paint a slightly different picture. Repeatedly David speaks of God as the one who supports him and gives him victory. This view of God emerges most strikingly in David's response to the promise oracle (2 Sam 7:18–29, a prayer longer than the oracle itself) and his psalm and "last words" in 2 Samuel 22 and 23. The wordiness

---

14. David speaks of God in 1 Sam 17:26, 37, 45–47; 20:3, 8; 22:3; 23:10–12; 24:6, 9–15, 22; 25:22, 32–24, 39; 26:9–11, 16, 19–20, 23–24; 30:23, 26; and 2 Sam 1:14, 16; 2:1, 5–7; 3:28, 35, 39; 4:9–11; 5:12, 20; 6:8–9, 18, 21–22; 7:18–29; 9:3; 12:5–6, 13, 22; 14:11; 15:25–26, 31; 16:10–12; 19:13, 23; 21:3; 22:2–51; 23:2–7, 17; 24:10, 14, 17, 21, 24.

of these compositions leaves the impression that David thinks God susceptible to courtly rhetoric (Eslinger 1994: 65–88).

On three occasions we see a distinctly abashed David (2 Sam 6:8–9; 12:13; 24:10, 17). His comments and actions in these cases make it clear that, in David's view, God is someone before whom you had better not try to hide your guilt. He speaks several times in terms that show he does not simply presume God's assistance (1 Sam 22:3, 26:19–20; 2 Sam 12:22, 15:25–26, 16:10–12). David's speech suggests a God who does not care to be taken for granted, even—or especially?—by a favorite.

Like David, the minor characters of the Samuel books invoke God rather freely.[15] Sometimes they use God-language for rhetorical emphasis, for instance when Joab exclaims, "As God lives, if you had not spoken, the people would have continued to pursue their kinsmen, not stopping until morning" (2 Sam 2:27). Sometimes such emphasis accompanies flatly inaccurate statements, for instance when Achish tells David: "As the LORD lives, you have been honest" (1 Sam 29:6; contrast 27:8–11). Israel's elders express quite mistaken assumptions about what will happen if they bring the ark to battle (1 Sam 4:3), in contrast to the Philistine conclusions in 1 Samuel 4 (however, the Philistines speak of "gods" rather than "God") and 5. The single most common topic in connection with which God is mentioned is David's destiny—no surprise, but further reinforcing our image of God as the one who backs David.

1 and 2 Samuel contain three extended theological statements in addition to those made by prophets and kings; all three come from women. Hannah's song in 1 Sam 2:1–10 makes two strong thematic points. First, it celebrates God as one who reverses earthly fortunes, breaking the bows of the mighty and strengthening the feeble. Second,

---

15. In 1 Samuel, Hannah speaks of God in 1:11, 27; 2:1–10; Elkanah in 1:23; the elders in 4:3; the Philistines in 4:7–9; 5:7, 10, 11; Phineas's wife in 4:21–22; the people of Beth-shemesh in 6:20; Israelites in 7:8; 12:19; 14:33, 45; Saul's servants in 16:15–16, 18; David's men in 24:4; Abigail in 25:24–31; Achish in 29:6, 9; and an Egyptian servant in 30:15. In 2 Samuel comments come from Joab in 2:27, 10:12, 19:7, 20:21, and 24:3; Abner in 3:9–10, 18; Baanah and Rechab in 4:8; an anonymous rumor in 6:12; the wise woman of Tekoa in 14:11, 13–17, 20; Absalom in 15:7–8; Ittai in 15:21; Shimei in 16:7–8; Hushai in 16:18; Ahimaaz in 18:19, 28; the Cushite runner in 18:31–32; Abishai in 19:21; Mephibosheth in 19:27; the woman of Abel in 20:19; Gibeonites in 21:6; and Araunah in 24:23.

it speaks of God's support for the king. (Both of these themes are reprised in David's psalm near the end of the Samuel books, 2 Samuel 22). Tension already exists between these themes as I have stated them, for insofar as the king is mighty he is also a candidate for being brought low. Tension also exists between the themes and the narrative they introduce: we see the mighty fallen (2 Samuel 1!) and another king upheld—but do we in fact see the feeble strengthened? We can point to the Goliath story and say "yes," but David had already been introduced to us in 16:18 as a young nobleman of valor and military skill. Perhaps it is significant that even the poetic line that most pertains to Hannah herself, "the barren has borne seven" (2:5), is not quite fulfilled by the prose that follows (according to 2:21 she bears five children after Samuel).

Abigail's flowery speech in 25:24–31 rings with much sharper irony as she praises David's forbearance, bribes him to forsake his contemplated vengeance, and closes with a strong hint of willingness to join him in his success. She speaks of God as one who restrains the king from vengeance—at no loss to the king, since God himself will "sling out" the lives of the king's enemies. Abigail plays royal theology to her own advantage.

Tekoa's wise woman, like Abigail, exonerates David from all guilt (2 Sam 14:9) before beginning her theological speech (14:11–20, preceded by a presumably fictitious case presentation in vv. 4–7). She too focuses on issues of bloodshed and counsels David to forego vengeance. She too sweetens her words with flattering phrases and talk of God's support for David. Twice she tells the king that he is "like an angel of God" (14:17 and 20, a phrase used also by Achish in 1 Sam 29:9 and Mephibosheth in 19:27)—a troublesome comparison, considering that the only other angel of God mentioned in 1 and 2 Samuel is the plague-angel of 2 Samuel 24. Her tongue portrays God as one who "will not take away a life," but the very need for this contrived confrontation shows that the point is not as obvious as she would like.

Conclusion

Our study of God's character in the books of Samuel, moving from the most secure layer of clues (narratorial reports of God's inner life) to the least reliable (God-talk by human characters in Samuel) has yielded a disturbing picture. God's inner life, at least to the extent that the narrator reports it, is dominated more by anger than by love, motivated more often by desire to destroy than desire to build up. God acts primarily through destructive means such as war, plague, and obstruction of good advice. In cases in which God does act constructively (for instance, aiding conception or halting plague), the action often simply ameliorates a prior harm caused by God (closing a womb, sending plague).

God's own words reinforce the picture just given: condemnations outnumber and outweigh commendations. The divine speeches in 1 and 2 Samuel further reveal a problem with divine integrity: God sometimes prevaricates and openly declares that a promise "forever" remains subject to cancelation.

Readers often excuse God's punishing behavior on the grounds that the humans in question deserve it. Furthermore, they may say, God's ultimate concern is to support Israel. But our survey of the relative merits of Eli, Samuel, Saul, and David has shown no just reason why Eli and Saul should be so vehemently rejected while Samuel and David receive such loyal divine support, and we have discovered a goodly number of reasons to question whether God's relationship to David redounds to Israel's benefit.

When we compare what human characters in 1 and 2 Samuel say about God to what the narrator has told us, we discover that not everything prophets say about God is true, although formal prophetic oracles do seem to render God's words reliably. The darkest picture of God comes from the prophet Samuel, who nonetheless receives consistent divine support—even thunderstorms on demand.

Saul seemingly tries to manipulate God with a series of oaths in 1 Samuel 14, then loses confidence during his confrontation with Samuel in the following chapter. Yet, despite the persecution he endures from God, he still seeks God's word in the final hours of his life. David utters oaths more casually than Saul and sometimes reverses them, but his language shows a keen awareness of the need to respect God's freedom.

What are we to make of this picture? One might be tempted—especially in light of historical-critical arguments that much of the Samuel material is very old, perhaps even from David's lifetime—to write it off as a "primitive" view of God. If one lives in a world of war, famine, and plague, the reasoning goes, then one's idea of God is likely to be rather

dark. In fact, most interpreters, assuming that the narratives were written to defend David, have gone a step further and supposed that 1 and
2 Samuel's picture of David—and his God—is *brighter* than the actual
events (whatever they were).

But recent voices have begun to question this consensus. Gunn
(1978) and Van Seters (1977: 277–91) propose that the "succession narrative," which contains many of the most openly damning stories about
David (such as 2 Samuel 11), is not "firsthand historical writing . . .
from one who was a contemporary of David" (Anderson 1986: 228) but
a written (Van Seters) or orally composed (Gunn) narrative from a
much later period.

What has this to do with a final-form literary reading such as the one
I have presented in this essay? While my observations are not dependent
on a particular understanding of the text's compositional history, pro-
posals like those of Gunn and Van Seters do help free us from the auto-
matic assumption that the picture in Samuel must be pro-David and
pro-God. They raise the possibility that the Samuel narratives do not attempt to create bright legend from murky fact but may instead deliberately *darken* an existing legend.[16]

One can imagine that in either monarchic Judah or in Second Temple
Yehud (when, as can be seen in Psalms and Chronicles, priests portrayed
themselves as David's spiritual heirs), a writer might wish to probe not
only the idealization of a human king but also the theology entailed in
that idealization. Too often we have assumed that the dark picture of God
in 1 and 2 Samuel just could not be, and so we rationalized it away. Could
the problematization of God in 1 and 2 Samuel instead be intentional, as
Delekat sensed when he wrote of a "deep-seated grudge of the narrator
against Yahweh" (Delekat 1967: 34, my translation)?

Intentional or otherwise, the shadows continue to haunt us. My
seminary students will need to preach about this material. What, if anything, constructive can they say? I offer in closing some thoughts about
the appropriation of the Samuel books, with their problematic God.

---

16. Noth supposed such a deconstructive attitude toward the post-David kings
when he described the "Deuteronomistic History" as an exposé of the failings for which
God had totally annihilated Judah (Noth 1981: 89). Yet he understood the picture of
David's own reign as largely positive (pp. 54–55) and assumed that the history defended
God's justice.

First, the Samuel books do not stand alone in the canon. If we set them within the framework of the Primary History (Torah and Former Prophets), rather than in isolation as I have by and large done in this essay, we not only have additional texts to consider, but within the Samuel books themselves our working assumptions may change. In such a reading one might—among other things—see God's struggles in Samuel as part of an ongoing learning process (a dynamic hinted at when God shows more forbearance toward Samuel than Eli, more patience with David than with Saul).[17] Nor is the Primary History our only portrait of God's workings with David and Israel; Chronicles and Psalms give us quite a different picture (Steussy 1999). Perhaps we need to rethink lectionaries and curricula that emphasize the Primary History at the expense of these other biblical materials.

Second, within this complex canonical picture the Samuel books may serve a very important function, reminding us that when human leaders assert authorization by God, the assertion reflects upon God's own character. It costs something to let God be claimed by special interests.

Third and finally, whatever the merits of this picture of God, let us at least show Job's honesty in dealing with it. However much it bothers us to call the God-portrait of 1 and 2 Samuel a troubling one, it is worse to offer such a picture with the explanation "this is love."

---

17. Miles moves this direction in *God: A Biography* (1995). I find myself in basic agreement with his interpretation, although I consider him a little too optimistic about the picture in Samuel.

Works Cited

Alter, Robert
1981   *The Art of Biblical Narrative.* New York: Basic Books.
Anderson, Bernhard W.
1986   *Understanding the Old Testament.* 4th ed. Engelwood Cliffs, N.J.: Prentice-Hall.

Brueggemann, Walter
1990   *First and Second Samuel.* Interpretation. Atlanta: John Knox.
Delekat, L.
1967   Tendenz und Theologie der David-Salomo-Erzählung. Pp. 26–36 in
        Das ferne und nahe Wort, ed. F. Maass. Berlin: Alred Töpelmann.
Eslinger, Lyle M.
1985   *Kingship of God in Crisis.* Bible and Literature Series. Sheffield: Al-
        mond.
1994   *House of God or House of David: The Rhetoric of 2 Samuel 7.* Journal for
        the Study of the Old Testament Supplement Series 164. Sheffield:
        JSOT Press.
Fokkelman, J. P.
1986   *The Crossing Fates.* Volume 2 of *Narrative Art and Poetry in the Books of
        Samuel.* Assen: Van Gorcum.
1993   *Vow and Desire.* Volume 4 of *Narrative Art and Poetry in the Books of
        Samuel.* Assen: Van Gorcum.
Gunn, David M.
1978   *The Story of King David: Genre and Interpretation.* Journal for the Study
        of the Old Testament Supplement Series 6. Sheffield: JSOT Press.
1980   *The Fate of King Saul: An Interpretation of a Biblical Story.* Journal for the
        Study of the Old Testament Supplement Series 14. Sheffield: JSOT
        Press.
1988   2 Samuel. Pp. 287–304 in *Harper's Bible Commentary,* ed. James L.
        Mays. San Francisco: Harper & Row.
Humphreys, W. Lee
1985   *The Tragic Vision and the Hebrew Tradition.* Overtures to Biblical The-
        ology. Philadelphia: Fortress.
McCarter, P. Kyle
1980   *I Samuel: A New Translation with Introduction, Notes and Commentary.*
        Anchor Bible 8. Garden City, N.Y.: Doubleday.
Miles, Jack
1995   *God: A Biography.* New York: Random.
Miscall, Peter
1987   *First Samuel: A Literary Reading.* Indiana Studies in Biblical Literature.
        Bloomington: Indiana University Press.
Noth, Martin
1981   *The Deuteronomistic History.* Journal for the Study of the Old Testament
        Supplement Series 15. Sheffield: JSOT Press. Translation of *Überliefer-
        ungsgeschichte Studien.* 2d ed. Tübingen: Max Niemeyer, 1957.
Polzin, Robert
1989   *Samuel and the Deuteronomist: A Literary Study of the Deuteronomic His-
        tory.* San Francisco: Harper & Row.

1993   *2 Samuel.* Part 3 of *David and the Deuteronomist: A Literary Study of the Deuteronomic History.* Indiana Studies in Biblical Literature. Bloomington: Indiana University Press.

Steussy, Marti J.
1999   *David: Biblical Portraits of Power.* Studies on Personalities of the Old Testament. Columbia: University of South Carolina Press.

Tsevat, M.
1980   The Biblical Account of the Foundation of the Monarchy in Israel. Pp. 77–99 in *The Meaning of the Book of Job and Other Biblical Studies.* Hoboken, N.J.: KTAV.

Van Seters, John
1997   *In Search of History: Historiography in the Ancient World and the Origins of Biblical History.* Winona Lake, Ind.: Eisenbrauns. Originally published, New Haven: Yale University Press, 1983.

"Why, O Lord, Do You Harden Our Heart?"
A Plea for Help from a Hiding God

WALTER HARRELSON

Southport, North Carolina

Isa 63:7–64:12 has analogies in other psalm texts, but few texts contain such a sustained cry to God to take note of a suffering people, unable to claim righteousness but equally unable to bear the plight in which they find themselves. This cry reminds readers today of situation after situation in which this plea for help would seem to be entirely appropriate. The psalm, as I shall note below, also gives eloquent testimony not only to God's joint responsibility with the community for what the community suffers but also to God's own suffering with the community. The text addresses issues that James Crenshaw has addressed over and again in his numerous and seminal publications.

Translation in Seven Strophes

I. *God's Past Deeds of Mercy* (63:7–9)

I will call to mind the merciful deeds of the LORD,
  the praises of the LORD,
in accordance with all the LORD has given us,
  God's great goodness shown the house of Israel,
granted them out of the divine mercy,
  the abundance of God's love.
God said:
"Surely they are my people,
  children who will not deal falsely."
So God became their Savior.
In their suffering, God also suffered,
  the angel of the Presence saved them.
In love and compassion God redeemed them,

lifted them up and carried them
all the days of old.

II. *Israel Rebelled, but God's Mercy Continued* (63:10–14)

But they rebelled and grieved God's Holy Spirit,
    so God turned, becoming their enemy,
    and fought against them.
Then God remembered the days of old,
    the days of Moses, God's servant.
Where is the one who brought up out of the sea
    the shepherds of the flock?
Where is the one who planted in their midst
    the Holy Spirit,
who made the Arm of Glory
    go forth at Moses' right hand,
who divided the waters before them—
    making an everlasting name—
leading them through the depths?
Like a horse in the desert, they did not stumble;
    like cattle going down into the valley,
    the Spirit of the LORD refreshed them.
Thus you led your people,
    making for yourself a glorious name.

III. *The Great Reversal* (63:15–19)

Look down from heaven, and see,
    from your holy and beautiful residence.
Where is your zeal, your power,
    the longing of your heart, your mother-love?
    These are withheld from me.
But you—you are our Father,
    even if Abraham should not know us,
    even if Israel should not acknowledge us.
You, O LORD, are our Father,
    our Redeemer from of old—that is your name.
O LORD, why do you make us stray from your ways,
    and harden our hearts, so that we do not fear you?
Return, for the sake of your servants,

for the sake of the tribes of your heritage.
Your holy people possessed your sanctuary for a little while;
   our adversaries have trampled it down.
For a long time it has seemed that you did not rule over us,
   as if we were not called by your name.

IV. *A Plea for God to Act* (64:1–5a)

If only you would rip open the heavens and come down,
   so that the mountains might quake at your presence!
Just as fire kindles brushwood,
   and fire causes water to boil,
so make known your name to your adversaries,
   and the nations will tremble at your presence!
Once you did awesome deeds,
   deeds that we did not expect;
you came down,
   the mountains quaked at your Presence.
From ages past no one has heard,
   no ear has understood;
no eye has seen a God other than you,
   One who works for those who wait faithfully.

V. *Confession of Sin* (64:5b–7)

See, you were angry, and we sinned;
   we have been in our sins for a long while—
   and shall we be saved?
We have become like those who are unclean;
   all our righteousness is like a filthy rag.
We all fade like a leaf,
   and like the wind, our iniquities take us away.
There is no one who calls on your name,
   who reaches out to grasp you;
for you have hidden your face from us,
   and handed us over to our iniquities.

VI. *Confession of Faith and Renewed Plea for Help* (64:8–12)

Yet, O LORD, you are our Father;
   we are the clay, and you are our potter.

We are the work of your hand.
Do not be so terribly angry, O LORD;
   do not remember iniquity forever.
See and consider: We are all your people!
Your holy cities have become a wilderness;
   Zion has become a wilderness,
   Jerusalem a desolation.
Our holy and beautiful house,
   where our ancestors praised you,
has been burned by fire;
   and all our pleasant places have become ruins.
Will you restrain yourself at these things, O LORD?
   Will you keep silent, and punish us so grievously?

VII. *God's Response* (65:1)

I was ready to be sought, but you did not even ask for me;
   ready to be found, but you did not even seek me out.
I said, "Here I am, here I am,"
   to a nation that did not even call out my name.

There are some difficult verses in the lament, the most problematic of which is 63:9. Should the first clause of v. 9 be read with the last clause of v. 8, thus yielding the following line?

and he became their Savior in all their distress.

With this reading, we would continue v. 9 as follows:

It was no messenger or angel,
   but God's own Presence that saved them.

This reading, widely adopted today, is less plausible, I believe, than the one I have given above. The Masoretic tradition supports the reading "In their suffering, God also suffered; the angel of the Presence saved them." Textually, the question is whether to read the particle *lōʾ* ('not') or the parallel reading preserved by the Masoretes, *lô* ('to him'). In my judgment, the latter reading makes the better sense, although either reading can be defended. There are no other textual problems that significantly affect the interpretation of the lament.

Using the seven divisions of the lament, I will now offer comments about each part.

I. God's Past Deeds of Mercy (63:7–9)

The lament clearly begins with v. 7. The grim theophany found in Isa 63:1–6 portrays the God of Israel as Warrior, returning from the battlefield in Edom, with blood-stained garments, having won the battle without the aid of any human army. The contrast between this vengeful deity and the compassionate LORD who begins to speak in v. 7 is striking. The collector of the traditions assigned to the book of Isaiah probably intended to underscore this contrast.

Many laments begin with words of praise to God, who in past times has been gracious and merciful to the people. Such a beginning is striking in Psalm 44, with which psalm this lament bears comparison at several points. In Isa 63:8, the love and mercy of God are singled out for special emphasis. God anticipates complete faithfulness from a people so beloved, so well cared for by the covenant partner. Surely they will not deal falsely (v. 8)! The contrast with Ps 44:17 must be intentional; there, the community flatly insists to God that it has not been false (the verb *šqr* is used in both texts). God thus became the Savior of Israel, sharing their trials and their sufferings, and by the agency of the Angel of the Presence, saving them. God's love and compassion are revealed in the intimate association of deity and people (v. 9), reminiscent of Isa 40:1–11.

No other text in the Hebrew Scripture expressly affirms that God suffers with the suffering people. This occurrence is, however, laying its weight on the presence of the deity in all of the joys and trials of the people of the covenant; it is not a text that sets out to teach that God suffers with the sufferers of earth. But the fact that the occurrence is not underscored only makes it the more striking and worthy of note. A. J. Heschel emphasized that the God of the prophets was characterized by divine pathos, a sharing of the lot of the people to such an extent that the idea of a suffering God clearly applied to Israel's God.[1]

II. Israel Rebelled, but God's Mercy Continued (63:10–14)

The next section contains two of the three references in the entire Hebrew Bible to the Holy Spirit (the other is in Psalm 51). Despite God's confidence that Israel would prove faithful to the covenant, Israel

---

1. See A. J. Heschel, *The Prophets* (Philadelphia: Jewish Publication Society, 1962).

in fact rebelled, grieving God's Holy Spirit. Here again the intimate portrayal of the deity as one who grieves over Israel's failings is noteworthy. Although the text notes that God turns against the faithless covenant partner, becoming the enemy of Israel, this hostility is portrayed as lasting only for a brief interval, for God remembers the early days of Israel, not underscoring the faithfulness of the people in the wilderness, as Hosea and Jeremiah did (Hosea 11; Jeremiah 2 and 31) but, rather, underscoring God's own deeds of love and mercy.

It is God who raises the rhetorical questions of vv. 11–13: "Where is the One who brought up out of the sea the shepherds of the flock?" This is of course a reference to the crossing of the Red Sea (Exodus 14– 15). "Where is the One who planted in Israel's midst the Holy Spirit?" The Holy Spirit is not localized in any of the holy objects of the wilderness period—not the Ark of the Covenant, not the Tabernacle, not even the rod of Moses or of Aaron. The Holy Spirit is present expecially in the whole persona of Moses (see Exodus 34, where the face of Moses is suffused with divine glory). Moses' upraised arm becomes, by the Spirit, the Arm of Glory. But this presence of the Spirit also refreshes and guides the whole people, making their wilderness march like that of cattle marching down into a valley or like the stride of a horse in the wilderness that has nothing in the terrain to cause it to stumble.

This look back into Israel's history draws the usual contrast between God's deeds of salvation in past times and God's refusal or inability to act for Israel's salvation in the present time. But the deity's presence in past times here is portrayed as extraordinarily intimate, close, refreshing. And the rhetorical questions are posed, as it were, by the deity: It is *God* who remembers the days of old, not the prophet who speaks for the people. It is God who remembers mercy, deliverance, the planting of the Holy Spirit, the raising of the Arm of Glory. God remembers the features of a saving God that Israel regularly recalls to the deity's notice.

III. The Great Reversal (63:15–19)

The description of Israel's contemporary plight has distinctive and powerful features, like the shift in Psalm 44 at v. 9, which is more abrupt, less well prepared for, literarily and psychologically. The poet in Isaiah 63 calls on God to look down from heaven, from that glorious residence far above and beyond the harsh realities of earth, and see what is going on. It is implied that God must surely not know what in fact is transpiring among the communities and nations of earth, for otherwise surely God would have taken action. God is portrayed as a *deus otiosus,* a deity in retirement. Such theological understandings were widespread in the ancient world, as we see most clearly in the literature from Ugarit. There the deity El is in retirement at the source of the Two Rivers, far to the north atop the mountains that touch heaven. Baal is the active deity, but El can be appealed to on occasion.

Our poet, however, can only speak of a deity who is in retirement, but who of course has no successor to take over, since by definition the God of Israel is the one deity of the universe. The result is that which the poet portrays in what follows. For now, God's zeal, God's power, and (worst of all) God's love and compassion are simply nowhere in evidence. God resides in the splendid divine house in the heavens, but the earth threatens to lapse back into chaos. The term translated 'mother-love' is the Hebrew noun *raḥămîm,* which has that connotation, as one can see in 1 Kgs 3:26, though of course it refers more generally to human compassion and love. The repeated designation of God as father is also without precedent in the Hebrew Bible.[2] The poet lays the groundwork for the coming appeal to God by insisting that the parental love that binds God and Israel is surely more enduring than even the love of Abraham or of Jacob/Israel. Surely, Abraham and Israel will never forget their offspring; how much less can the God of Abraham and of Israel do so? The thought is of course reminiscent of Isaiah 40–55, with its repeated reminders to Israel that God will come to save, for God could not possibly forget the people of the covenant (see especially Isaiah 43).

In the context of a divine love that no other nation can claim, the poet begins the lament proper (v. 17). The question places God squarely in the circle of responsibility for Israel's plight: it was the LORD who caused Israel to stray from the true path, the LORD who hardened Israel's hearts so that they no longer showed due reverence to the deity. The theme is familiar from the stories of the plagues in Egypt (Exodus 7–11). In Exodus, three ways of referring to the hardening of Pharaoh's

---

2. The other occurrences comparable with the three in our passage are found in Deut 32:6; Jer 3:4, 19; Jer 31:9; Mal 1:6, 2:10.

heart are found. In some texts, God hardens Pharaoh's heart so that he will not repent too quickly and be spared due punishment. In other texts, Pharaoh hardens his own heart, stubbornly refusing to let Israel leave Egypt, even after it has become evident that it is folly for him to continue his resistance. And in a third set of texts, the heart of Pharaoh is said simply to get hard—with no reason given. It just happens. Here in our Isaiah text it seems that we have another instance of this last kind of hardness of heart.

The poet cannot believe that God quite deliberately set out to lead Israel astray, but the effect is the same: since Israel's love for God has grown cold, God's love for Israel must have grown cold. We remember the pathos-laden line from Psalm 77: "Has God forgotten to be gracious?" (v. 9). God must be called on to return, to repent (as in Psalm 90, another communal lament). God must do so out of divine mercy, for anything else is a monstrous refusal to be the divine parent that God in fact is. God must do so also because Israel's need is so great.

God's inattentiveness has lasted long enough. It is now time for God to remember that in fact Israel is called by God's name, is God's child, is beloved, is known, and no other action than return in mercy and love is acceptable. Israel's poet serves notice on God!

IV. A Plea for God to Act (64:1–5a)

The powerful opening of this fourth section of the lament cuts into the world of sixth–fifth century B.C.E. Judaism. The poet calls for a theophany, a divine appearance that will give the lie to the notion that Israel's God no longer has interest in the community of the covenant: Let it be a divine appearance like those known in times past: with the mountains quaking and the entire earth set in motion. Let God come with the same inevitability discerned when fire is set to kindling and when water is set and left upon a burning flame. God's enemies, the nations that hold Israel captive—let them tremble as the mountains quake! In earlier times you came unexpectedly, without warning, causing all to fear and tremble. Do so again! Come to the aid of your suffering people, just as you did in those wonder years about which we have heard so much. Again we think about Psalm 44. The opening lines of Psalm 44 speak of how the lamenting community has heard *with its ears* of how once God came to save, came to deliver an endangered people. The reference to hearing with the ears may contain a tone of irritation: we have heard that ancient story until we are sick of hearing it, for it is given the lie by current events.

V. Confession of Sin (64:5b–7)

This profound confession bears comparison with Psalm 51, though once again the poet manages to indicate that to some extent the deity shares the people's sin. God's very anger, it seems (v. 5b), contributes to Israel's sin. It is not just that we failed the divine partner and exile befell us, which is the common line taken by many prophets (Jeremiah and Ezekiel in particular). God was angry, God began to turn against the people, and this made the people all the less ready to be faithful. "You were angry, and we sinned!" How subtly does our poet bring God into the circle of responsibility for the people's plight.

The subtle presentation continues: For a long while we have been in our sins; is it believable that we can, on our own initiative, repent, turn to God for forgiveness, and be saved? No, Israel has become odious to itself and to the deity: this once-beloved community, our poet dares to say, is like a filthy rag—no doubt a reference to cloth used during the menstrual cycle and then discarded.

Shifting the image, the poet portrays Israel as a leaf, dried up, and borne away on the wind. The wind that bears faded and dried-up Israel away is—Israel's iniquities! And, as this long time of sin continues, drying Israel out, turning the community into a loathesome thing fit only for discarding, what has Israel's loving and beloved parent done? God has hidden the divine face, *handing Israel over to its iniquities.* Here again, we see how the author of the lament places responsibility on the deity. God has not simply looked the other way as Israel sinned and became odious to the deity. God has, either by direct action or at least by failure to intervene, handed the people over to their iniquities.

VI. Confession of Faith and Renewed Plea for Help (64:8–12)

The impassioned plea with which the poet concludes the lament renews the identification of God as Father. It also uses the image of potter and clay in a way quite different from the way found in Jeremiah 18 or in Isa 29:16. Our poet notes that God is the creator of this sinful and suffering people, is intimately related to them as one who shaped them entirely. The fault in the creature Israel, accordingly, must surely owe something to the divine shaper. "We are the work of your hand!"

On the basis of this argument, the poet goes on to plead with God not to be so outraged, not to let the divine anger go on and on. Does God not see that it must surely mean something that Israel is the work of the divine hand, of the potter who fashioned the clay, of the parent who brought the child into existence? And *all* of us, the poet notes, the faithful and the apostate, all of us are your people. There is nothing of the argument here that Amos and other prophets condemn: the notion that God is partial to Israel, or should be, because Israel is after all God's chosen race (see Amos 3:2 and 9:7). On the contrary, the appeal in this lament is for God to let divine love and compassion, divine craftwork and creativity, divine intimacy and parent-love have their proper sway in dealing with an errant community.

The final appeal is to call to God's attention just what has happened to entities dear to God's heart. The land of Israel has been turned into a wasteland. Even Zion, the place where our ancestors praised you, has been destroyed by fire. Note that the poet calls the Temple, not the house of God, God's earthly dwelling, but "our" holy and beautiful house. How could the poet miss the opportunity to try to shame the deity by pointing out that the very abode of God on earth has been burned, and God has not lifted a finger? This poet knows well enough that God's own being and character are not tied to the continuation of the earthly Temple. It is enough to speak more generally of "your holy cities," scattered throughout the land of the promise and to include Zion among these cities. The destruction of the Temple is immensely grave, of course, but it is the Temple as the place of prayer and praise to God, the place that helps to affirm and to maintain the intimate association of people and God that this poet speaks of over and again.

In view of all the above, the poet finally asks: will God continue to refuse to intervene, keep silent, and let the punishment run its course?

VII. God's Response (65:1)

Chapters 65–66 may have several elements that comprise what the collectors of the Isaiah traditions understood to be God's response to this long lament. In my judgment, one critically important part of that divine response has been preserved in its proper location. Isa 65:1 contains four half-lines that may be the best and most potent response that the Israelite community could have come to treat as God's response. These lines present a deity who has been waiting for the community of Israel to take with proper seriousness the fate of the community of the covenant, a fate on which, by Israelite belief, the fate of the entire world hangs. What has been wrong with Israel's response to the community's sufferings, so well laid out in this lament? The community has not been sufficiently incensed, not sufficiently ready to accept responsibility and, above all, not sufficiently subtle in bringing the deity into the picture as one who must be implicated. Ps 44:23[22] insists that it is 'on your account' (Hebrew *'ālêkā*) that Israel is killed all day long, treated as sheep to be slaughtered. Our poet, in the many subtle ways we have noted above, both affirms Israel's sin as a causal factor and insists that God too is involved in the blows that Israel has suffered—not, however, as righteous judge who rightly punishes evildoers but as loving parent who has gone through these times of travail with Israel and who now, given the seriousness with which the community cries out for help, demanding that God act as God should and must act, is ready to act.

The words only begin the story, of course. God affirms Israel for this bold attack upon the deity, for God has been waiting for just such seriousness of purpose to emerge. Israel had precluded God's help by not having asked for it with boldness, with language and commitment that disclose the true partnership that exists between potter and clay, between parent and child. The LORD looked for Israel's prayers, and Israel did not pray, did not cry out, did not show that their plight was simply unendurable, unacceptable. God was ready to be found, but Israel did not seek God out. And more: God was reaching out, crying out, "Here I am, here I am!" Israel, however, did not even name the name of God.

The poet has taken us through a long journey of faith. From a beginning in which God's past acts of graciousness were sketched, the author led us through forms of Israelite response that grieved the deity to events that brought humiliation and disgrace not alone on Israel but on God as well, events that Israel's God had shared at every point with the people. The most striking theological affirmation of the poet, I believe, is that the very intimacy of God and people that this poet knows and must have personally shared is the chief argument used to claim God's saving help. There is no abject denigration of the people, not even for rhetorical effect. The shocking line "all our righteousness is like a filthy rag" is an appeal to the God who loves Israel to heal and mend this loathesome situation into which the community has come. The appeal for aid is quite simply and strikingly that divine love prompt divine action. The first verse of Isaiah 65, I believe, is to be understood as the affirmation the poet receives that God agrees with the poet's argument and affirms it.

Later on in Isaiah 65 is a second divine response, this one focused on the coming triumph of the divine purposes for the universe. Most clearly set out in vv. 17–25, where we have one of the many versions of prophetic sketches of the consummation of God's work for Israel and the world that dot the prophetic corpus,[3] these pictures of the future consummation not only give the people assurance that things will get better one day but they also offer the incentive and the blueprint for action in the here and now to work with God for the visions' realization.

Why, then, does God make us stray from the divine ways, hardening our hearts so that we lose our fear of deity? God does not cause us to stray, and God does not harden our hearts. Even so, in the pilgrimage of faith, our poet teaches us, stray we will, and our hearts will indeed become calloused so that we can bear what the course of life brings. Through it all, our poet insists, the hidden God is present, encouraging both faithful lives and cries of outrage at life's injustices, insanities, and foulness. To the cries of outrage, God says, "Good! Now you are finally calling for action. Be assured that I will act."

---

3. I have sketched the import of these promises most recently in R. M. Falk and W. Harrelson, *Jews and Christians in Search of Social Justice* (Nashville: Abingdon, 1996), chapter 7.

The God Who Loves and Hates

PAUL L. REDDITT
Georgetown College

Mal 1:2–3 contains an assertion attributed to God: "I have loved Jacob, but Esau I have hated." The word ʾhb ('love') designates the close human relationships of choosing someone in particular (Prov 8:17), cleaving to someone (for example, God, Deut 11:22), knitting person to person (1 Sam 18:1), or feeling strong desire (Cant 5:8), as well as taking conscious action on behalf of someone (Gen 29:18, 30). It can also be applied to Yahweh's relationship with Israel, as here.[1] The word śnʾ ('hate') designates revulsion against persons (family or enemy) or behaviors. God, too, is said to hate—to hate the strongholds of Jacob (Amos 6:8), wickedness (Ps 5:6), idolatry (Jer 44:4), and—in Malachi 1—Esau.

The ascription of such a powerful, negative emotion as hate to God gives most commentators pause. This is particularly so in Mal 1:3, for the verse gives no reason for this hatred. Indeed, in his commentary on Malachi, John Calvin relates love and hate, not to differences in the origins of Jacob and Esau, still less to the deeds of their lives, but to predestination—that is, to God's secret election of Jacob and rejection of Esau.[2]

Contemporary commentators shrink from such a view[3] and explain the ascription of "hatred" to God in some other way. In this paper I will review these explanations and seek to build on them by understanding

---

1. M. E. Tate, "Questions for Priests and People in Malachi 1:2–2:16," *RevExp* 84 (1987) 392–33.

2. J. Calvin, *Commentaries* (Library of Christian Classics 23; Philadelphia: Westminster, 1958) 288–95.

3. See, for example, P. Verhoef (*The Books of Haggai and Malachi* [NICOT; Grand Rapids: Eerdmans, 1987] 201), who explicitly distances himself from Calvin on this point, despite agreeing with him on much else about these verses. Cf. G. J. Botterweck, "Jakob habe ich lieb: Esau hasse ich," *BibLeb* 1 (1960) 37.

the antonyms in terms of God's fidelity to Israel within the context of their covenant. I will then evaluate this theology, raising the issue of an appropriate criterion for this evaluation and suggesting a modified form of "perfect-being theology." Finally, I will argue that this kind of an evaluative program should be part of the task of studying the theology of the Hebrew Scriptures.

Proposed Solutions to the Problem of God's Hating Edom

Scholars have offered a variety of solutions to the problem of God's hating Esau, solutions that are not necessarily mutually exclusive. One of the more popular solutions is to understand the antonymic pair as "prefer/not prefer"; that is, the terms only bespeak a relative difference in God's feelings toward the sons.[4] The scarcity of adjectives in Hebrew is said to cause the use of so strong a verb as śnʾ. Marvin E. Tate, for example, points to instances in which the pair is used elsewhere in the sense of love more / love less: for example, Gen 39:30–31, where the word śnʾ is used of Leah, but the translation 'hate' is clearly too strong. Tate also connects this understanding of "love/hate" to the concept of election when he writes: "Thus Yahweh affirms that he has shown love for Israel by his choice of Jacob/Israel rather than of Esau/Edom."[5]

Even so, unless there was some basis for preferring Israel, God could be understood as acting in an arbitrary fashion. Hence, scholars understanding the words to mean "prefer/not prefer" often appeal to the history of Edom (which is said to have descended from Esau) to justify God's relative preference for Israel. Relationships between Edom and Israel might never have been very good, but after Edom betrayed survivors from Jerusalem and after its capture by Nebuchadnezzar,[6] the Hebrew Bible never again had a good word for Edom.[7]

---

4. See Botterweck, "Jakob habe ich lieb: Esau hasse ich," 35–36; K. Elliger, *Das Buch der zwölf kleinen Propheten* (ATD 25; Göttingen: Vandenhoeck & Ruprecht, 1982) 189; Tate, "Malachi 1:2–2:16," 394–95.

5. Ibid., 395.

6. The extent to which Edom participated in the sack of Jerusalem, if at all, is difficult to determine. The (N)RSV translation of Obadiah 11–15 suggests Edom participated in the looting of the city, but even if this translation is correct, there is reason to be cautious in accepting those verses as an account of what Edom actually did. J. R. Bartlett

A second solution is to understand "love/hate" in terms of "elect/ reject."[8] This understanding is based on God's covenant with Israel (Gen 25:23). The word "hate" is understood in the sense of "not chosen," and any moral blame for God's rejection of Esau is ascribed to Esau. Joyce G. Baldwin's comment is typical:

> The verb "hate" is to be understood in the light of God's electing love. The very fact that Jacob was chosen, "loved," meant that Esau was rejected, "hated," rejection being implicit in the exercise of choice. Personal animosity towards Esau is not implied. Esau and his descendants, however, by nurturing resentment and showing hostility towards Jacob, did bring God's punishment on themselves.[9]

While the notion of covenant does seem to be at work in Mal 1:2–3, Baldwin's explanation will not otherwise bear close scrutiny. According to Gen 12:3, God's election of Israel had a broad purpose: "by you all the families of the earth shall bless themselves," a purpose not reflected in Mal 1:2–3 or by commentators who argue that the election of Jacob/ Israel necessarily implied the rejection of Esau/Edom.

Third, Rex Mason argues that, while the terms constitute an idiomatic way of saying that God had chosen Jacob instead of Esau, the main emphasis lay on God's freedom to choose one or the other. Just as God is free to choose Israel in a covenant relationship, so also God is free to

---

(*Edom and the Edomites* [JSOTSup 77; Sheffield: Sheffield Academic Press, 1989] 154–55) argues that these verses imagine Edom taking part in the looting of Jerusalem and warns against it. Either way, the verses evidence harsh feeling toward Edom, which is the issue here.

7. See B. C. Cresson, "The Condemnation of Edom in Post-exilic Judaism," in *The Use of the Old Testament in the New and Other Studies: Studies in Honor of William Franklin Stinespring* (ed. J. M. Efird; Durham, N.C.: Duke University Press, 1972) 125–48.

8. See, for example, D. R. Jones, *Haggai, Zechariah, Malachi* (Torch Bible Commentaries; London: SCM, 1962) 182; J. Kodel, *Lamentations, Haggai, Zechariah, Second Zechariah, Malachi, Obadiah, Jonah, Baruch* (Old Testament Message; Wilmington, Del.: Glazier, 1982) 97; R. A. Mason, *The Books of Haggai, Zechariah, and Malachi* (The Cambridge Bible Commentary on the New English Bible; Cambridge: Cambridge University Press, 1977) 141; E. Sellin, *Das Zwölfprophetenbuch übersetzt und erklärt* (KAT 12; 2d–3d ed.; Leipzig: Scholl, 1930) 591; R. L. Smith, *Micah–Malachi* (WBC 32; Waco, Tex.: Word, 1984) 305.

9. J. G. Baldwin, *Haggai, Zechariah, Malachi* (Tyndale Old Testament Commentaries 24; London: Tyndale, 1972) 222–23.

reject Israel. Even so, Mason argues, as does Baldwin, that God does not reject people arbitrarily but rejects those who "create a domain for wickedness."[10]

Similarly, David M. Bossman understands the verbs in terms of the relationship between a father and his sons: "the opposition between God's love of the two brothers Jacob and Esau suggests an inegalitarian relationship, in which Jacob remains in union with God, i.e., at home, while Esau is separated and placed in a lower rank than his brother."[11] One should note, however, that this understanding reverses the portrayal of the two brothers in Genesis in two respects: (1) the earthly father Isaac seemed to prefer Esau over Jacob, and (2) Jacob fled to his mother's family in Haran, while Esau remained near his father's home. Even so, Mason and Bossman seem correct to emphasize the role of covenant in Mal 1:2–5.

A fifth possibility is to emphasize love and downplay the aspect of hate. S. D. Snyman argues that the context within which the antonyms occur is God's love for Israel. Hence, "not too much should be made of Yahweh's hate for Esau/Edom in this pericope. . . ."[12] Steven L. McKenzie and Howard N. Wallace combine this solution with the second listed above—namely, the appeal to the covenant. They relate the terms to the concept of the "love of God" in Deuteronomy, which is defined in terms of loyalty, service, and obedience—that is, terms with a treaty or covenant background.[13]

A sixth possible understanding of the antonyms may be added to those derived from a review of scholarship on Mal 1:2–3: namely, to see them as a projection of the author's feelings onto God,[14] a view not

---

10. Mason, *Haggai, Zechariah, Malachi,* 141.
11. D. M. Bossman, "Kinship and Religious Systems in the Prophet Malachi," in *Religious Writings and Religious Systems* (Brown Studies in Religion 1; ed. J. Neusner; Atlanta: Scholars Press, 1989) 132.
12. S. D. Snyman, "Antitheses in Malachi 1, 2–5," *ZAW* 98 (1986) 438. See also his review of scholarship on 1:2–5 on p. 437.
13. S. L. McKenzie and H. N. Wallace, "Covenant Themes in Malachi," *CBQ* 45 (1983) 555.
14. If L. Feuerbach is correct that "*Theology is anthropology,*" every statement about God is really a statement about humanity. If true, this option for understanding Mal 1:2–3 does not help very much because it would apply equally well to all statements about God and would yield no basis for distinguishing among such statements. What is intended here, rather, is something more like the transferring of a human wish onto God.

adopted explicitly by any scholar I have reviewed.[15] Such projections seem to appear elsewhere, however, for example, in Nahum's depiction of God gleefully throwing filth at Nineveh (Nah 3:6). In any time, distinguishing one's own feelings about one's enemies from how one's God feels toward those same people is fraught with difficulty, and authors of scripture, including the author of Mal 1:2–3, do not seem to have been immune to this difficulty.

This brief survey has yielded the following basic result: one may well suppose that the prophet's perspective on Jacob and Esau seems (1) to have been informed by his understanding of God's fidelity to the covenant with Israel and (2) to have been colored by his own emotions toward Edom.

The Crux of the Issue

These views for the most part operate on the assumption (sometimes unacknowledged) that God must act morally, an assumption that this article ultimately will affirm. The crux of the issue for the audience of Mal 1:2–3, however, was not some abstract notion of the nature of God as a moral being but, as Snyman points out,[16] with the existential question of whether God still loved Israel. The collapse of the Davidic dynasty in 586 had called into question God's covenant with it (2 Samuel 7), and the conditions of the postexilic period probably seemed to call into question God's promises to restore the community, such as promises found in the book of Ezekiel and in Deutero-Isaiah. The answer to the question of God's relationship to Israel in the larger passage Mal 1:2–5 was that, though Israel (priests and people alike) had broken the covenant with God, God had not, would not, indeed must not break covenant with Israel.

The next question to raise is simple: could God have changed with respect to Israel? Do these verses imply God's immutability?[17] Mal 3:6

---

15. Verhoef (*Haggai and Malachi*, 200) rejects this possibility, arguing instead that the antonyms represent God's own feelings.

16. Snyman, "Antitheses in Malachi 1, 2–5."

17. See my use of the word "immutability" in "The Book of Malachi in Its Social Setting," *CBQ* 56 (1994) 247; and *Haggai, Zechariah, Malachi* (NCB; London: Harper-Collins, 1994) 155.

reads: "For I the Lord do not change" (NRSV).[18] It is sometimes understood to say he could not change, but probably only means that he had
not. If God had ceased loving Israel, the people would have been con-
sumed for their sin. God, however, had remained faithful to them. Israel, by contrast, had violated God's decrees, the stipulations of God's
covenant, so Israel needed to repent. According to 3:7, if they turned
(*šûb*) toward God, God would turn (*šûb*) toward them (presumably with
forgiveness). Thus the covenant would remain in force.[19]

Walter Brueggemann argues that immutability is foreign to the entire Hebrew Bible's presentation of God: "It is more appropriate to
speak of this God in the categories of *fidelity* than of *immutability*, and
when fidelity replaces immutability, our notion of God's sovereignty is
deeply changed."[20] In the context of Mal 1:2–3, then, the people of Israel feared that God had changed with respect to Israel and no longer
loved them. The prophet's response was that God had not.

Prior to the writing of Mal 1:2–5, destruction had come to Edom,
presumably (for the author) the consequence of conflicts with Judah
(compare Judg 11:17; Amos 1:11; Ezek 25:12). Edom, unlike Judah, was
not in a covenantal relationship with God and would not be rebuilt. Further, the prophet seeks justification for and/or anticipation of God's hatred of Edom in the prior revelation and finds it in (or reads it into) the

---

18. Because of the apparent connection between Mal 1:2–5 and 3:6, Sellin (*Zwölfprophetenbuch*, 588) argues that 1:2–5 originally belonged with 3:6–12. I argue instead
(*Haggai, Zechariah, Malachi*, 155) that 3:8–12 seems self-contained and has no connection with 3:6–7, which did originally conclude 1:2–5.

19. In the Hebrew Bible, God did not always forgive Israel. J. L. Crenshaw (*A
Whirlpool of Torment* [OBT 12; Philadelphia: Fortress, 1984] 54–56) calls attention to Jer
15:1–9 as an example of God's refusal to do so. Following upon an account of the apparently genuine, but tardy, repentance of the people of Judah (14:19–22), God gave
them over to pestilence, sword, famine, and captivity (15:1–4). In 15:5–9 one encounters a divine soliloquy to the effect that constant rejection of God will now be met by
"grim determination to oversee their total eradication" (p. 56).

20. W. Brueggemann, *The Message of the Psalms: A Theological Commentary* (Minneapolis: Augsburg, 1984) 52. Compare J. Miles (*God: A Biography* [New York: Knopf,
1995] 12): "there is virtually no warrant in the New Testament for any claim that God
is immutable, and there is equally little in the Hebrew Bible. . . . Were it not so, he
could not be surprised; and he is endlessly and often most unpleasantly surprised. God
is constant; he is not immutable."

story of Jacob and Esau, most likely in Gen 25:23.[21] There God promises
that Jacob would be stronger than Esau, who would serve his younger
brother. Mal 1:2–5 then recasts this relationship and projects it into the
fifth century and beyond in terms of love for Jacob and hatred for Esau.[22]

God's fidelity to Israel, then—not immutability—provides the context in which Mal 1:2–5 demonstrates God's love for Israel by proclaiming God's hatred for Esau. The issue is not so much what the word *śn'*
means (this is fairly clear) but how one understands the text when it says
God "hates" Esau. The verse actually makes two claims. First, it claims
that the harm Edom had experienced was God's punishment for its mis-
conduct toward Judah; God's love for and fidelity toward Israel would
not allow God to overlook Edom's actions.[23] Second, it claims that the

---

21. Scholars routinely assign Gen 25:21–26 to the Yahwistic source of the Pentateuch (for example, W. Harrelson, *Interpreting the Old Testament* [New York: Holt, Rine-
hart and Winston, 1964] 488) or some other early source (for example, G. Fohrer,
Introduction to the Old Testament [Nashville: Abingdon, 1968] 161; and O. Eissfeldt, *The
Old Testament: An Introduction* [New York: Harper & Row, 1965] 195).

22. What is striking is how little, if at all, such sentiment pervades the Jacob/Esau
stories in the book of Genesis. Esau rather than Jacob is Isaac's preferred son. He is a
hunter who is bribed by Jacob to sell his birthright for a mess of pottage (Gen 25:29–
34) and is cheated out of his father's blessing by his mother and his trickster brother
(Gen 27:1–45). Even in the (presumably later) Priestly account of Esau's marriage to
Canaanite wives (who make life miserable for Isaac and Rebekah, Gen 26:34–35), he
tries to make amends by marrying a descendant of Abraham (28:6–9).

When the brothers meet again after years of separation, Esau welcomes Jacob back
home, declines his gifts, and offers him protection (33:4–17). When Isaac dies, Jacob
and Esau together bury their father (35:29).Not even the crucial text Gen 25:23 states
that God hates or rejects Edom, though it might be said in the context of the longer
Pentateuchal narrative to imply God's preference for the younger twin. It can, however,
be read simply as a statement of the future relationship between the boys. (See the discussion by G. von Rad, *Genesis* [OTL; Philadelphia: Westminster, 1961] 260–61). Either way, Gen 25:23, which neither mentions election nor labels Edom as immoral,
becomes the proof text for the assertion of God's love and hate in Mal 1:2–3, because
God's fidelity to postexilic Judah seemed to demand it.

23. Neither could fidelity to Israel take God's actions as far as Mal 1:2–5 envisions,
however. Such wholesale punishment would affect the innocent and the marginally
guilty in Edom along with those fully responsible for the action against Judah. Thus,
while Mal 1:2–5 does not take such nuances into calculation but paints destruction in
sweeping strokes, God as a moral being presumably could neither act as depicted here
nor allow evil to continue unchecked.

motivation for this punishment was hatred, which is better seen as the author's projection of his own feelings onto God.

The issue of whether God is immutable also surfaces in other places in the Hebrew Bible. It will be useful, then, to examine the classic case of 1 Samuel 15 in this connection. The key word in the chapter is *nḥm* which, when used with reference to past events, signifies the changing of God's mind in the sense of 'regret' and, when used with reference to future events, signifies the changing of God's mind in the sense of 'relent'.[24] According to v. 11, God regrets having made Saul king because of Saul's disobedience and sends Samuel to tell him so. God also would not relent and reinstate Saul, despite Saul's plea for forgiveness, since (v. 29) "the Glory of Israel will not lie and will not relent; for he is not a man to relent" (*nḥm* both places). Verse 29 would sound like an affirmation of God's immutability were it not for verse 11, which says God regretted making Saul king.

How is one to resolve this dilemma? Verse 23 elaborates on verse 11. Saul by his rejection of God's commands earned God's rejection of his kingship. In other words, God's relationship with Saul was conditional; if Saul broke that relationship, God had no further obligation to him. (One might note in passing that Mal 1:2–5 did not draw this same conclusion about the people of Judah as a whole; instead, God continued to love Judah.) The word *nḥm* in v. 29, moreover, is used in association with the word *šqr*, which means 'lie' (RSV) or 'deceive' (NRSV, footnote w). Apparently the author of 1 Samuel 15 thought that as conditions changed God's mind could change too; what God could not do was deceive people or act unfaithfully toward them.[25]

---

24. J. M. Sasson, *The Book of Jonah* (AB 24B; New York: Doubleday, 1990) 262.

25. Not every biblical author shared this conviction. Jeremiah, for example, could call God a "deceitful brook" (Jer 15:18), a charge that brought the prophet a sharp rebuke from God! In addition, God is said also to have deceived his people. J. L. Crenshaw (*Prophetic Conflict* [BZAW 122; Berlin: de Gruyter, 1971] 84) calls 1 Kgs 22:1–40 the crucial text on this issue: "There can be no question about the fact that this story depicts the 'false prophets' as men who gave in good faith the message conveyed to them, and portrays God as the source of this lie, even if mediated by a spirit." Crenshaw (p. 88) resolves the problem in this narrative with three observations. (1) This portrayal of the demonic in Yahweh is the price Israel paid for rejecting dualism. (2) The demonic in Yahweh is to be subsumed under the larger rubric of divine providence. (3) The demonic should be understood as God's means of testing Israel.

An Evaluation of the Theology of
Malachi 1:2–3

What has emerged from this study thus far is not a static picture of God defined in terms of the perfection of immutability but a dynamic picture of God struggling for fidelity toward the wayward people of Israel. This conclusion is not novel, either in biblical theology or systematic theology. Karl Barth says,

> There is such a thing as a holy mutability of God. He is above all ages. But above them as their Lord, . . . and therefore as the one who—as Master and in His own way—partakes in this alteration, so that there is something corresponding to that alteration in his own essence.[26]

This conclusion does, however, raise the larger theological question that surfaces in the study of texts like Mal 1:2–3, namely: what kind of being is God?[27]

The issue is basic to theism. If one claims that a god is worthy of worship (a claim basic even to polytheism), it is necessary to say in what that being's worth-ship consists. If one goes further to claim that a god is the being most worthy of worship (monolatry) or that a god is the only being worthy of worship (monotheism), the superiority of that god to (all) others requires explication and defense. Upon what basis would such a defense rest? By what criterion might one evaluate claims about the divine?

Historically, both Judaism and Christianity, under the influence of Greek thought, have appealed to the perfection of God. As an example, one may focus on the classic monotheistic claims in the Hebrew Bible in Isa 44:24, 45:5–7, and 46:5–11, where Deutero-Isaiah attempts to justify monotheistic claims on behalf of Yahweh. These verses claimed that Yahweh was superior to the Babylonian gods because Yahweh created the world and all peoples in it and was active (even proactive) in it, unlike the Babylonian gods, which were created by people and could do nothing, not even move about without being carried by human beings.

---

26. K. Barth, *Church Dogmatics* (New York: Scribners, 1957) 2/1.496; quoted by J. L. Mays, "Response to Janzen: 'Metaphor and Reality in Hosea 11,'" *Old Testament Interpretation from a Process Perspective* (*Semeia* 24; ed. W. A. Beardslee and D. J. Lull; 1982) 50.

27. This is the opening question by T. Fretheim, *The Suffering of God: An Old Testament Perspective* (OBT; Philadelphia: Fortress, 1984) 1.

The particulars of Deutero-Isaiah's argument are not the issue here. Instead, the point is that these verses constitute part of the biblical root of "perfect-being theology." Its other root for modern Westerners is Greek thinking. As early as book 2 of *The Republic*, Plato could assume agreement with this sentiment: "But surely God and the things of God are in every way perfect?"[28]

Since perfect-being theology does have roots in Hebrew thinking, it might serve as a criterion for the evaluation of biblical statements about God, particularly if it is refined somewhat. The classical formulation of perfect-being theology, in Christianity at least, came from Anselm: God is "that than which a greater cannot be thought."[29] This formulation has been criticized as a proof for the existence of God since the time of Immanuel Kant, but it still retains force as a statement about God. Thomas V. Morris has recently restated Anselm's dictum as follows: "God is a being with the greatest possible array of compossible great making properties."[30] Simply put, God is the being with the greatest number of moral characteristics that do not cancel each other out logically.[31]

While such properties would be intrinsically good, Morris notes that a precise list of these properties exceeds unaided human intuition. Consequently, one has room to appeal to the biblical record to correct the list.[32] As seen already, one property that would seem to fail the biblical test is immutability. Another would be impassibility,[33] if one recalls A. J. Heschel's description of God as the Most Moved Mover.[34]

---

28. Plato, *The Republic and Other Works* (Anchor Books; Garden City, N.Y.: Doubleday, 1973) 67.

29. Anselm, "Proslogion," in *Anselm of Canterbury* (3 vols.; 2d ed.; Lewiston, N.Y.: Edwin Mellen, 1975) 1.94.

30. T. V. Morris, *Our Idea of God: An Introduction to Philosophical Theology* (Downers Grove, Ill.: InterVarsity, 1991) 35.

31. The effects of perfect-being theology sometimes have been viewed as detrimental to both biblical anthropology and theology. Consequently, this paper is not a call to adopt any particular statement of perfect-being theology. Rather, its value for this discussion is that perfect-being theology raises the issue under discussion here: the worthship of God, particularly as God is described in the Hebrew Bible.

32. Ibid., 41–43.

33. Ibid., 43. See more fully, N. Wolterstorff, "Suffering Love," in *Philosophy and the Christian Faith* (ed. T. V. Morris; Notre Dame: University of Notre Dame Press, 1988) 196–237.

34. Heschel, however, held that the divine pathos, expressed in terms of the pairs love and anger, mercy and indignation, kindness and wrath, was an expression only of

Terrence Fretheim has moved this discussion forward by showing that the Hebrew Bible, in contrast to the Greek ideal of God, records that Yahweh does not always know what will happen in the future (for example, Ezek 12:13), participates within the created order instead of standing aloof from it (for example, Ps 139:13–16), limits his power (for example, Gen 8:21), graciously declines to exact full punishment on sinners (for example, Hos 11:8–9), and suffers with (Isa 54:7–8; Jer 48:30) and on account of (Jer 15:6; Mal 2:17) the people of Israel.[35] Likewise Paul S. Fiddes speaks of the God who suffers change and yet remains God.[36]

Once the notion of a perfect being has been corrected by reference to biblical theology, particular claims within the biblical record itself in turn should be subjected to careful scrutiny as to the appropriateness of the Bible's depictions of God as that perfect being. In the case of Mal 1:2–3, as long as Yahweh was conceived only or primarily as the God of Israel, God's relationship to Israel could be expressed ethnocentrically. Even today, one can acknowledge the negative emotions of the author of Mal 1:2–5 and perhaps even grant that Edom's sin against Jerusalem might have been morally repugnant without at the same time accepting the nationalistic bias of the passage, in which exilic and postexilic animosity was read back into the past and justified as God's verdict against Edom.

Contemporary readers should question such theology, however, not simply because they do not share Malachi's nationalistic perspective, but because this perspective is incompatible with the claim in passages such as Isa 45:18–22 that the sole God of all peoples is Yahweh, or Isa 56:1–8, which invites God-fearing foreigners to worship in the Temple,[37] and because the perspective of Mal 1:3 is incompatible with

---

God's relationship to Israel, and not an expression of God's essence. See *Between God and Man: An Interpretation of Judaism* (ed. F. A. Rothschild; New York: Harper, 1959) 123.

35. Fretheim, *The Suffering of God*, 45–46, 74–78, 107, and often.

36. P. S. Fiddes, *The Creative Suffering of God* (Oxford: Clarendon, 1988), chaps. 3 and 5.

37. To be sure, Isa 44:9–20 and similar passages can ridicule idolatry, but monotheism involves the claim of exclusive worth-ship. Also, Isaiah 47 predicts God's overthrow of Israel's enemy Babylon, but Babylon's own deeds warrant her downfall (v. 10). Whether Deutero-Isaiah himself steps over the line of nationalism in passages like 43:3 may be left open here with only the comment that his expressions are subject to the same review as other biblical authors.

the notion of God in the Hebrew Bible as the only being deserving of human worship.[38]

What kind of a picture of God might emerge from this mutual correction? Charles Hartshorne suggests the following as philosophically acceptable: "God requires *a* world, but not *the* world. By contrast, what the world requires is not simply *a* God but *the* one and only possible God, the Worshipful One."[39] His answer implies that the Hebrew Bible's view of God as unified and as the sole, wise, and powerful "creator"[40] who is righteously related to his whole creation is on target. (On the other hand, Hartshorne implies that God *had* to create, while the Hebrew Scriptures do not seem to see God under any such compulsion.)

Hartshorne continues, arguing that one should conceive of God as "unborn and immortal,"[41] omnipresent,[42] and also loving, "because in any world God alone could and would be universally loving, universally lovable, and everlasting."[43] God is not "the transcendental snob, or the transcendental tyrant, either ignoring the creatures or else reducing them to his mere puppets, . . . [but] the unsurpassingly interacting, loving, presiding genius and companion of all existence."[44] One could then infer, over against Mal 1:2–3, that God would also be a merciful judge who is neither petty nor biased but who does judge human behavior. Such a God is indeed great and greatly to be praised (Ps 48:2).

---

38. K. Armstrong (*A History of God: The 4000-Year Quest of Judaism, Christianity, and Islam* [New York: Knopf, 1993] 19) writes of this same type of portrayal of God in Exodus as follows: "He is passionately partisan, has little compassion for anyone but his own favorites and is simply a tribal deity. If Yahweh had remained such a savage God, the sooner he vanished, the better it would have been for everybody."

39. C. Hartshorne, *A Natural Theology for Our Time* (La Salle, Ill.: Open Court, 1967) 64–65.

40. Hartshorne, of course, would think of God as the necessary being who brings order to the world (an idea in keeping with the Genesis accounts of creation), not as one who created *ex nihilo*. One must leave open the possibility, however, that both Genesis and Hartshorne need to be corrected by something like the idea of *creatio ex nihilo*.

41. Ibid., 127.

42. Ibid., 131. Hartshorne even uses the term "ubiquitous."

43. Ibid., 56.

44. Ibid., 137.

Implication for the Task of Studying the Theology of the Hebrew Scriptures

These observations raise the issue of the task of studying the theology of the Hebrew Scriptures. This task can be confined to delineating the various theologies within these writings: "This subject matter which concerns the theologian is . . . simply Israel's own explicit assertions about Jahweh."[45] This subject matter can be expanded to include the religion of Israel and its piety; the thoughts about God contained in the Hebrew Scriptures; even the sum of all of its statements about God, cast into a kind of system; and an all-embracing theological principle.[46] A review of the major treatments of "Old Testament" theology available today shows that they adopt basically a descriptive stance.[47] Even when they move beyond description, they debate issues like the relationship of Old Testament theology to other disciplines and the relationship of Old Testament to New Testament theology. Not one calls for a critical appraisal of the adequacy of the theological statements of the Hebrew Scriptures themselves.

---

45. G. von Rad, *Old Testament Theology* (2 vols.; New York: Harper & Row, 1962–65) 1.105.

46. C. Westermann, "The Interpretation of the Old Testament," in *Essays on Old Testament Hermeneutics* (ed. C. Westermann; Richmond: John Knox, 1964) 47.

47. Works reviewed include the basic German Old Testament theologies or outlines by W. Eichrodt (*Theology of the Old Testament*; OTL [2 vols.; Philadelphia: Westminster, 1961–67]), L. Köhler (*Old Testament Theology* [London: Lutterworth, 1957]), von Rad (*Old Testament Theology*), Westermann (*Elements of Old Testament Theology*), and W. Zimmerli (*Old Testament Theology in Outline* [Edinburgh: T. & T. Clark, 1978]); other continental theologies, including T. C. Vriezen (*An Outline of Old Testament Theology* [Wageningen, Holland: Veenman, 1960]), and E. Jacob (*Theology of the Old Testament* [New York: Harper & Row, 1958]); and English-language theologies by A. B. Davidson (Edinburgh: T. & T. Clark, 1904]) and B. S. Childs (*Old Testament Theology in a Canonical Context* [Philadelphia: Fortress, 1985]); and books about Old Testament theology by W. Brueggemann (*Old Testament Theology: Essays on Structure, Theme, and Text* [Philadelphia: Fortress, 1992]), Childs (*Biblical Theology in Crisis* [Philadelphia: Westminster, 1970]), R. C. Dentan (*Preface to Old Testament Theology* [rev. ed.; New York: Seabury, 1963]), G. Hasel (*Old Testament Theology: Basic Issues in the Current Debate* [4th ed.; Grand Rapids: Eerdmans, 1991]), L. G. Perdue (*The Collapse of History: Restructuring Old Testament Theology* [OBT; Minneapolis: Fortress, 1994]), and H. G. Reventlow (*Problems of Old Testament Theology in the Twentieth Century* [Philadelphia: Fortress, 1985]).

The omission of such an enterprise is all the more remarkable in view of the sensitivity of the authors of these books to subjects such as the historicity (or lack of same) of the events of Israel's life before God. In addition to Fretheim, whose work was mentioned above, five authors surveyed for this article do raise the type of question being raised here. The first is Dale Patrick, who emphasizes the consistency of God's character. He focuses on the incomparability of God, who thus possesses such characteristics as power, wisdom, justice, righteousness, loyal care, majesty, and mystery to a superlative degree.[48] Similarly C. L. Labuschagne emphasizes the incomparability of Yahweh in terms of God's holiness, redoubtableness, greatness, maintenance of justice, succor, and rescue of Israel through wars and wonders.[49] Third, John Goldingay raises the question of diversity and contradiction. He distinguishes among formal contradictions (which involve differences at the level of words but not substance), contextual contradictions (which reflect a variety of circumstances), substantial contradictions (which involve true disagreement), and fundamental contradictions (which involve substantial contradictions at the level of one's ethical stance or religious outlook).[50]

Fourth, Rolf P. Knierim argues for systematizing the variety of theologies found in the Hebrew Bible and not merely describing them.[51] He also offers as the central organizing rubric "the universal dominion of Yahweh in justice and righteousness,"[52] a rubric that allows for choos-

---

48. D. Patrick, *The Rendering of God in the Old Testament* (OBT 10; Philadelphia: Fortress, 1981) 46–60, esp. 51. It will be helpful at this point to examine briefly the last-mentioned phrase, "the mystery of God." If one means by it that God is infinite and beyond a human's capacity to understand fully, the phrase is clearly appropriate. If, however, one means that God is completely inscrutable, this definition would leave God's people without a clue as to what pleases God. Surely, however, the Hebrew Scriptures often remind the reader of what pleases God (e.g., Mic 6:8). Finally, if God is arbitrary, even knowing what God says to do would be useless, since God would reward, punish, or ignore people based on whim.

49. See C. L. Labuschagne, *The Incomparability of Yahweh in the Old Testament* (Pretoria Oriental Series 5; Leiden: Brill, 1966) 98.

50. J. Goldingay, *Theological Diversity and the Authority of the Old Testament* (Grand Rapids: Eerdmans, 1987) 16–24.

51. R. P. Knierim, *The Task of Old Testament Theology: Method and Cases* (Grand Rapids: Eerdmans, 1995) 16.

52. Ibid., 15.

ing "theologically legitimate priorities"[53] among the plurality of theologies. For Knierim, the task is "the examination of the correspondence or relationship of the Old Testament's theologies themselves."[54]

Finally, the exhaustive new study by Brueggemann, *Theology of the Old Testament: Testimony, Dispute, Advocacy,* also is sensitive to the diversity of theologies in the Hebrew Bible and to unresolved tensions in the metaphors used for Yahweh (for example, "judge," "king," "warrior," and "father," to choose but one set of the metaphors Brueggemann discusses).[55] Still, he is content to reflect the diversity within the Hebrew Bible; he seems to prefer to hold fast even to more or less contradictory theologies rather than succumb to "reductionism."

The point in this paper, however, is that all theological claims should be evaluated on the basis of their appropriateness for describing the being with the "greatest possible array of compossible great-making properties." This issue is different from Brueggemann's concern that the exegete and pastor examine all of the claims. It is also different from the familiar question of whether "Old Testament" theology should be descriptive or normative.[56] The claim here is that either should be evaluative, and the criteria for this evaluation ought to be transcultural and transtemporal as far as possible.

Perhaps biblical scholars assume that such reflections belong to the philosophy of religion, which assuredly they do. I am attempting here to show that they also belong to the task of studying the theology of the Hebrew Scriptures. It is one thing for an exegete to expose "ungodlike" attitudes and behaviors attributed to God in biblical texts. It is quite another thing to assume that they should be included in a valid picture of God's character. If modern readers do not expect the Bible always to be without scientific or historical error, they also need not expect it to be without theological error. If modern exegetes are prepared to acknowledge the gender and economic biases of the text, why not acknowledge

---

53. Ibid., 9.

54. Ibid., 7.

55. W. Brueggemann, *Theology of the Old Testament: Testimony, Dispute, Advocacy* (Minneapolis: Fortress, 1997) 247–49.

56. See the review of the whole subject of "Old Testament" theology by W. E. Lemke, "Theology (OT)," *ABD* 6.448–73, particularly the discussion of "Descriptive and Normative Dimensions," pp. 454–56.

the theological biases as well? R. N. Whybray, in his article in this volume, points to places where the biblical writers or narrative voices within a text reject the theology in or the theological spin put on a particular passage. Why should the Old Testament theologian do less, where appropriate?

Wisdom and Yahwism Revisited

ROLAND E. MURPHY, O. CARM.

Washington, D.C.

Some years ago I struggled to argue for the compatibility of Yah-wism and biblical wisdom.[1] At the time, and perhaps still today, the two seemed incompatible, as if one were comparing apples and oranges. Not only was the theological neglect of or indifference to wisdom literature a sign of this, but as recently as 1987 the divorce between the two was vigorously defended.[2] Perhaps now it is not too bold to say that some props have been knocked out from under those who considered wis-dom a foreign body within the Bible. These props I would characterize as the tunnel vision of biblical wisdom provided by the Egyptian "win-dow," the "ma⁽atizing" of wisdom.[3] Second, there has been a weaken-ing in the ranks of those who adhered to the *Tat-Ergehen Zusammenhang* or deed/consequence theory of biblical reward and punishment.[4] It was the use made of this viewpoint, first seriously advanced by K. Koch, that was misleading. As an argument, it seemed to lock God into a me-chanical system contrary to genuine Yahwism; the sages were all lumped

---

1. See my "Wisdom and Yahwism," in *No Famine in the Land* (ed. J. Flanagan and A. Robinson; J. L. McKenzie Festschrift; Missoula, Mont.: Scholars Press, 1975) 117–26.

2. The outspoken representative was the late H. D. Preuss; see his *Einführung in die alttestamentliche Weisheitsliteratur* (Stuttgart: Kohlhammer, 1987).

3. See my "Religious Dimensions of Israelite Wisdom," *Ancient Israelite Religion* (F. M. Cross Festschrift; ed. P. D. Miller et al.; Philadelphia: Fortress, 1987) 449–56, esp. 449. Since then a devastating blow to glib parallels between Israel and Egypt has been given by M. V. Fox, "World Order and Ma⁽at: A Crooked Parallel," *JANES* 23 (1995) 37–48.

4. For details on the ongoing discussion of Koch's famous theory, see the remarks of J. Hausman, R. Clements, and B. Janowski indicated in my *The Tree of Life* (2d rev. ed.; Grand Rapids, Mich.: Eerdmans, 1996) 224–27. To these can be added R. van Leeu-wen, "Wealth and Poverty: System and Contradictions in Proverbs," *Hebrew Studies* 33 (1992) 25–36; and the discussion in M. V. Fox, "World Order," esp. pp. 39–40.

together with Job's dubious friends. A third consideration may also be added: there is growing respect for the religious values of the wisdom literature and hence the possible compatibility with Yahwism.[5]

The discussion is far from over. The difference between the two seems so striking, and almost from the beginning of the modern discussion of biblical theology they have been in two separate camps. Not too long ago my esteemed colleague and sage, James L. Crenshaw, described the situation in these words: "For me, the crucial issue concerns whether or not ancient sages accepted the world view of Yahwism." He went on to add, "Murphy thinks they did; I am not able to accept that position."[6] I would like to take up again this topic as a tribute and compliment to him and attempt to justify the compatibility of ancient wisdom and Yahwism—in other words, the ancient sages shared the world view of Yahwism. Basically, this is not a question of time—that is, a question of just when the ancient sages become Yahwists—but of mentality or conceptuality. A specific determination of time would lead to a hypothetical discussion (for example, when did Israel become "monotheistic"?). The issue is simply the inclusion of ancient (that is, preexilic) wisdom within the religious world view of the people who worshiped YHWH.

We cannot escape a discussion of time altogether, but we can perhaps avoid the pitfalls of uncertain dating. All would agree that "ancient wisdom" would predate the exile and much of it could go back beyond Solomon, with whom the Bible associates wisdom (for example, 1 Kgs 5:14[4:34]) and who became the standard-bearer of von Rad's ill-fated "Enlightenment." This means that for all practical purposes we are dealing with Proverbs 10–31, allowing for a few late items such as the poem in 31:10–31. The period of the early monarchy, Saul and David, represents a time of centralization, and one does not have sufficient evidence of education in schools during this period.[7] Some sort of training or edu-

---

5. See, e.g., L. Boström, *The God of the Sages: The Portrayal of God in the Book of Proverbs* (ConBOT 29; Stockholm: Almqvist & Wiksell, 1990), esp. 236–43.

6. J. L. Crenshaw, "Murphy's Axiom: Every Gnomic Saying Needs a Balancing Corrective," in *The Listening Heart* (R. E. Murphy Festschrift; ed. K. Hoglund et al.; JSOTSup 56; Sheffield: JSOT Press, 1987) 1–17; see esp. p. 13.

7. The heated discussion about the role (or even the existence) of schools in the transmission of Israelite wisdom has been raised to a new level by M. V. Fox, "The Social

cation there had to be. One may point to the practical advice concerning the explanation of the Passover to children (Exod 12:28, 13:14)—some kind of religious training united the family. While these examples refer to what may be called Yahwism, they provide a realistic means by which any kind of training would have been communicated. Moreover, the lessons were garnered from observation and experience—the ethos of the family and tribe in a society like early Israel. These lessons for life would also have found an entree into the hearts and minds of the young (see Prov 10:1) and would have developed into *bons mots* and admonitions regarding world and neighbor, as well as personal conduct. Eventually the transmission of the material found itself packaged and written down in collections (this is perhaps not unlike the history of the transmission of the Psalms, which has inspired so much recent research). The relationship of Prov 22:17–23:11 (24:22) to the teaching of Amenemope is a case by itself. It clearly indicates loose Israelite dependence, but it does not follow that wisdom sayings and instructions were the gift of Egypt to the Israelite establishment.

Before any further discussion, a certain caution is in order. Is it legitimate to separate Yahwism and wisdom from each other and then discuss whether they are compatible? In other words, does the very discussion concede more centrality, more importance, to Yahwism (understood as the Exodus-Sinai revelation and all that this involved), making it the criterion by which everything else is to be judged? On these terms, the issue is already predetermined. If I am correct in this, one must stay open to a more balanced and even evaluation of wisdom.

The question of outside influence is a question for Yahwism as well as for wisdom. When one examines the highly volatile relationship of YHWH to the *baʿalim* in the history of Israel, there can be no denying the

---

Location of the Book of Proverbs," in *Texts, Temples, and Traditions: A Tribute to Menahem Haran* (ed. M. Fox et al.; Winona Lake, Ind.: Eisenbrauns, 1996) 227–39. He points out that the existence of schools has been the wrong question. In the ill-focused debate, "school" was never really defined. Specifically, the scribal school in Egypt was not a "wisdom school." All kinds of literature were cultivated there, and wisdom literature served also as scribal exercises. But the wisdom teachers were fathers who taught their sons: Ptahhotep and Amenemope, for example. The transmission is a family thing in its origins at least, and this is what is reflected in Proverbs 1–9 and in parts of 10–31. To put it succinctly: "The self-presentation of Wisdom Literature is as paternal teaching" (p. 232).

influence of Canaanite religion. A whole world of Canaanitisms, from the innocuous world view of "Sea" and "Leviathan" on through fertility cults, influenced the way in which Israel understood the Lord. It took a long time before Israel could become convinced of the words in Hos 2:10–11, "It was I who gave her the grain and wine and oil. . . . I will take back my grain in its time, and my new wine in its season. . . ." The figure of Yhwh was considerably modified over the years in which the people honored him as Lord. I do not mean merely the Elijan choice between Yhwh and Baal, but the traits of Baal that were assimilated into the understanding of the Lord, such as epithet of cloud-rider or the adaptation of the Canaanite ideas that lie behind Psalm 29. This is not derogatory; rather, the point is that Old Testament faith showed itself resilient in many areas and faithful in areas that counted. Israel overcame and incorporated into itself many strange factors over the centuries. It had less trouble with wisdom that was indigenous to the Israelite tribes and that flowered into the wisdom literature of the Bible.

The homey origins (one is hard put to distinguish family from tribal ethos here) of early Israelite wisdom has been emphasized recently by C. Westermann.[8] He stresses oral transmission, and this has the practical effect of showing that wisdom admonitions were built into the family/ society. This "wisdom" derived from the experience and standards that the early Israelites settled upon. They were not "laws" in the same sense as the Decalogue and other codes (which were certainly influenced by such elementary wisdom sayings). But they were important for coping with life and achieving the success and prosperity that was part of the divine blessings of the Lord upon the people.

At least for early wisdom, the scenario of Israelite dependence on Egyptian wisdom is misleading. I have no intent to sever Israelite wisdom from any outside source. Wisdom was truly an international commodity, and each culture developed its own, with or without outside influence. But it is arguable that the early wisdom of Israel was at least "home-grown," and it need not be separated from Yahwism. In other words, an-

8. Cf. C. Westermann, _Wurzeln der Weisheit_ (Göttingen: Vandenhoeck & Ruprecht, 1990) 51–83; idem, _Roots of Wisdom_ (Louisville: Westminster/John Knox, 1995) 38–67; see also my "Israelite Wisdom and the Home," in _Où demeures-tu: La maison depuis le monde biblique_ (G. Couturier festschrift; ed. C. Petit et al.; Montreal: Fides, 1994) 199–212.

cient wisdom was the way early Israelites interpreted the world and themselves in the light of their experience. These were Yahwists who did this—whether fervent, orthodox, or on the fringe. They had traditions about a God named YHWH who had done marvels for them, and part of their *Weltanschauung* or world view was their reaction to the world that the Lord had created and to the human beings who populated it.

H. Delkurt, in a recent study of the ethical aspects of Prov 10:1–22:17 and 25:1–29:27, investigates four key areas of human conduct: parent and children; the lazy and diligent; the rich and the poor; man and woman.[9] These topics are far from exhaustive. He claims that it is no surprise that wisdom is silent about the *Heilsgeschichte*, since it deals explicitly with the everyday experience of the individual and not with the cultic traditions. The fact that the wisdom ideals do not contradict those of the rest of the Old Testament suggests that the early sages or teachers were aware of the religious premises that undergirded formal "religion." One cannot attribute wisdom and Torah to the guidance of different deities (for example, an undefined *Urhebergott* and YHWH) as some have attempted to do. The God of Israel heard prayers (Prov 15:29) and was responsible for both good and evil (Prov 16:4, 18:22). Experience itself was not regarded as the final arbiter (Prov 16:1, 33)

One may even suspect that behind the separation of Yahwism and wisdom lies a modern presupposition, the distinction between revelation and natural theology. That is to say, revelational theology is the view of God and world that can be derived from Torah and Prophets; God revealed self to Israel in history through the promises, deliverance from Sinai, and so on. But wisdom, or the human experiences reflected in the wisdom literature, are not truly revelation. They fall supposedly into the category of "natural theology" that in recent times was the *bête noire* of Karl Barth. James Barr has argued against Barth, claiming that there is natural theology in the Bible (for example, the Areopagus speech of Paul).[10] This is not the place to discuss this issue. More to the point is the question whether the "natural theology" contained in the Bible, or even construed outside of biblical revelation, is truly "natural."

---

9. Cf. H. Delkurt, *Ethische Einsichten in der alttestamentlichen Spruchweisheit* (Biblisch-Theologische Studien 21; Neukirchen-Vluyn: Neukirchener Verlag, 1993), esp. 143–61.

10. Cf. James Barr, *Biblical Faith and Natural Theology* (Oxford: Clarendon, 1993).

Properly understood, natural theology is an analysis of God from the point of view of reason, leaving aside the biblical data. It received tremendous impetus in scholasticism and on up to modern times. As a concept or a field of investigation, it has its own rules, as it were. It confines itself to the realm of creation, including human experience. This kind of study is respectable and logically based. But is it realistic, *actual?* Does it deal with the reality that humans find themselves in? From a biblical point of view, the action of YHWH penetrates all things; nothing and no person escapes the divine sovereignty and power. Hence the Old Testament is not talking about natural theology as later philosophers have conceived it (abstracting from biblical data). It is talking about the one order of things, the order of concrete human beings, who all stand in some relation to the ruler of the universe, drawn in by history and by experience. Therefore we should recognize the correctness that biblical revelation is more than the Torah and the Prophets. It includes the Writings and wisdom. God reveals self in the historical events of Sinai and the prophets. Indeed this revelation in historical events can be seen as comparatively rare. To be sure, the events are rehearsed in the cult, but where are human beings to be reached? In the relatively rare occasions of cultic worship or in the daily events of human life, where do they relate to each other, to the world, and ultimately to God? Even in the cult, there are Psalms like 8, 19, and 29 that speak more broadly than normal Israelite "orthodoxy." They are open to the experience of every human being, even people beyond Israel. The ecumenicity of the Psalms, describing human suffering and religious jubilation, points to a world outside of a narrow Yahwism and ultimately to a universal revelation through creation as well as history.

The issue of revelation has been raised by the penetrating questions posed by James Barr: "If one believes that God has revealed himself in his creation and continues to do so, why is that 'natural' theology and not 'revealed'? . . . If one believes that God was revealing himself in ancient Israel, why is this not 'natural' and 'revealed'?"[11] This is more than

---

11. Ibid., 115. The same point is made by Karl Rahner: "From a theological point of view, the *concrete* process of the so-called natural knowledge of God in either its acceptance or its rejection is always more than a merely natural knowledge of God. . . . The knowledge of God we are concerned with, then, is that concrete, original, historically constituted and transcendental knowledge of God which either in the mode of its

a matter of terminology. When initial presuppositions support the superiority of the historical over the experiential (as if the experiential was outside of history), the division between Yahwism and wisdom is inevitable. This is precisely the division that governs the exposition of wisdom literature by the late H. D. Preuss. It is as though the incarnational model of revelation of God in history is the only model that the Bible tolerates. Of course, this fits a Christian approach and can be supported by the historical interventions recorded in the Bible. But is it the only model?

There is another model, and it can be termed canonical, for want of a better word. By this I mean the fact that the wisdom phenomenon was included in the Bible as part of the written record, as testimony to God's revelation. This tells us something about the theological position of the ancient sages. One cannot disregard the fact that during a certain undefinable period wisdom was being transmitted and developed until it was finally secured in the eventual closing of the canon of books that "soiled the hands." It would not make sense to think that Israel treasured wisdom if it was contrary to or not in harmony with its total religious understanding. There is general agreement that Ben Sira and the author of the Wisdom of Solomon reflect the influence of the traditional *Heilsgeschichte* (Ben Sira 44–50; Wisdom 10–19), and they have been interpreted (by H. D. Preuss) as a movement that secured and ennobled wisdom literature for the Jews of a later historical period. This is a gratuitous assumption, even a circular argument. It is extremely unlikely that the three wisdom books of the Hebrew Bible would have been accepted and transmitted only to be "saved" by two books that were never accepted into the Hebrew Bible.

From an academic viewpoint, one can make logical and theoretical definitions of Yahwism. The absence of such staples as the promises, covenant, and so on can become the yardstick to separate "authentic" belief from a real and human understanding of the Lord. This is a theoretical and theological classification with logical validity. Yet one must

acceptance or of rejection is inevitably present in the most ordinary human life. It is at once both natural knowledge and knowledge in grace, it is at once both knowledge and revelation-faith. . . ." Cf. K. Rahner, *Foundations of Christian Faith* (New York: Seabury, 1978) 57.

question if Israelites ever lived this way, compartmentalized into Yahwists for "religious" reasons of a historical and cultic nature and sages for
pursuing ways to cope with daily life. They had only one world view,
not two, in which the Lord they worshiped was also the God recognized
in their experience of each other and the world. O. Plöger has expressed
this well: "Would it not be astonishing if an Israel that meets us primarily
as the people of its God, Yahweh, in the Old Testament, would have
pursued questions about life style with a conscious exclusion of Yahweh?
Even in the old wisdom period Yahweh will have certainly been known
to sapiential thought, to the consideration of the expert sages, even
though they will not always have used the name so readily."[12] Plöger
grants that the profile of the Lord may differ in wisdom literature from
that in other books. But this fact should not be overestimated any more
than one might draw conclusions from the differences recognizable between the Lord who was worshiped in the Temple and the God of judgment proclaimed by the prophets. I do not think it is exaggeration to say
that the eventual definition of wisdom as fear of the Lord (Prov 1:7 and
often) makes explicit what was there from the beginning. Or to put it
concretely, one can say that the religious wisdom of old comes to full
expression in the work of Ben Sira (Sir 33:16–17; 24:24, 30–34). This
claim does not rest only on Sirach's identification of wisdom and Torah
but also on his use of wisdom tropes.

It has long been noticed that Proverbs 10–16 abound in Yʜᴡʜ sayings and that there is a strong emphasis on the contrast between the just
and the wicked, the wise and the foolish. This equation is a primary
perspective in evaluating human conduct, and it is also found extensively in the Psalter. Two important points appear: (1) There is a striking
emphasis on the *ṣaddîq* and *rāšāʿ*. This is an important element in wisdom thinking, linking it to the central demands of the Lord. (2) There
is also the profound insight here: that righteousness is wisdom; wrongdoing is folly. Prov 10:16–17 provides an instructive example:

---

12. O. Plöger, *Sprüche Salomos (Proverbia)* (BKAT 17; Neukirchen-Vluyn: Neukirchener Verlag, 1984) xxxv.

The wage of the righteous leads to life,
the gain of the wicked to sin.
Whoever heeds instruction is on the path to life,
but one who rejects a rebuke goes astray. (NRSV)

The righteous of v. 16 is the one who heeds instruction in v. 17; both are destined for life. The wicked of v. 16 and the one who ignores a rebuke (practically, a fool by definition) are parallel; they end up badly. The same parameters of righteous/wisdom and wrong-doing/folly appear again in 15:2, 28. Where the identification is not explicit, it is implicit countless times.

It is important also to recognize that the agony and suffering of the Israelite is a primary theme in the wisdom literature, as the essays in this volume in honor of Professor Crenshaw demonstrate. Why there? One cannot of course exclude the Psalms, especially the psalms of lament. But even in the case of the Psalms, there is very little reference to so-called yahwistic factors. Psalm 89 is a communal lament over the divine failure to observe the Davidic covenant. But it has not the agony of Lamentations 3 (influenced by wisdom?) or of the standard laments of Job, and we may also include the suffering servant of Isaiah 53, however it be interpreted. One can point to other examples of grief in which the sacred traditions are reflected. But the real agony seems to be featured only in the wisdom literature and Psalms. I find this rather astonishing and yet to be expected if one does not relegate theology to abstraction but rather looks into the human heart, as wisdom does.[13] But can this theme of agony become an exclusive window on wisdom because it is something that we moderns find congenial to our human condition? Surely, this approach can be defended as true reader-response interpretation, but are we separating it from its moorings within wisdom?

---

13. In this connection, I find the study of Dorothea Sitzler provocative. See her *Vorwurf gegen Gott* (Studies in Oriental Religions 321; Wiesbaden: Harrassowitz, 1995). She studies this motif in Egypt (for example, Ipuwer) and Mesopotamia (for example, the *ludlul*). Her conclusions make one wonder if we are on the right track in analyzing biblical reproaches. She concludes (see pp. 119–230 and esp. 231–33) that the complainer is not "just" but, rather, an "ideal type," whose essence as it were lies in loyalty to the god. The occasion has not been provoked by a personal crisis. Hence the reproach is accompanied by a *Bekenntnis* (compare the typical Old Testament psalms of "thanksgiving"). There is no true dialogue; the sufferer is challenging the divinity and seeking revelation. The real issue is divine loyalty.

In a recent study, W. P. Brown has taken an original approach: to find within biblical wisdom its proper focus—moral formation.[14] He gives full attention to the agony of Job and the questioning of Qoheleth but progress in building moral fiber is achieved here. There is a wisdom context in which they are to be understood. The relationship of the Bible to ethics is difficult to pin down, but Brown has indicated the essential role of the wisdom tradition. Moral rules of dos and don'ts "cannot operate independently of the formation of character in traditions transmitted and shaped by the community." Can Wisdom and Sinai go hand in hand?

---

14. See W. P. Brown, *Character in Crisis: A Fresh Approach to the Wisdom Literature of the Old Testament* (Grand Rapids, Mich.: Eerdmans, 1996); the quotation is from p. 14. See also the description in my *Tree of Life*, 199–200.

Revelation and the Problem of the Hidden God in Second Temple Wisdom Literature

LEO G. PERDUE

Brite Divinity School

Introduction:
Revelation in Ancient Israel and Early Judaism

Biblical theologians for the past century have taught us that ancient Israel and early Judaism viewed the revelation of the character, will, and activity of God in at least four distinct ways: (1) the narratives and songs of ancient storytellers who speak and/or sing of the mighty acts of God in creation and in history on behalf of the chosen people, whether household, clan, tribe, or nation (for example, narratives of the Yahwist, the Elohist, the Priestly School, the Deuteronomic sermons of the prophet Moses, and the great hymns of the Psalter that include Psalms 33, 78, 104, 105, 106, 135, and 136); (2) the inspired oracles of the prophets deriving from a state of ecstasy in which God or the divine word was encountered (the major and minor prophets); (3) priestly oracles deriving from theophanies in the sacred sphere of divine presence, especially during certain holy occasions (the priestly tradition in Exodus 20–40, Leviticus); and (4) sapiential sayings embodying an incipient form of natural theology in which humans through sense perception and reason, sharpened by study illuminated by the charisma of divine insight, have observed the order of creation and then articulated its revelation of the divine will, actions, and character (the wisdom corpus).[1]

---

1. E.g., see W. Eichrodt, *Old Testament Theology* (2 vols.; Philadelphia: Westminster, 1961–67) 2.15–45; and H. D. Preuss, *Old Testament Theology* (2 vols.; Louisville: Westminster/John Knox, 1995–96) 1.200–263.

201

These distinct though divergent understandings of revelation existed side by side in the Hebrew Bible, apparently without creating significant discord, although there were obvious efforts both to interpret the problems associated with each and to correlate two or more understandings into a more systematic representation. Second Isaiah, for example, integrates in a most compelling fashion the forms of prophetic pronouncement and hymnic articulation with the content of revelation in creation and history. However, it is perhaps the sages of ancient Israel and early Judaism who struggle the most to find ways of dealing with the discordant notes of revelation, especially when divine presence is difficult to ascertain in human life or when the traditional teachings of earlier generations fail to correlate with experience carefully considered. These various understandings of revelation and the problems they posed have entered and subsequently shaped in different ways the construing of contemporary theological discourse.

During the reign of neoorthodoxy in Continental and American theology from the 1930s into the 1960s, Old Testament theology underwent a dramatic transformation from its earlier configuration that was largely influenced by the characteristic features of old liberalism with its central emphases on the astuteness and reliability of human reason, the openness to truth wherever its location, great confidence in nineteenth- and early-twentieth-century scientific method, skepticism concerning the certainty of knowing ultimate truth, an abiding assurance of the goodness of humanity, and a high degree of faith in human progress. Many in this theological tradition emphasized the immanence of God in the world, who was universally open to human reason and experience. Humans thus required no means of special revelation to come to a knowledge of God. This spirit of confidence in humanity and liberalism's larger world view of an evolving reality in which civilization continued to make progressive strides in increasing significantly its moral and humane character, so pervasive in Christianity in Europe and America, began to totter as a result of the human slaughter of trench warfare during World War I and ultimately received its *coup de grace* from the devastation incurred by World War II and the atrocities of the Nazi death camps.[2]

---

2. J. Dillenberger and C. Welch, *Protestant Christianity Interpreted through Its Development* (2d ed.; New York: Scribner's, 1954) 179–231.

The dominant themes of this "new" orthodoxy, shaped by such influential theologians as Karl Barth and Emil Brunner, took root in Europe between the two great global conflicts and entered America especially after the conclusion of the Second World War. Chastened by the ghastly destruction of world war, this new theology embraced and proclaimed the themes of the sovereignty and transcendence of God, divine providence in guiding creation and history, salvation through encounter with the divine Word, God's greatest and final act of revelation and redemption in Jesus Christ, the centrality of Christ in the expression of Christian faith, and a much darker view of human nature. In particular, faith in human ways of knowing God, in particular reason and natural theology, and the affirmation of the goodness of human nature were largely subdued and at times even disavowed.

While revelation among neoorthodox theologians came to be understood in several ways, there was a common consensus that the knowledge of God was not accessible to human reason and the observation of nature. Thus revelation was not universally available to all humans. Human nature was, after all, depraved, and humanity was estranged from the creator. The modes of divine revelation included the direct encounter of a human being with God through, for example, proclamation of the divine word rediscovered in scripture and activated by God in the act of proclaiming. But revelation ultimately is not equated with scripture, tradition, or creeds but with the self-manifestation of God, whose ultimate disclosure came in the form of the incarnation—that is, in Christ, in whom God was fully present.[3] This encounter requires of one a decision—an either-or—either of faith or a turning away in disbelief. Significant here is the emphasis placed on God's initiating act of self-disclosure to estranged humans and not on their own attempts to penetrate the veil of divine mystery.[4]

Neoorthodoxy during this period signficantly affected both the understanding and place of scripture in Christian faith and the theological character of biblical interpretation given shape by what Brevard Childs called, in a reductionistic fashion, the Biblical Theology movement in America (see, for example, G. Ernest Wright) and by the traditio-

---

3. Ibid., 273–76.
4. Ibid., 255–83. For a survey of important theologies developing since the decline of neoorthodoxy, see L. Kliever, *The Shattered Spectrum: A Survey of Contemporary Theology* (Atlanta: John Knox, 1981).

historical approach of the leading German Old Testament scholars (for example, Albrecht Alt, Martin Noth, and Gerhard von Rad). This new, often compelling, and eventually dominant theology began to appear in Old Testament scholarship prior to the outbreak of World War II and came to shape much of the contours and content of biblical interpretation well into the 1970s.[5]

The proclamation of the biblical word and the confessional response of the community to this message became the center of life and faith for the Western church. The revelation of God in the Hebrew Bible came to be construed in two ways: as the word of God, spoken especially by the prophets and encapsulated in the law,[6] and as the mighty acts of God in history on behalf of Israel captured in the stories and songs of narrators, poets, and minstrels.[7] God's acts of creation and divine blessing were not ignored, but they were often understood by leading Old Testament theologians of the day either as a pagan influence on Israelite belief[8] or as a prolegomenon to salvation history and not as a separate tradition of faith. Creation theology was viewed with some suspicion due to its connection in the ancient Near East with fertility and fertility religion.[9] The major exception to this insignificant role given to creation faith was expressed in the work of Claus Westermann, who argued that Israelite theology consisted of two interactive poles: salvation (history) and blessing (creation).[10] Old Testament theologians influenced by neoorthodoxy also view revelation through human reason and experience largely as il-

---

5. For a survey, see B. S. Childs, *Biblical Theology in Crisis* (Philadelphia: Westminster, 1970). Also see J. Barr, "The Theological Case against Biblical Theology," *Canon, Theology, and Old Testament Interpretation* (B. S. Childs festschrift; ed. G. M. Tucker et al.; Philadelphia: Fortress, 1988) 3–19.

6. For the prophets and the revelation of God, see G. von Rad, *Old Testament Theology* (2 vols.; Philadelphia: Westminster, 1965) esp. 2.80–98. For a critical review of von Rad's theology, see L. G. Perdue, *The Collapse of History: Reconstructing Old Testament Theology* (OBT; Minneapolis: Fortress, 1994) 45–68.

7. See in particular G. E. Wright, *God Who Acts: Biblical Theology as Recital* (SBT 8; London: SCM, 1952). See Perdue, *The Collapse of History*, 23–44, for a summary and critique of Wright's theology.

8. Wright, *God Who Acts*; idem, *The Old Testament against Its Environment* (SBT 2; London: SCM, 1950).

9. Von Rad, *Old Testament Theology*, 1.136–65.

10. C. Westermann, *Theologie des Alten Testaments in Grundzügen* (ATD Ergänzungsheft 6; Göttingen: Vandenhoeck & Ruprecht, 1978); and *Creation* (Philadelphia: Fortress, 1974).

legitimate. True revelation, so they contended, came to a limited few through divine proclamation. Authentic knowledge of God was neither accessible universally nor open to rational and analytical inquiry.

The part of scripture that proved more than problematic for neo-orthodoxy and those biblical scholars who approached biblical theology by the avenue of salvation history was wisdom literature. Except for the critical sages (Agur, Job, and Qoheleth), this corpus posed no significant theological problem for old liberalism, for indeed the teachings of the sages, their epistemology and emphasis on the order of creation, and their understanding of revelation through the order(s) of creation, conformed nicely with late-nineteenth- and early-twentieth-century Protestant theology. However, neoorthodoxy was perplexed by this part of the Hebrew canon and came to reduce severely or even dismiss its authenticity. Lacking any mention of redemptive history until Jesus ben Sira in the early part of the second century B.C.E., sapiential literature could not be successfully positioned within the framework of the dominant biblical theology of the period so shaped by Barthian theology.

In a rather obvious misplacing of the wisdom corpus, Gerhard von Rad positioned the biblical wisdom texts (prior to Ben Sira) within the final section of the first volume of his Old Testament Theology. He called this section "Israel before Jahweh (Israel's Answer)" and placed the wisdom texts alongside the Psalter. This decision largely lacked credibility, since wisdom texts were not responding either positively or negatively to the theology of God's mighty acts in history. Indeed, prior to Ben Sira, there is no mention of covenant and salvation history in sapiential literature. By contrast, wisdom was firmly grounded in creation theology and saw the knowledge of God deriving from human experience, the empirical observation of world order, and the conclusions of reasoned reflection.[11]

The Problem of Revelation in Wisdom Literature: Major Approaches

J. Coert Rylaarsdam

Professor Crenshaw is not the first among the major interpreters of Israel's wisdom corpus to grapple with the issue of divine revelation in

---

11. See my *Wisdom and Creation: The Theology of Wisdom Literature* (Nashville: Abingdon, 1984).

the writings of Israelite and early Jewish sages. J. Coert Rylaarsdam devoted an entire monograph to this topic in a classic study that continues to retain its significant value.[12] In this volume he raises the question: did the sages claim primarily a "natural endowment of reasoning and purposive consciousness" granted by the creator to all humans, though certainly not developed at least not equally by everyone, or are some humans, at least those elected by God, provided a special gift that enables them to rise above the ingenerate properties of intellect and reason, common to human nature, in order that they alone might attain special insight into divine nature and human existence?[13] If the first is true, argues Rylaarsdam, then authority for the sages issues from knowledge attainable by all and thus is largely social. But if the latter proves correct, then authority is a matter that is both social and theological.

Thus for Rylaarsdam, a key, perhaps *the* key, question that arises in interpreting the wisdom texts is the means by which the wise claimed to come to a knowledge of the goals of life and how they were to be obtained, either from natural reason and collective human experience or from God through one or more means of divine enlightenment. A secular answer would suggest that the sages derived their insights through the acuity of analytical and integrative reasoning that responds to empirical observation and experience. Settling this question from a theological perspective, one needs to ask: how did those who wrote the wisdom literature "think that God and his ways became known to them?"[14] Rylaarsdam contends, as does von Rad later on, that over the six centuries in which this literature was produced the answer changed from an emphasis on individual freedom and the use of the human natural resources of reason and experience to an emphasis on God's special revelation, obtainable only through the divine gift of wisdom that ultimately was seen to be embodied in the Torah (Ben Sira) or the Spirit of God (Wisdom of Solomon). In other words, the movement was from "the sufficiency of nature, reason, creation . . . [to] an assertion of the necessity of grace, faith, redemption. It opens in a spirit of indifference toward the national cult, including the Law; it closes in glorification of the cult

---

12. J. C. Rylaarsdam, *Revelation in Jewish Wisdom Literature* (Chicago: University of Chicago, 1946).

13. Ibid., vi.

14. Ibid., ix.

and absorption by it."[15] Wisdom begins with the belief that the world is rational and moral in its design, moves into a period in which reality is irrational and lacking in moral reference, and concludes with the affirmation that the sapiential meaning of existence and the cosmic and social setting for human life became identified with the nationalization of human knowledge in the form of the Jewish Torah and Temple cult, the Jewish nation, and the creedal confession of the redemptive acts of God on Israel's behalf.

For Rylaarsdam the traditional sages of Israel and Judah generally recognized the limits of human understanding, including their own, even though they still affirmed a providential design for and guidance of the world that still remained partially hidden.[16] There were exceptions among the sages to this candid, though still positive affirmation. Qoheleth, says Rylaarsdam, denies that there is any providential design discernible to human observation and study but concludes rather that there is only the operation of blind fate without reference to moral standards. However, Rylaarsdam denies that the "loss of moral direction," the "deep pessimism," and the admission of the human failure to obtain the knowledge of God and the divine will for human life expressed in sapiential texts like Job, Agur, and Qoheleth, ever achieved a final, normative status in Jewish teachings.

Rylaarsdam asserts that what finally prevails in Jewish wisdom, especially as detailed in the writings of Ben Sira and Wisdom, is the confidence that the knowledge of God and the goals of human life may be obtained through the divine gift of wisdom, not to all, but only to the Jewish sages.[17] The optimistic view of reality as a moral order that reveals the character of God and is ascertainable by the human intellect begins with early wisdom's affirmation of natural endowment and concludes with late wisdom's belief that divine revelation is given to the chosen few. The pessimistic outlook in the writings of the cynics and skeptics, which doubts the possibility of revelation and greatly lessens the certainty of human knowledge, enters the sapiential tradition between these two poles. Rylaarsdam argues that these two positions

---

15. Ibid., x.
16. Ibid., 15.
17. Ibid., 16.

found in sapiential literature represent not simply a contrast but more a major, linear development in the thinking of Israelite and Jewish sages.

Gerhard von Rad

In his *tour de force* on the thought of the sages entitled *Weisheit in Israel*, Gerhard von Rad devoted an entire chapter to the topic "Die Selbstoffenbarung der Schopfung" (The Self-Revelation of Creation) in Israelite and early Jewish wisdom literature. Here he traces the theme of revelation under three subheadings ("Die weltimmanente Weisheit" = Wisdom Immanent in the World; "Der Anruf" = The Call; and "Der geistige Eros" = Intellectual Love).[18] According to the sages, Wisdom, personified as a goddess in the compelling didactic poems of Proverbs 8, Job 28, and Ben Sira 24, was present in creation as the revelatory voice of Yahweh. For von Rad, scholars were not to concern themselves primarily with the tracing of the *religionsgeschichtlich* background of Woman Wisdom, an objective that heretofore had been the major interest of interpreters of these and similar texts, but with the theological theme of divine revelation. For von Rad, history of religions always takes a back seat to theology.

In the subheading "Wisdom Immanent in the World," von Rad provides an incisive look at Job 28, Proverbs 8, and Prov 3:19–20. In the first poem, he notes that the point is clearly made that human beings, in spite of their great achievements, cannot discover the location of wisdom. This knowledge is limited to God alone. Implied by this poem is the understanding that Wisdom, created by God, assisted him during creation. This likely intimates that she is the means and power by which he created and sustains the world as well as the knowledge by which God and providence are known. In addition, divine wisdom, or knowledge, goes back to primeval origins.

For von Rad, this representation of wisdom has nothing to do with the process of hypostatization, that is, the giving of independent life and a distinct character to a divine attribute, or with a divine, mythological figure based on an ancient goddess in Near Eastern mythology. Indeed, there is not even present in these poetic ruminations the notion of a

---

18. G. von Rad, *Weisheit in Israel* (Neukirchen-Vluyn: Neukirchener Verlag, 1990) 189–228 = *Wisdom in Israel* (Nashville: Abingdon, 1972) 144–76.

mere literary personification. Rather, von Rad's explication of wisdom may be summarized as follows: While wisdom is "in" the world, it is not a part of creation. Wisdom is something like the "meaning" that God has placed within creation—that is, the "divine mystery of creation." What this poem says, then, is that the knowledge of wisdom, the most precious thing in the world, is denied to human beings, meaning that they do not have access to understanding the nature and operation of creation. Humanity's inability to gain access to the location of wisdom means that no one can understand the mystery of creation and thus have power to master it, a teaching that earlier sages had believed was possible. For von Rad, the poem is saying that "the world never reveals the mystery of its order."[19] To correct this negative conclusion to the human quest for wisdom, a later editor inserts the final verse (v. 28), which asserts that the way to wisdom is through the fear of Yahweh (that is, religious piety). This later sage-redactor concludes that the truly wise person is the one who abandons the quest for a comprehensive meaning of the world in order to retreat into the unfathomable mystery of divine praise.

Proverbs 8 is comprised of three parts: vv. 4–21, in which Wisdom summons the unlearned to follow her and declares her worth; vv. 22–31, where Wisdom proclaims her primeval origins; and vv. 32–36, in which Wisdom issues a paraenetic ultimatum of life or death residing in the decision of the student to follow or not follow her teaching. Here, von Rad incorporates in his exposition the neoorthodox tenet that the Wisdom who calls to humanity is the self-manifestation or self-revelation of God.

Von Rad focuses more of his attention on the richest, most intriguing theological section, vv. 22–31, where, in his judgment, the poet depends on Egyptian mythological representations of Maʿat as the daughter of Re and the goddess of order. However, this recognition is of little significance to von Rad. For him, Wisdom is neither divine in nature nor a hypostatization of an attribute of God. Rather, "she" is created by Yahweh and is the first work of all creation. What is spoken of here, however, is no heavenly undertaking far removed from the place of human habitation, but a cosmic event that happens to humanity—

---

19. Ibid., *Wisdom in Israel*, 148.

that is, an event that is brought upon human beings by and through the world. This means that this poem speaks of an ordering power that affects human beings and directs their lives. As noted elsewhere (Prov 3:19–20, Sir 1:9), God has bestowed wisdom on the whole of creation—that is, wisdom is and becomes a righteous power that shapes the prudent and just behavior of human beings. Von Rad asks the distinguishing question, "What is Israel's contribution to this ancient notion of a cosmic order or a collage of orders?" The answer is that Wisdom calls and woos humans to her embrace that they may have the benefit of a wise and righteous order to envelop and guide their lives. Wisdom, this world reason that humans may incorporate into their character and behavior, was presented in the form of a personal being, a favorite child, in whom God found delight and who in turn delights in the world of human habitation. Wisdom becomes, then, for the sages of Israel's wisdom school, an object of focused, even intense, contemplation.

The "call" of Wisdom is briefly but significantly mentioned in various locations in the didactic poems of Proverbs 1–9 (Prov 1:20–21; 8:1, 4; 9:3). Whom she calls, of course, are humans, that is, all humankind. Wisdom is not esoteric knowledge revealed only to a select few initiants but is open and publicly accessible to all who would heed her voice. She is available to human beings both to possess and to know. She offers, not hidden knowledge, but the way to life and well-being. Thus for Israel's teachers, humans are "addressed from creation by a desire for order" that is inescapable, a desire that resides not only within their own being but also within the nature of reality itself. This order is the basis for ethical existence (Prov 2:9–20), but it is also an active force, a power (8:14) that reaches beyond private life to embrace the totality of human society, indeed all of creation, both human and nonhuman (Sir 24:3–6). Wisdom, still a creation of God, not only covers the entire earth but also rules it, indeed speaks to its various entities. Yet this same Wisdom, who addresses humans and offers them life, may also withdraw her call (Prov 1:24–31) from those who have not listened, dooming them to destruction. Creation, encompassed and imbued by Wisdom, becomes the teacher of humans who accept her call and take up her course of study (12:7–9). Humans are invited to allow primeval Wisdom, the first of God's mighty works in creation, to be their teacher and to guide them in all of their decisions and, in making "correct" choices, they discover the fruits of salvation.

It finally becomes clear that the Voice who addresses humanity is God himself, the One who is "the mystery inherent in the creation of the world."[20] God speaks through the mouth of creation and opens the eyes and ears of humans to divine instruction. Yet it was Ben Sira who, for the first time, directed this voice of Wisdom in creation specifically to Israel, where she eventually took up her dwelling (Sir 24:7–11). Only in Israel were there humans who opened their minds and their hearts to Wisdom's call and thus her teachings, which eventually became embodied in the Torah.

But perhaps the most incisive insight of von Rad is the recognition that for Israel's sages, this creation, which through the voice of Wisdom calls out to humans and offers them salvation, also loves them. This is no passive love waiting to be requited by the passionate search, discovery, and finally embrace of those smitten by the charms of Woman Wisdom. Rather, Wisdom, with seductive speech and erotic dress, is pictured as actively searching out her lovers, and at times she goes into the world in pursuit of even the reticent of heart and the simple of mind. On occasion, Wisdom assumes the guise of a fertility goddess and commissions her maidens to invite humans to join her in her love feast (Prov 9:1–6). This contrasts with the invitation of the woman who sought to fulfill her fertility vow in Proverbs 7 and with Woman Folly who, presented in the guise of a harlot, attempted to seduce the wayward young men of Israel to her bed and thus to their death (9:13–18). Von Rad describes this yielding to Wisdom's alluring voice as a mystical bonding to the glory of creation, much like the uniting of a man and a woman in the sweet embrace of sexual ecstasy (Prov 8:17, Wis 6:12–16, Sir 15:2). Humans love and in turn are loved by this life-giving order of creation that reveals itself in the voice of Woman Wisdom. It is this order of creation that becomes the mediator between God and humanity and not the great traditions of salvation history and the cult or their representatives and voices, the court historians, the priests, and the prophets. Through Wisdom, humans discover the world to be not an alienated place where they wander, rootless and estranged but a home that is comfortable, secure, and sustaining.

---

20. Ibid., 163.

Roland Murphy

Some fourteen years after the appearance of von Rad's *Weisheit in Israel*, Roland Murphy delivered before the Society of Biblical Literature his presidential address, entitled "Wisdom and Creation."[21] He began this probing and provocative speech by posing a rather comprehensive question: "How has the biblical data on creation been integrated into OT Theology?" The typical answer of biblical scholars, at least since World War II, has been that creation needs some special pleading to be included in a genuine "Yahwism" since, in the view of many, Old Testament theology is centered on redemptive acts of history, including the revelation and covenant at Sinai. This tradition of the mighty acts of God and the events of Sinai was articulated in the great narratives and hymns of Israel's storytellers and poets and was later reshaped and re-articulated by the prophetic tradition.

In rehearsing the views of Gerhard von Rad, Claus Westermann, and Walther Zimmerli, Murphy notes that all three secured for the wisdom literature creation as its special home, even though the writings of the sages have often been regarded by many as marginal to true Yahwistic religion. Yet for Murphy there is no evidence that creation, or for that matter, even wisdom ever resided outside the sphere of ancient Yahwistic faith. Indeed, the Israelites shaped their own understanding of wisdom and creation as a significant element of their religious system of piety and belief. They did so in two major ways: creation as the story of "beginnings" and creation as the location for the acting out of human life.

The first way ("creation as beginnings") is present in numerous sapiential texts, including wisdom's representation as the *'āmôn* ('artisan' or 'nursling') in Prov 8:30. Indeed, in the magnificent poem in Prov 8:22–31, Wisdom, while not clearly revealed, nevertheless is portrayed as divine in origin and as having something to do with creation. She delights in humans and offers them the gift of life. Who is this enigmatic Lady Wisdom? For Murphy, von Rad is correct at least to a degree in his assertion that she is the "self-revelation of creation."[22] Yet, Murphy parts company with von Rad and others who contend that wisdom is

---

21. R. Murphy, "Wisdom and Creation," *JBL* 104 (1985) 3–11.

22. See the title of chapter 9: "The Self-Revelation of Creation" in von Rad, *Wisdom in Israel*, 144–76.

some kind of "order," regardless of how mysterious its nature. Murphy prefers the metaphor of wooing and marriage in place of the abstract and bloodless term "order." This Lady Wisdom goes in pursuit of human beings, and in the encounter they recognize her as the revelation of God, not simply of creation. "She is the divine summons issued in and through creation, sounding through the vast realm of the created world and heard on the level of human experience."[23] Here Murphy is close to von Rad's category of wisdom as eros or "intellectual love," though he parts company with von Rad's understanding of the wisdom teaching of "order" or "orders" of creation.

The second way ("creation as the setting for human existence") is found in texts that point to the continuing and sustaining of creation as the place where humans carry on their lives. The sage's experience of creation is no less an avenue for the expression and living out of faith than is the hymnic praise of the God of providence and salvation in community worship. In affirming von Rad's conclusion,[24] Murphy argues that for the sages the experience of the world is also an experience of God. This world of divine making is not silent but addresses its listeners with a language about God and human life that can be "heard" (Psalm 19; Job 38–41). Murphy concludes that wisdom is not to be reduced simply to a teaching. Rather, wisdom is as much a dialogue with the created world as it is an array of admonitions that broach the topics of ethical behavior. Humanity has, for the sages, an existential relationship to creation that includes both life and death, well-being and suffering. Yet knowledge of the world possessed no aura of human certitude, since the ambiguities of life issuing from this dialogue opened the sages to various, even conflicting, views of many matters. Indeed, residing within creation was the mystery of God, who transcended all human attempts to comprehend.

According to Murphy, the sages made no real distinction between the rational knowledge of God and revealed knowledge. The new point made by Ben Sira in his exquisite poem on Woman Wisdom in chapter 24 is the identification of cosmic wisdom with the Torah, for both have

---

23. Murphy, "Wisdom and Creation," 10.
24. Von Rad, *Wisdom in Israel*, 62.

now become the Word of God. The revelation of the Word and the testimony of creation have merged into one.

James L. Crenshaw

Throughout his many influential writings on the wisdom texts, James L. Crenshaw has often noted that revelation is a significant issue in both the wisdom literature and its interpretation.[25] For example, in his essay on the portrayal of God in wisdom literature, he argues that the deity of the sages is typically represented as removed from the ken of direct human observation and experience and thus from immediate sapiential knowledge.[26] This is true even in the conservative tradition and not just the more radical wisdom of Agur, Job, and Qoheleth. However, what may be known about God is universal; that is, the knowledge of God is open to all human beings and is not limited simply to Israel, though its sages and wisdom's residence in their national domain are argued to have the advantage over and to be superior to foreign wise men and women, their teachings, and their cultures.[27]

Crenshaw suggests that there are two indirect means of divine revelation, or ways that God is known, in the wisdom texts. The first is

---

25. Among the major writings of Crenshaw that address the issue of revelation, see "Popular Questioning of the Justice of God," *ZAW* 82 (1970) 380–95; "Review of Gerhard von Rad, *Wisdom in Israel*," *Religious Studies News* 2 (1976) 6–12; "In Search of Divine Presence: Some Remarks Preliminary to a Theology of Wisdom," *RevExp* 74 (1977) 353–69; "Human Dilemma and Literature of Dissent," in *Tradition and Theology in the Old Testament* (ed. D. Knight; Philadelphia: Fortress; 1977) 235–58; "The Birth of Skepticism in Ancient Israel," in *The Divine Helmsman: Studies on God's Control of Human Events, Presented to Lou H. Silberman* (ed. J. L. Crenshaw and S. Sandmel; Philadelphia: Fortress, 1984) 1–19; "The Expression *mî yôdēaʿ* in the Hebrew Bible," *VT* 36 (1986) 274–88; *Theodicy in the Old Testament* (ed. J. L. Crenshaw; Philadelphia: Fortress / London: SPCK, 1987); "The Acquisition of Knowledge in Israelite Wisdom Literature," *Word and World* 7 (1987) 245–52; "Clanging Symbols (Prov. 30:1–14)," in *Justice and the Holy: Essays in Honor of Walter Harrelson* (ed. D. Knight and P. Paris; Atlanta: Scholars Press, 1989) 51–64; *Trembling at the Threshold of a Biblical Text* (Grand Rapids: Eerdmans, 1994); "Wisdom and the Sage: On Knowing and Not Knowing," in *Proceedings of the Eleventh World Congress of Jewish Studies,* Div. A: *The Bible and the World* (ed. D. Assaf; Jerusalem: World Union of Jewish Studies, 1994) 137–44; "The Contemplative Life in the Ancient Near East," *Civilizations of the Ancient Near East* 4 (ed. J. M. Sasson; New York: Scribner's, 1995) 2445–57.

26. Idem, "The Concept of God in Old Testament Wisdom," in *The Search for Wisdom* (ed. L. G. Perdue, et al.; Louisville: Westminster/John Knox, 1993) 1–18.

27. Idem, "The Contemplative Life in the Ancient Near East," 2450.

through acts in history—not the great deeds of redemption of Israel (for example, the exodus from Egypt), at least not until their inclusion in the ruminations of Ben Sira in the early second century B.C.E.—but the divine blessings meted out to the wise who engage in deeds of righteousness and God's punishments inflicted on the fools who practice wickedness. This theology is sometimes named retributive theology or, in German, *Vergeltung*, which argues that there is a direct correlation between deed and consequence, though the role of God in this process is understood in different ways by wisdom scholars.[28]

The other avenue of divine revelation open to the sages is creation, where God not only originates the world and all of its creatures but also oversees the maintenance of life for every living thing. The sages believed that a divine order permeated both the cosmos and human society and that, as long as this affirmation remained intact, even occasional assaults of chaos in the form of such disturbances as evil, suffering, and death did not undermine the religious system of meaning that sages imposed on the world. Only significant disruptions led to the radical questioning of the justice of God and the emergence of doubt about both a righteous order divinely secured and even divine righteousness (see Job, Qoheleth, and Agur).[29]

Crenshaw argues that, in their characterizations of God and these acts of redemption, blessing, and punishment, the sages spoke both of divine mercy and justice. However, the tension between God's mercy and justice is ever present in their writings, for the reasons for divine actions or the reticence to act are not clearly explained, not even within the framework of a sometimes present or at least implicit theory of retribution. Even with the revelation of the "Voice from the whirlwind" to Job, Crenshaw observes that "at best, we intuit the silencing effect of new insight on a chastened sufferer."[30] Still, the definition of this "insight" is not at all clear. While the boastful Elihu (chaps. 32–37) may claim to possess perfect knowledge, observes Crenshaw, his fearful observation of divine power in the dramatic effects of a thunderstorm does

---

28. See, for example, K. Koch, "Gibt es ein Vergeltungsdogma im Alten Testament?" *ZTK* 52 (1955) 1–42.

29. Crenshaw, "Introduction: The Shift from Theodicy to Anthropodicy," *Theodicy in the Old Testament*, 1–12.

30. Idem, "The Concept of God in Old Testament Wisdom," 5.

not reveal the reason for God's actions in nature (37:13 = Qoh 9:1).[31] Thus, God in wisdom literature remains at least to some extent hidden and enigmatic and is only indirectly known through the activities of blessing and punishment and the order and maintenance of creation.

However, what appears to be God's failure to act, especially when the righteous suffer and the wicked prosper, became especially troubling to the sages, whose reflections eventually move from outspoken assurance to quiet confidence to gnawing doubt to intense questioning of divine mercy and justice.[32] This finally led to what Crenshaw has at times called the "birth of skepticism in ancient Israel."[33] Skepticism, according to Crenshaw, incorporates both a denial of or doubting thought about a theological affirmation and a positive affirmation of a "hidden reality" that resides beyond the ken of human knowing. A correct understanding acknowledges that the skeptic witnesses a disparity between theological assertion and contemporary existence, proclaims and laments this incongruity, and yet through hope looks to a better world where compatibility between belief and reality will emerge. When this hope disappears, skepticism becomes cynicism, in which the transformation of the tragic present is no longer expected. Cynicism contains no compelling, anticipatory vision of a new heaven and new earth. There is only the skeptic's doubt and not the hope.

Theologically speaking, the gulf that separates the world of God from that of human dwelling is the difficulty that gives rise to skepticism and even eventually cynicism in some elements of the Hebrew canon. Indeed, skepticism represents a crisis of faith in God, not in divine existence, but in the lack of coincidence between affirmations about the mercy and justice of God and human experience of the world. While permeating much of the Hebrew Bible, indicating that it is intrinsic to Israelite religion, skepticism finds its prime examples, not only in the questioning "why" of Job's lament and in his accusation against divine justice, but also in Qoheleth's more resigned conclusion that the hidden God remains beyond the ability of even the wisest sages to comprehend. Yet Crenshaw also argues that skepticism involves a loss of faith in hu-

---

31. Ibid.
32. See Crenshaw's classic essay "Popular Questioning of the Justice of God in Ancient Israel." Also see his "Human Dilemma and Human Dissent."
33. Idem, "The Birth of Skepticism in Ancient Israel."

man beings, especially in their ability to know what is true, the future, and God himself. This low view of human knowledge is expressed also in a variety of texts, with one of its greatest expressions encapsulated in the poem on Wisdom in Job 28.

Crenshaw recognizes that even the earliest sages contained a degree of skepticism, for they openly admitted that there were major limits to what they could know about reality in general and God in particular. Indeed the juxtaposition of credal affirmation of the goodness and justice of God and the denial of the same in sapiential literature is one of its most striking features. This said, Crenshaw focuses much of his attention on the increasing intensity of the problem of the hidden God in the texts of Agur (Prov 30:1–14), the poetry of Job (chaps. 3–27, 29–31; and 38:1–42:6), the poem on the inaccessibility of wisdom in Job 28, and the book of Qoheleth. In Job 28 human knowledge is limited to the point that humans cannot discover Wisdom, the source of understanding of God, reality, and proper human behavior that leads to life. In Job the limits of human knowledge are affirmed and, from the poet's perspective, ever fixed. For Qoheleth, God is indifferent to the plight of human beings and their knowledge that is limited to a world where things are never permanent. God and the divine world are off-limits to human knowing. In Agur one finds the most pessimistic view of human knowledge couched in the form of impossible questions about key matters of God and the world, which from this sage's viewpoint have no answer. This increasing crescendo built to the point that skepticism even threatened to overwhelm the entire wisdom movement. Thus, while God's existence in Israelite wisdom was not denied, some sages did disavow his goodness. And the skeptical sages denied that humans possessed the cognitive ability to discover and know the truth. Crenshaw notes that even with the turn of the sages toward a more chastened, yet still conservative, wisdom tradition in the writings of Jesus ben Sira and the Wisdom of Solomon, this problem of the hidden God, while lessened, still continued unabated. Indeed, the theme of the hidden God continued in the teachings, not just of the sages, but also of other social and religious groups who helped shape emerging Judaism in the Second Temple period.[34]

---

34. Ibid.

Finally, Crenshaw recognizes, as do most wisdom scholars, that the personification of wisdom, especially in the erotic form of an alluring woman with seductive lips and beautiful charms, became the literary and theological instrument by which the knowledge of God was made accessible to human beings. This lovely figure, who embodied the wisdom tradition, became the chosen metaphor by which a transcendent deity came to reveal himself and the rewards he offered to those who followed her path.[35] Ben Sira was the one responsible for identifying this personification of divine attribute and the wisdom tradition with the written Torah (Ben Sira 24). Divine revelation has now entered into a written text and is open to the understanding of the learned scribe. Natural theology has been replaced with the divine revelation of the written word.

Constructing a Typology for Views of Revelation in Wisdom

Scholars of the wisdom texts have continued to struggle with the question of revelation in the literature of Israelite and early Jewish sages. The dominance of neoorthodoxy for the better part of almost 40 years in the middle of this century led to the diminishment of the theological place and importance of the wisdom texts in the Hebrew Bible, since this corpus had no place for the mighty acts of God until Ben Sira in the early second century B.C.E. Subsequently, revelation through reason and creation, as seen through the eyes of the sages, was viewed at best as secondary and at worst as "natural" theology or even an expression of pagan religion.

Among the scholars of Israelite and Jewish wisdom who dispelled the enchantment with neoorthodoxy's influence on biblical theology is Crenshaw, but he has been joined by several others who have strived to give voice to the ancient sapiential texts, often ignored, silenced, or even discarded by those who saw in redemptive history the key to Old Testament theology. The scholars we have examined have provided greater clarity about the major understandings of revelation in Second Temple Wisdom and about its important role in Old Testament theology. Perhaps a simple typology will serve as a summary of their important assessments of this topic.

---

35. Idem, "The Contemplative Life in the Ancient Near East," 2452–53.

Dynamic Understandings of Revelation in the Wisdom Corpus

It is commonplace among most wisdom scholars, including the scholars we have reviewed, to note that there were numerous understandings of revelation, which continued to change. Rylaarsdam's sequential tracing of the three major stages of natural reason (later enhanced by the notion of the divine gift of insight), irrationality, and the nationalization of wisdom has largely been embraced, though with minor adjustments from time to time, by most scholars. This is not to say that these four scholars we have just examined have reached exactly the same conclusions about this evolution.

Reason and Revelation

Rylaarsdam examined the issue of revelation in wisdom chiefly in terms of the traditional categories of reason and revelation, with the first pointing to the human intellect as the means to ascertain the nature and will of God, while the latter moved beyond this intrinsic ability to the notion of a divine gift of insight that enhanced native reason and enabled the sage to gain a deeper and more complete understanding of divine mystery. For Rylaarsdam, revelation in wisdom literature finally came to be viewed as a combination of salvation history, cultic theophany, and sapiential observation, but only after a period of significant struggle and doubt evidenced in the writings of Job and Qoheleth. While there was a steady movement from the first understanding to the last, the sages finally arrived at the conclusion that divine mystery was not so readily accessible even to the most astute sages.

Revelation as Intellectual Eros

Von Rad, while arguing for a similar understanding of progression proposed by Rylaarsdam and others, introduced the new category of intellectual eros—that is, wisdom was the meaning of reality, hidden at first, that became both the voice of God calling to those who would learn of her and the alluring representation of divine mystery, capable of being embraced but never fully known. This portrayal of the lovers' embrace, while not abandoning reason, adds to the sages' understanding of revelation the religious category of mysticism. Indeed, this Wisdom not only ordered and directed human lives in the paths of righteousness but also offered to those who took her in their arms the gifts of blessing and life. However, von Rad concluded that the sapiential promises of blessings and life for the wise and righteous and of cursings imposed on the foolish and the wicked, couched within either an explicit or implicit understanding of retribution, ultimately failed. This failure, in view of the holocaust of exile and the suffering of the innocent, became clear to all. The uncertainty about divine involvement in human (cosmic as well as individual) affairs finally led to the emergence of apocalyptic and its emphasis on esoteric knowledge and divine mystery.[36] The failure of wisdom led to the rise of apocalyptic.

Murphy borrowed from von Rad's understanding of wisdom as intellectual eros and his argument that the knowledge of creation was not differentiated from the knowledge of God. However, Murphy parted company with von Rad when it came to the theme of order or orders of creation. While rejecting the common argument that wisdom is somehow connected with a world order or orders, Murphy contended that in wisdom literature creation is understood both as "beginnings" and as the "context" of acting out human life. These two understandings were in no way disconnected from Israel's fundamental understanding of faith in God. Like von Rad, Murphy argued that wisdom is the divine voice that calls the willingly obedient to life and addresses humanity about the character, will, and action of God. Ultimately, in Ben Sira the revelation of the divine Word is one and the same with the revelation of the witness of creation.

The Hidden God

Crenshaw agrees that wisdom underwent important changes in its thinking about revelation. The arenas for divine action and thus revelation were creation and human experience in both cosmos and society. However, perhaps more than his colleagues, he has underscored the sages' recognition that human experience did not always easily correlate with the teachings of retribution and that even in the more traditional and conservative wisdom texts God continues to remain somewhat hidden. According to Crenshaw, the eventual failure of correlation between human deed and ultimate outcome led to a "crisis" in wisdom thinking in which eventually an attack on divine justice was only partially quieted by Qoheleth's teaching about a mysterious, hidden deity.

---

36. Von Rad, *Old Testament Theology*, 2.307–8.

For Qoheleth, "the God" was not only hidden and incapable of being known, he was to be feared. While Crenshaw does not agree with von Rad that this disjunction between divine activity and human experience was the major stimulus for the development of apocalyptic, he does reach the conclusion that even the efforts of the theological syntheses of salvation history, cultic theophany, and human reason and experience in the writings of Ben Sira and the Wisdom of Solomon did not quell the disquietude emerging from the admission of divine mystery. Even the later movements of apocalyptic and Jewish mysticism, with their emphasis on esoteric knowledge, did not eliminate the troubling unease in theological reflection on the hidden God.

Conclusion:
Revelation and the Hidden God

Rylaarsdam, von Rad, Murphy, and Crenshaw have made important contributions to our understanding of divine revelation in wisdom literature. Yet, one might sharpen the point, as Crenshaw does, that the sages engaged in an enormous intellectual and passionate struggle of wit and pathos long before Jewish sages (especially Ben Sira and the author of Wisdom) forged a correlation of the means of revelation: native reason and the divine gift of insight to those who "feared God," the careful and astute observation of providence in nature and history, human experience in all of its contexts, and divine inspiration that included not only the gift of wisdom but also cultic theophany and sacred texts. Even then, this synthesis did not remove all of the skeptic's doubt. Crenshaw's frequent reminder of the continuing presence of the hidden, at times silent, God in Jewish literature enables us to experience the pathos of these existential wrestlings, seeking to come to a knowledge of God.

By way of conclusion, one might say that Israel's sages, struggling with the problem of divine revelation, found a partial solution in the entwining of the reason of Apollo with the dance of Dionysus. This is to say that reason and passion, experience analytically examined and the ecstasy of mystical love, are both constituent elements of the human creature who is intent on finding wisdom and thus the pathway to a rational understanding and experiential knowledge of God. Even so, Crenshaw's contention proves to be correct as later sages, teachers, and seers demonstrate: the variety of the approaches to God do not strip

away the outer veneer of divine enigma. The mystery of the hidden
God finds no closure in Jewish thought. This view continues to be a
dominant theme in Jewish literature throughout the centuries and poses
a challenge to those theologies, modern as well as ancient, that too easily
base their claims of revelation on this or that means of access to the
knowledge of the hidden God.

Job's Wife: The Satan's Handmaid

DAVID PENCHANSKY

University of St. Thomas

In a talk he gave at the University of St. Thomas, Holocaust survivor Elie Wiesel stated, "For years and years I am waiting for a student to take up the theme of Mrs. Job for a Ph.D. dissertation. . . . I would accept this invitation perfectly. So if there is one among you who will do the dissertation, I will be the advisor."[1] Although it is too late for me to accept this invitation, I too am intrigued by Job's wife and here offer some of my thoughts concerning her.

First, to summarize the text: Job has been severely afflicted to his breaking point, having lost his wealth, his social position in the community, his children, and finally his health. The one thing he holds onto in the midst of his suffering is his integrity, his motivation to speak only well of Yahweh, regardless of his own personal experience.

And now his wife attacks him, saying, "How long will you hold on to your integrity? Curse God and die."

What do we make of this woman? How are we to think of her? Is she an evil woman doing the Satan's bidding, as St. Augustine was the first to suggest,[2] or is she some sort of feminist saint, someone to be admired, bringing a breath of fresh air to the maudlin piety of the first few chapters of the book of Job?

---

1. E. Wiesel, "The Eternal Question of Suffering and Evil," *Proceedings of the Center for Jewish-Christian Learning* 3 (Spring 1988) 16.

2. S. Terrien, "The Book of Job: Introduction and Exegesis," *IB* 3.921. See also N. Habel, *The Book of Job* (OTL; Philadelphia: Westminster, 1985) 97, where he quotes Augustine's term as *diaboli adjutrix*. I have not, however, been able to find any reference to the original quotation. Neither Terrien nor Habel gives a reference.

There have been two traditional understandings of Job's wife, strongly at odds with one another. Many have tried to defend her reputation. They claim that she means Job well and has just been misunderstood, since it is clearly God who is afflicting him and there is no hope of respite, and since suicide does not seem to be an option.[3] She encourages Job to do the one forbidden thing that would assure his immediate destruction and the end to his interminable agony.[4] Job's wife then is helping him, not damning him. The Septuagint and the *Testament of Job* expand on her role, trying to evoke more sympathy for this woman. Clearly, they say, she has sacrificed and suffered for Job. She shares his pain and takes care of him. But the text, I contend, will not allow us this sympathetic view. Job's wife tells him to "curse God," an activity so dangerous, many biblical texts imply, that immediate death results.

To continue this composite traditional reading, Job rebukes his wife, characterizing her statement as "foolish woman-talk." This rather harsh and sexist attack on her cognitive abilities and theological acumen is softened somewhat by pious interpreters who see her as a faithful and devout helper to her tortured husband. They stress that she is only speaking *like* the foolish women, not that she herself *is* a foolish woman. This interpretation, however, is at odds with most careful encounters with Job's wife in the biblical text.

The other traditional reading of Job's wife, as was mentioned earlier, was introduced by St. Augustine.[5] Job's wife, he says,[6] has left her proper state to sell herself over to sin, hubris, and rebellion, and she thereby becomes the instrument of the Satan to further attack and afflict Job. The merits of this position will be discussed in more detail shortly.

---

3. We are not quite sure exactly why it is not an option, but it never seems to be seriously considered by any of the participants. Life, it would seem, according to the biblical text, is a given until God takes it away.

4. M. Weiss, *The Story of Job's Beginning* (Jerusalem: Magnes, 1983) 70; Terrien, "The Book of Job."

5. See Habel, *Job*, 96; M. H. Pope, *Job: A New Translation with Introduction and Commentary* (AB 15; Garden City, N.Y.: Doubleday, 1965) 21; E. Dhorme, *A Commentary on the Book of Job* (London: Nelson, 1967) 19. Other early interpreters also supported this conclusion. Terrien ("The Book of Job," 921) quotes Chrysostom and others who maintain that the narrator meant thereby to increase the sufferer's torture to a climactic degree.

6. Tertullian, Jerome, and others made similar comments.

I wish to devolop an alternative reading based on the work of Phyllis Trible[7] and others who have taken obscure female characters and examined them in the light of contemporary concerns for woman's social and ideological position. I will use this approach as a model for a different reading of this text. Because I am aware of no feminist reading of the story of Job's wife to contrast with the traditional readings, I will endeavor to construct one. My methodology will be as follows:

1. I will expose the pervasive influence of the patriarchal narrative focus and the patriarchal readings of the text.
2. I will seek to take the perspective of the female characters, asking how they experienced the narrative action and how their insights expose hidden or supressed textual activity.
3. I will try to unleash the text's liberating and transformative character; that is, this reading will seek to promote and highlight the humanizing tendencies embedded in the text.
4. I will reverse the existing textual polarities by making the minor character in the male-oriented narrative a major literary force and by taking the supposed bad character and making her good.

To begin this reading, Job's wife is a female victim of an oppressive male-oriented social structure and a male-oriented narrative. She is unnamed. Her name, and therefore her identity, is not important. She appears as a stock character. Her pain is neither acknowledged nor described, although she too has lost her social position and her children. She is not even the subject of God's attention but, rather, suffers incidentally because of the wager concerning Job's integrity. She is compelled to see her husband suffer terribly.

Those who look for the hidden story of women concealed within the text of the Bible must immediately take notice of this unnamed woman, whose desolation reminds us of two other anonymous female characters, the wife of Judah whose mysterious loss of two sons is quickly passed over by the narrator (and then she dies), and the unnamed concubine of the beastly Levite who threw her to the mob to be

---

7. See especially P. Trible's work in *God and the Rhetoric of Sexuality* (Philadephia: Fortress, 1978); and *Texts of Terror* (Philadephia: Fortress, 1984).

gang-raped and murdered and then dismembered her as an example to
Israel of the offense against *his* honor.[8]

But the feminist identification goes far beyond the pain and isolation
of this woman. Job's wife models independence of thought. She is not
limited by the narrow views of piety and respect of deity so prevalent
both in the words of Job in the prologue *and* of his friends in the poetic
dialogues. She is not afraid to commit the unpardonable sin—to encourage blasphemy. She rebels openly against a patriarchal, triumphalist
God, having nothing else to lose. The patriarchal religion can offer her
nothing.

She is strong and forceful, unwilling to bow down in her pain and
misfortune. She stands proud, gazing angrily at her husband and his creator, and refuses to accept the rightness and morality of their religious
activities. She reacts to her pain not with cowering servility but with
arrogant rejection of the religious norms of her society.

This feminist reading would present the narrative in the following
fashion: a woman through the pain of her grief and loss, a previously
comfortable woman, complacent perhaps, finds the strength to stand up
to the deity that afflicts her and her family. The story might then diverge
in two directions. In one version, Job's wife dismisses the pious senti-
mentality of Job with contempt. She rejects him along with his theologically precise (though experientially incorrect) answers to their situation.
Her statement might then be translated as an expletive: "Curse God and
drop dead!"

The other version allows her to retain a benevolent relationship to
Job. She becomes Job's teacher, or more correctly, Job's spiritual mother,
birthing Job into a new level of understanding, insisting on the necessity
of theological suspicion and asserting the validity of the human perspective in one's dealings with God. This, however, does not fully represent
my preferred reading because I find a richer and more suggestive way to
understand Job's wife, one that produces a more authentic experience of
Job's, and his wife's, development as characters. I consider that this second reading employs the feminist perspective as well, but it seeks to incorporate some of the earlier traditional understandings.

---

8. One might also consider the unnamed wife of Phineas, son of the high priest,
who died in childbirth, naming her son Ichabod, capturing the essence of her evil age.

I suggest a reading that holds these other two in tension, both the Augustinian and the feminist. Augustine was to a significant degree correct in calling Job's wife "the Satan's handmaid." I would like, however, to put a more contemporary (and I hope more sensitive) spin on his characterization.

The oppression and affliction of Job is what the first two chapters of the book are about.[9] Nature deserts Job. Community deserts Job. Security has deserted him. *God* has deserted him. He has been left his wife. Only she and the Satan remain to keep him company.[10]

Now his wife deserts him as well, not by dying and disappearing from the narrative, as did the rest of Job's family, but by staying and attacking him. This, the final and most brutal insult of all, embodies all of Job's painful abandonments. Her rejection of Job and her insistence that he curse God and die[11] attack Job at his weakest and most vulnerable point, the only thing he has left—his integrity. His notion of integrity is inextricably linked with his pious refusal to curse God under any circumstances. Job's wife, however, insists that his integrity should instead be linked to the *necessity* of his rejection of the God who has stricken him.

Job's wife personifies the universe that has turned against Job. She transforms herself into the crone, the destroyer, the despair who swallows everything up. Perhaps, even greater than the Satan's handmaid, she is herself the gnawing absence of a benevolent God in the world, reaching to the very bones and marrow of Job's experience.

One must also note that the wife's comments do effect the birthing of Job's new stance (as evidenced in the poetic center of the book of Job), wherein he rediscovers his integrity through promethean valor. She embodies what Job becomes or what he wishes to become. She is Dame Wisdom, teaching Job a hard lesson, one that he finally seems to learn. This too brings us to the very core of Job's pain.

---

9. For a fuller discussion of this, see my *The Betrayal of God: Ideological Conflict in Job* (Louisville: Westminster / John Knox, 1990).

10. There have been many who observe the many parallels between the activities of Satan and the role of Job's wife. Aquinas posits that Satan spares Job's wife (though not the rest of his family) so that she might tempt him (Dhorme, *Job*, 19). Habel calls Job's wife "the incarnation of Satan" on earth (*Job*, 81).

11. Thus reflecting both Job's fastidious concern with his children's speech, the narrator's references to Job's perfection, and the Satan's boast that he will make Job curse Yahweh.

Job's wife offers him a new response to the quality of terror that life offered. She turns to her suffering husband and says to him, "You still keep your integrity! Blaspheme God and die!" We are stunned by the callousness of her remarks. But perhaps by encouraging him to strip away everything that shielded him, she enabled him to see the desperation that was always there. He had been too self-satisfied in his piety (even *after* his affliction) ever to see it.

But one must take care not to domesticate this fearsome woman falsely. Her words are so malicious and carefully chosen. She disparages his efforts at integrity, calling them pointless, having no effect. She tells him to blaspheme, the very thing he had always been so scrupulous to avoid. But she encourages him to tear apart and cast away the last vestiges of his pious rationalizations, the final barrier between him and the fearful void.

I suspect that most ancient Israelites shared knowledge of a terrible, public secret, one that they would not dare to utter aloud: that outside of the ancient stories (and even in some of them[12]) people were not struck dead when they cursed God. Not all were like the sons of Korah or Nadab and Abihu or Uzzah or the children who mocked Elisha.[13] There were certainly people in Israel who did curse God, and not just the unrighteous. Job could not face this fearful truth. Job's wife gave him courage to accuse deity and *he does it well.* He curses God with an artistry and passion that is unsurpassed.

Job's wife made him aware of the issues that are at the heart of communal life: personal integrity and human discourse. On this ash heap he faced the precariousness of being human. When he was robbed of everything, he finally tasted the absence at the heart of things, and the utter fragility of all human knowledge. With her words, so brutal and cutting, she comes close to personifying all of the abuse that Job received from the universe. If Job embodies the experience of human pain and abandonment, Job's wife represents the source of all human suffering. Eliphaz, Bildad, Zophar, and even young Elihu argue with Job, annoying and angering him, but Job's pain was magnified and illuminated through the lens of *her* abuse. Job did blaspheme God: but did not die. Finally, *this* is his integrity.

---

12. Jeremiah, Qoheleth, Job, and some Psalms, for instance.

13. See my *What Rough Beast? Images of God in the Hebrew Bible* (Louisville: Westminster / John Knox, 1999) for a fuller discussion of these passages.

The Verb hāyâ in Qoheleth

ANTOON SCHOORS
Catholic University of Leuven

Taking into account Qoh 2:22 *hwh* and 11:3 *yhw[?]*,[1] the verb *hyh* occurs 49 times[2] in Qoheleth, which is exactly the same frequency as for *[?]dm* and the highest frequency of any word in the book. As is the case with *[?]dm*,[3] this frequency can be accounted for by the philosophical genre of the book, since philosophy is about "being." However, M. V. Fox has correctly pointed out that "this verb is often best translated 'to happen.' This is a well-established sense of *hāyâ* (BDB, pp. 224–25[4]). The concept of 'being' is not, of course, entirely distinct from 'happening,' and often a translation can use either verb."[5] Without doubt the verb can have the meaning 'to happen', and it seems always to have

---

Author's note: It is a privilege and a pleasure to offer this short article as a modest tribute to James Crenshaw, the prominent interpreter of Qoheleth, whom I appreciate very much as a competent colleague and a friend. Translations in double brackets in this essay have been added by an editor, unless otherwise indicated.

1. See my *The Preacher Sought to Find Pleasing Words* (OLA 41; Leuven: Peeters, 1992) 42–43.

2. Qoh 1:9 (twice), 10 (twice), 11 (three times), 12, 16; 2:7(three times), 9, 10, 18, 19, 22; 3:14, 15 (three times), 20, 22; 4:3, 16; 5:1; 6:3 (twice), 10, 12; 7:10 (twice), 14, 16, 17, 19, 24; 8:7 (twice), 12, 13; 9:8; 10:14 (twice); 11:2, 3, 8; 12:7, 9.

3. On *[?]dm*, see my "Word *[?]dm* in Qoheleth," in *Immigration and Emigration within the Near East: Festschrift E. Lipiński* (OLA 65; ed. K. van Lerberghe and A. Schoors; Leuven: Peeters, 1995) 299–304.

4. Cf. also H. Ringgren, "*hāyāh*," *TWAT* 2.397 = *TDOT* 3.372–73.

5. M. V. Fox, *Qohelet and His Contradictions* (JSOTSup 71; Sheffield: JSOT Press, 1981) 151–52.

meant 'to be' in the sense of 'to exist' and in the sense of 'to come into existence, to happen' at the same time.[6] But in Biblical Hebrew the meaning is not very often 'to happen'.[7]

Many attestations of the verb *hyh* in Qoheleth have a commonplace meaning. Quite often it has the function of a copula. This is the case in Qoh 1:12, 15: *'ny qhlt hyty mlk*; but the problem here is whether the perfect tense has the force of a present or of a past. With a nominal predicate, the "auxiliary" verb expresses the modal or temporal nuance, and therefore in BH *hyh* is normally not used as a copula when the sentence has in view a present situation. But B. Isaksson, who defends the present force of many perfect forms of *hyh* in Qoheleth on good grounds,[8] states that "the stative aspect of *hāyîtî* in 1:12 obviously must not be construed as an actual (cursive) present. It involves at the same time a perfect and a present: 'I have been, and still I am.'"[9] Other instances of the term functioning as a copula are found in 1:10, 16; 2:7, 10, 18, 19; 5:1; 6:3; 7:10, 14, 16, 17, 19;[10] 9:8; 11:8; 12:9. In this category, Qoh 4:16 is a problematic text: *'yn-qṣ lkl-hʿm lkl 'šr-hyh lpnyhm*. At first sight, the persons comprised in v. 16b are the subject of the relative clause. Thus, R. Gordis renders the relative clause 'who lived before them', with the comment: "i.e., the old king and his young successor."[11] In that case the clause is comparable to 1:18; 2:7, 9; and *lpnhm* has a temporal meaning. But most commentators regard the young king as the subject of the relative clause, and the suffix of *lpnyhm* could then refer to the antecedent of the relative: "There was no end to all the

---

6. Ringgren, "*hāyāh*," *TDOT* 3.372: "It appears, however, that from the very outset *hāyāh* was used to refer to 'being' in the sense of 'exist, be present' (= what has come into being) and of 'come into being, happen' (= what is coming into being)." *TWAT* 2.397: "Immerhin hat es den Anschein, als habe *hājāh* von vornherein zugleich 'sein' im sinne von 'existieren, vorhanden sein' (= Gewordenes) und im sinne von 'entstehen, geschehen' (= Werdendes) bezeichnet."

7. Ibid., *TWAT* 2.398 = *TDOT* 3.373.

8. See my *Pleasing Words*, 172–73.

9. B. Isaksson, *Studies in the Language of Qoheleth* (Studia Semitica Upsaliensia; Uppsala: University of Uppsala Press, 1987) 50; cf. H.W. Hertzberg, *Der Prediger* (KAT 17/4; Gütersloh: Mohn, 1963) 81–82.

10. Present tense; see my *Pleasing Words*, 173.

11. R. Gordis, *Koheleth: The Man and His World* (New York: Schocken, 1955) 236. Cf. C. F. Whitley, *Koheleth: His Language and Thought* (BZAW 145; Berlin: de Gruyter, 1979) 46.

people—all whose leader he was."[12] The expression then means 'to be in front of', which is a metaphor for leadership. Another problematic text, with which I dealt extensively in my book on the language of Qoheleth, is 11:3 *šm yhwʾ*.[13] H. Kruse has suggested that a root *hwh*, meaning 'to fall', is to be found here, and he has been followed by K. Galling.[14] But it is preferable to consider the verb as a copula with the predicate *šām*, expressing the place, 'In the place where the tree falls, *there it will lie*' (RSV), just as in 7:19, *ʾšr hyw bʿyr* 'that are in a city'.[15]

Sometimes *hyh l-* expresses possession or belonging, as in 2:7 *hyh ly* (twice), 6:3 *qbwrh lʾ-hyth lw*.[16] Also to be mentioned here are the phrases in 8:12–13, "it will be well with those who fear God," and "it will not be well with the wicked." The verb occurs with an analogous meaning in Qoh 1:11. The full significance of this verse is debated. The RSV renders the verse as follows: "There is no remembrance of former things, nor will there be any remembrance of later things yet to happen among those who come after." In doing so it follows one trend in exegesis, according to which the verse refers to things or events.[17] But according to

---

12. G. A. Barton, *Critical and Exegetical Commentary on the Book of Ecclesiastes* (ICC; Edinburgh: T. & T. Clark, 1908) 119 and 122; compare the RSV and "in quorum conspectu vel ante quos Rex hicce novus vivit ac est" in M. Geier, *In Salomonis Regis Israel Ecclesiasten Commentarius* (Leipzig, 1668) 153; and M. Thilo, *Der Prediger Salomo, neu übersetzt und auf seinen Gedankengang untersucht* (Bonn: Marcus & Webers, 1923) 35: "denen er zur Verfügung stand" [['at whose disposal he was']]. See also E. Elster, *Commentar über den Prediger Salomo* (Göttingen: Dietrich, 1855) 83; C. D. Ginsburg, *Coheleth Commonly Called the Book of Ecclesiastes* (London: Longman, Green, Longman, and Roberts, 1861) 333–34; A. H. McNeile, *Introduction to Ecclesiastes* (Cambridge: Cambridge University Press, 1904) 67; F. Zimmermann, "The Aramaic Provenance of Qohelet," *JQR* 36 (1945–46) 34–35; G. C. Aalders, *Het boek De Prediker* (Kampen: Kok, 1948) 101; Fox, *Qohelet and His Contradictions*, 208.

13. See my *Pleasing Words*, 42–43.

14. H. Kruse, "*Da partem septem necnon octo* (Qoh 11:1–6)," *VD* 27 (1949) 168; K. Galling, *Der Prediger* (HAT 1/18; Tübingen: Mohr, 1969) 118–19; cf. *HALAT*, 231 (s.v. הוה), where this root is accepted for Job 37:6 and other texts but not for Qoh 11:3.

15. Cf. Aalders, *Prediker*, 235; R. B. Y. Scott, *Proverbs, Ecclesiastes* (AB; Garden City, N.Y.: Doubleday, 1965) 250; R. Braun, *Kohelet und die frühhellenistische Popularphilosophie* (BZAW 130: Berlin: de Gruyter, 1973) 136.

16. Present tense according to Isaksson, *Language of Qoheleth*, 84. E. Podechard (*L'Ecclésiaste* [Ébib; Paris: Lecoffre, 1912] 355) says: "un fait présent et durable" [['a fact present and durable']]. See my *Pleasing Words*, 173.

17. S. H. Auerbach (*Das Buch Koheleth neu übersetzt mit einem hebräischen Commentar* [Breslau, 1837] 31) translates "Ereignisse" [['events']]. Cf. W. J. Fuerst, *The Books of Ruth,*

others "times" are meant,[18] and there are still others who think that the verse is about "people, generations."[19] In defense of the meaning "times," Aalders invokes the presence of the word עוֹלְמִים in the preceding verse. Gordis and C. Lepre object that "things" would have been expressed by the feminine plural and therefore prefer "people" as the referent. But this argument still leaves us with the "ages" of v. 10 or with "people." Because of the connection between vv. 10 and 11, "ages" has my preference. Thus the three imperfect forms of *hyh* refer to the future: *šyhyw* (twice) means 'that will be, exist', "the later ages" being the subject of the first one and "the people who remember" of the last one, and *lᵓ-yhyh lhm* expresses belonging or possession.

In Qoheleth several times we find the phrase *mh-šhyh* (1:9, 3:15, 6:10, 7:24) and twice its counterpart *mh-šyhyh* (8:7, 10:14). It seems that the first occurrence in 1:9 sets the lead for understanding the expression: *mh-šhyh hwᵓ šyhyh wmh-šnᶜšh hwᵓ šyᶜšh.*

The verb here clearly has a quite general meaning. It is in this kind of sentence that, according to Fox, the verb specifically means 'to happen'. Qoh 1:9 "does not mean that a certain entity will once again come into existence, a notion quite foreign to Qohelet. It means that *types of events* recur *ad infinitum*."[20] In this verse, the parallelism with ᶜšh confirms this thesis. N. Lohfink agrees and stresses that the sentence deals with what happens and in the second part with human activity.[21] And both Fox and Lohfink refer to 3:1–8, the "Catalogue of Times," for an illustration of the type of events Qoheleth has in mind. The idea of this catalogue is strikingly recapitulated in a sentence that is very close to 1:9—that is, 3:15: "Whatever happens (*hyh*) already has happened,

Esther, Ecclesiastes, the Song of Songs, Lamentations (Cambridge Bible Commentary on the NEB; Cambridge: Cambridge University Press, 1975) 104; J. A. Loader, *Ecclesiastes: A Practical Commentary* (NCB; Grand Rapids: Eerdmans, 1986) 23; Fox, *Qoheleth*, 173.

18. Cf. Thilo, *Prediger Salomo*, 30; Aalders, *Prediker*, 37–38; A. Strobel, *Das Buch Prediger* (Düsseldorf: Patmos, 1967) 32. In the Vg the neuter *quae postea futura sunt* can refer to things in general or to the *saecula* mentioned in v. 10. In the LXX the equivalent forms ending in -*ois* can be masculine or neuter.

19. Cf. Elster, *Commentar über den Prediger Salomo*, 46; Gordis, *Koheleth*, 198; C. Lepre, *Qoheleth, traduzione ritmica call originale ebraico e note* (Bologna: Libreria Palmaverde,1975) 32.

20. Fox, *Qoheleth*, 151.

21. N. Lohfink, *Kohelet* (Die Neue Echter Bibel; Würzburg: Echter, 1980) 22.

and what is to happen (*lhywt*) already has happened (*hyh*)."[22] The question again is whether the perfect forms of *hyh* in 1:9 as well as in 3:15 express the present tense. This question is not without importance in a study of the meaning of the verb in Qoheleth's language: does he only place past and future in opposition or does he put all that is in existence in opposition to what is still to come instead? In connection with 1:9, Isaksson is of the opinion that it is reasonable "to conceive the phrase *maśśœhāyā* as having reference to present time, or more properly, to any time (the general present)." This meaning would be confirmed by the general perspective of the text: "The interest is focused on the invariances of life in the midst of things which can be observed."[23] But if the present is here a general present and if the verb means 'to happen', the difference from a past tense is negligible, since the general present would also mean 'what has happened up to now', since it is in opposition to the future, *yhyh*. On the contrary, in 3:15 the opposition is between the present and the past, expressed by *kbr*, and then between the future and the past: *mh-šhyh kbr hw' w'šr lhywt kbr hyh*.

This verse has been much debated in scholarly literature, particularly because of the somewhat awkward construction with *kbr hw'*. According to C. D. Ginsburg, *mh-šhyh* refers to what has recently taken place, while *kbr hw'* should be completed with *hyh*, the clause *kbr hw'* (*hyh*) describing the same thing as already having occurred long before.[24] Within the Aramaic translation theory, H. L. Ginsberg regards v. 15aα as a mistranslation of the Aramaic *mh dy hāwē' kbr hwā',* and thus the meaning of v. 15a would be 'that which is and that which will be has already been'.[25] This emendation fails with the rejection of the theory in question, and the perfect of *hyh* can have present force anyway. Another unacceptable emendation has been proposed by P. Joüon, who reads,

---

22. Fox, *Qoheleth.*

23. Isaksson, *Language of Qoheleth,* 75–76. Cf. Podechard, *L'Ecclésiaste,* 52: "ce qui existe, ce qui arrive" [['that which exists, that which is happening']].

24. Ginsburg, *Coheleth,* 313.

25. H. L. Ginsberg, *qhlt* (Tel Aviv: Newman, 1961) 75. Cf. idem, *Studies in Qoheleth* (New York: Jewish Theological Society of America, 1950) 23; F. Zimmermann, "The Aramaic Provenance of Qohelet," *JQR* 36 (1945–46) 34. The suggestion is rejected by R. Gordis, "The Original Language of Qohelet," *JQR* 37 (1946–47) 79; M. Elyoenay, *mḥqrym bqhlt wmšly* [Studies on Qoheleth and Proverbs] (Jerusalem: Kiryat Sepher, 1977) 50–51.

"Ce qui arrive est déjà arrivé (*hyh*); / Ce qui arrivera arrive (*yhyh*) déjà."[26]

Gordis's translation 'what has been, already exists . . .' does not make sense, and his comment "the first clause asserts the identity of past and present" does not make it more acceptable.[27] And a rendering "Was gewesen ist war längst da" [['what has been was there long ago']], as suggested by Ringgren,[28] is not any better. Isaksson rightly remarks that Qoheleth is dealing here with the actual life under the sun, and therefore the perfect form does refer to a gnomic present, as already proposed by a number of critics and as I have also stated in my book on Qoheleth's language.[29] The result of this investigation is to confirm the RSV translation: 'That which is, already has been . . .' (compare also the NEB). The nominal clause *kbr hw'*, in which the past meaning is expressed by *kbr*, is a good Hebrew clause, and C. F. Whitley's translation very well renders its meaning: 'that which is, is of long ago'.[30] Of course, the second *hyh* in 3:15 has a past meaning because of its adjunct *kbr*. The same applies to 1:10 where the verb also means 'to happen', since it is a comment on v. 9. In sum, in Qoh 1:9 and 3:15, *mh-šhyh* refers to the general situation under the sun, in the more dynamic sense of 'what happens' rather than in the more static or ontological sense of 'what is'.

---

26. P. Joüon, "Notes philologiques sur le texte hébreu de l'Ecclésiaste," *Bib* 11 (1930) 420. [['That which happens has happened before; that which will happen is happening already'.]]

27. Gordis, *Koheleth*, 156 and 223. Cf. A. Chouraqui, *Les cinq volumes* (Paris: Desclée de Brouwer, 1975) 128: "Ce qui a été est déjà . . ." [['That which has been already is/exists . . .']]. Also see C. Bridges, *An Exposition of the Book of Ecclesiastes* (Geneva Series of Commentaries; London: Banner of Truth Trust, 1859) 73.

28. Ringgren, *TWAT* 2.398 = *TDOT* 3.373. Cf. D. Michel, *Untersuchungen zur eigenart des Buches Qohelet* (BZAW 183; Berlin: de Gruyter, 1989) 73: "Was war, ist längst schon gewesen" [['What was, has long ago already been']].

29. Isaksson, *Language of Qoheleth*, 82; compare my *Pleasing Words*," 174; Thilo, *Der Prediger Salomo*, 34: "Was ist (*hyh* presentisch), das war längst" [['what is was long ago']]; Podechard, *L'Ecclésiaste*, 300; D. Lys, *L'Ecclésiaste ou, que vaut la vie?* (Paris: Letouzey & Ané, 1977) 366; A. Lauha, *Kohelet* (BKAT 19; Neukirchen-Vluyn: Neukirchener Verlag, 1978) 62.

30. Whitley, *Koheleth*, 34. Compare E. S. Artom, *ḥmš mgylwt mpršwt* [The Five Scrolls Interpreted] (Tel Aviv: Yavneh, 1967) 77, who paraphrases the clause as follows: *hw' dbr šl kbr, klwmr kbr hyh qwdm lkn.*

The same analysis applies to the phrase as it occurs in Qoh 6:10. A plethora of exegetes render it with the verb 'to happen'.[31] And again many of them decide in favor of a present tense.[32] The adherents of the Aramaic translation theory here again invoke a mistranslation of Aramaic *hwʾ*, which was read as *hwāʾ* instead of the correct *hāwēʾ*.[33] The second half of v. 15a makes it clear that the whole verse is about humankind. This has been observed for a long time by several scholars,[34] and Isaksson has rightly underlined that "it is evident that the formally impersonal expression *maśśœhaya* in fact refers to mankind and its activities,"[35] even if his interpretation of *ʾdm* as a proper name is not necessarily correct.[36]

The last attestation of *mh-šhyh*, in Qoh 7:24, has been understood along the same lines as the previous occurrences. Again a number of scholars read the verb as meaning 'to happen'.[37] But I have the impression that, because of the highly "philosophical" character of the verse, the tendency is to understand the verb as referring to "existence."[38]

31. E.g., Ginsburg, *Coheleth*, 366; Thilo, *Prediger Salomo*, 37; Ginsberg, *qhlt*, 94; Galling, *Prediger*, 105. Braun (*Kohelet*, 119) translates "die ewige Gleichförmigkeit des Geschehens" [['the eternal uniformity of events']]. See also L. Alonso Schökel, *Eclesiastés y Sabiduría* (Madrid: Cristiandad, 1974) 43; Fox, *Qoheleth and His Contradictions*, 224; Michel, *Qohelet*, 161.

32. Besides Thilo, Ginsberg, Galling, Fox, and Michel, also Geier, *Ecclesiasten Commentarius*, 22; Podechard, *L'Ecclésiaste*, 360; Whitley, *Koheleth*, 60; J. L. Crenshaw, *Ecclesiastes: A Commentary* (OTL; Philadelphia: Westminster, 1987) 130; Isaksson, *Language of Qoheleth*, 88.

33. Zimmermann, "Aramaic Provenance," 35; C. C. Torrey, "The Question of the Original Language of Kohelet," *JQR* 39 (1948–49) 159; Ginsberg, *qhlt*, 94.

34. Geier, *Ecclesiasten Commentarius*, 221–22; J. Cotton, *A Brief Exposition . . . upon the Whole Book of Ecclesiastes* (London: T. C. for Ralph Smith, 1654) 112; E. H. Plumptre, *Ecclesiastes* (Cambridge Bible; London: Cambridge University Press, 1890) 158; G. Wildeboer, *Der Prediger* (Kurzer Hand-commentar zum Alten Testament 17; Tübingen: Mohr, 1898) 144.

35. Isaksson, *Language of Qoheleth*, 85–88.

36. See my "The Word *ʾdm* in Qoheleth," 303–4.

37. For example the NEB; Artom, *ḥmš mgylwt mpršwt*, 89: *mh šhtrhš kʿwlm*; L. Gorssen, *Breuk tussen God en mens: Onderzoek naar de samenhang en de originaliteit van de hoofdthema's uit het boek "Prediker"* (Brugge: Desclée de Brouwer, 1970) 104: "alles wat er gebeurt" [['all that happens']]; Fox, *Qoheleth and His Contradictions*, 240.

38. Cf. F. Delitzsch, *Hoheslied und Koheleth* (Biblischer Kommentar über die poetischen Bücher des AT 4; Leipzig: Dörffling & Franke, 1875) 324–25; V. E. Reichert, "Ecclesiastes," in *The Five Megilloth* (ed. A. Cohen; The Soncino Books of the Bible; London: Soncino, 1946) 157; Gordis, *Koheleth*, 271: 'all that exists'.

According to Barton, " 'that which exists' seems here to refer to the true inwardness of things, the reality below all changing phenomena," and further he explains that the expression "usually means events or phenomena which exist (1:9, 3:15, 6:10), but the context makes it necessary to understand it here as that which underlies phenomena."[39]

Thilo's insistence on "das Wesen der Dinge" [['the essence of things']] does not exclude the primarily dynamic aspect of what is meant here. Thilo himself opens his comment with the remark "Eigentl. 'was geschieht' " [['Actually, "what happens" ']].[40] And Isaksson correctly renders the bearing of the verse: "True wisdom, which would involve insight into the real nature of the things *going on* [emphasis mine] under the sun, is beyond the reach of human intellect, and this is exactly what is expressed in 7:24."[41] It is evident then that here again the perfect form refers to a timeless present.[42]

The phrase *mh-šyhyh* (Qoh 8:7, 10:14) undoubtedly has in view what will happen in the future.[43] A number of critics render it 'the future'.[44] In 8:7 this applies to the second occurrence of the word as well. As for 10:14, it has been suggested on the basis of a few manuscripts, the LXX, Sym, Syr, and the Vg, that *mh-šyhyh* be emended to *mh-šhyh*.[45] But this is based on a wrong understanding of the opposition between the two halves of the sentence. It is not necessary to posit an opposition, for a perfectly synonymous parallelism is possible. Some commentators see here a distinction between the "future in general" in the first member and "what will happen after his death" in the second.[46] A question quite similar to the one in 10:14bβ is asked in 3:22, "who can bring him

39. Barton, *Ecclesiastes*, 146 and 148.

40. Thilo, *Prediger Salomo*, 38.

41. Isaksson, *Language of Qoheleth*, 90–91.

42. See Gorssen, Fox, Gordis, Reichert, Delitzsch, Barton, and Isaksson in the preceding notes; also Ginsberg, *Studies in Qoheleth*, 102.

43. Cf. Podechard, *L'Ecclésiaste*, 396–97; Gorssen, *Breuk tussen God en mens*, 106–7; Braun, *Kohelet*, 84–86.

44. E.g., Plumptre, *Ecclesiastes*, 177; Wildeboer, *Der Prediger*, 150; Reichert, "Ecclesiastes," 162; H. Brandenburg, *Das Buch der Sprüche, der Prediger und das Hohelied* (Giessen: Brunnen, 1971) 168.

45. BHS; McNeile, *Ecclesiastes*, 155; D. Buzy, "L'Ecclésiaste," *La Sainte Bible* VI (ed. L. Pirot; Paris: Letouzey & Ané, 1941) 265. See the LXX, Syr, and Vg.

46. Ginsburg, *Coheleth*, 438; Delitzsch, *Hoheslied und Qoheleth*, 372; cf. Podechard, *L'Ecclésiaste*, 435.

to see what will be after him?" (RSV),[47] and in 6:12, "who can tell man what will be after him under the sun?" (RSV). J. L. Crenshaw rightly translates *yhyh ʾḥryw* 'what will *occur* after him/them' (3:22, 10:14), but his translation 'what will occur *afterward?*' in 6:12 is less felicitous.[48] Another verse that proclaims human ignorance about what will happen in the future is 11:2b: "for you know not what evil will happen on earth" (RSV).[49]

In Qoh 7:10 the beginning of the sentence is mostly translated 'How is it that . . .' or 'Why is it that. . .'. According to Zimmermann and C. C. Torrey, *mh hyh* would be a mistranslation of Aramaic *mh hwʾ*, whereas Isaksson remarks that, *hyh* having stative force, the perfect tense here refers to the present.[50] I have the impression, however, that the verb here again has the meaning 'to happen', and I suggest the translation 'Do not say: "What happened that the former days were better than these?" '

Sometimes the verb expresses more the durable quality of what God does. Thus in Qoh 3:14 *yhyh* appears in combination with *lꜥwlm*.

Qoh 2:22 poses a special problem, for here the participle of the root *hwh* is used: "what has a man for all his toil?" According to Lys the author has deliberately chosen this root because he wants to express something different from *hyh*, which would mean the banal 'being', whereas here Qoheleth means that toil makes a person participate in 'l'être'. Qoheleth would here pose the problem of ontological being.[51] Lys is right in remarking that this is the only place where Qoheleth employs this Aramaic root but not in looking for an ontological explanation. Instead, the explanation is grammatical: except for *hôyâ* in Exod 9:3, there is no

---

47. Cf. Ginsburg, *Coheleth*, 320.

48. Crenshaw, *Ecclesiastes*, 101, 130, and 168; cf. Aalders, *De Prediker*, 135.

49. Cf. Buzy, "L'Ecclésiaste," 267; Galling, *Der Prediger*, 118; Braun, *Kohelet,* 136.

50. Zimmermann, "Aramaic Provenance," 35; C. C. Torrey, "The Question of the Original Language of Kohelet," *JQR* 39 (1948–49) 159; Isaksson, *Language of Qoheleth*, 88–89.

51. Lys, *L'Ecclésiaste*, 274–75: "Qoheleth pose le problème que nous appellerions ontologique de l'être, qui se distingue des étants (cf. Heidegger)" [['Qoheleth poses what we call the ontological problem of being, which is distinct from the beings']]. Cf. idem, "L'être et le Temps: Communication de Qoheleth," in *La Sagesse de l'Ancien Testament* (Gembloux, 1979) 249–58; A. Neher, *Notes sur Qohélet (L'Ecclésiaste)* (Paris: Minuit, 1951) 93. See my *Pleasing Words*, 99. There I have also mentioned some attempts to dissociate the root *hwh* from *hyh*.

participle of *hyh* in Biblical Hebrew.[52] Michel is closer to the mark when he compares Qoh 2:22 to 1:3. This parallelism clearly shows that *hôweh* replaces *ytrwn* and that it is used here to stress the enduring character of the gain he is searching for. Michel goes somewhat in Lys's direction when he suspects the possible influence of Greek philosophical terminology.[53] This connection with *ytrwn* has already been noted by Ginsburg and in a less clear way by F. Delitzsch and, as a matter of fact, is reflected in the versions of the Vg and Tg.[54]

In Qoh 3:20, the context suggests that *hyh* here means 'to come from, to originate': "all are from the dust" (RSV). In 4:3, however, the verb expresses existence of a human person, and in its perfect tense "it is localized to the nunc-level by the adverb *ʿdn*."[55] Finally, the expression *kĕšehāyâ* in Qoh 12:7 expresses the former condition of man as far as he is dust.[56] There is no need to emend the text to *bšhyh*, as suggested by Galling, giving it a local meaning 'where it was'.[57]

In sum, what is typical for Qoheleth is the high frequency of the verb *hyh* and the fact that it rather often has the dynamic meaning 'to happen'. This illustrates that he is a real philosopher but more interested in human life than in an ontology of an unalterable metaphysical world. Therefore, the problem that Qoheleth, with all his wisdom, cannot fathom in a satisfactory way is this: the way God has preordained human life "under the sun," because God belongs to the metaphysical world.

---

52. Ibid., 99.

53. Michel, *Qohelet*, 33: "soll aber doch wohl das Dauernde, Bleibende betonen und damit die Vorstellung eines relativen *jitrôn* abweisen" [['however, that which lasts or remains should be emphasized and the suggestion of a relative *yitron* thereby rejected']]; he adds in n. 85: "Man kann sogar fragen, ob hier nicht Einfluß philosophischer Terminologie des Griechischen anzunehmen ist!" [['One can question whether the influence of Greek philosophical terminology should not be admitted!']].

54. Ginsburg, *Coheleth*, 298; Delitzsch, *Der Prediger*, 254: "Was ist dem Menschen werdend—*resultierend* bei all seiner Arbeit" [['What humanity gets—results from all his labor']]. Cf. Vg: *quid enim proderit homini*; cf. Tg.

55. Isaksson, *Language of Qoheleth*, 83. Cf. Lys, *L'Ecclésiate*, 366; Chouraqui, *Les cinq volumes*, 130.

56. Cf. Ginsburg, *Coheleth*, 468; Podechard, *L'Ecclésiaste*, 470.

57. K. Galling, *Der Prediger*, 120; Scott (*Proverbs, Ecclesiastes*, 254) translates the same way without comment. The ancient versions support the MT except for the Vg (*unde erat*), which suggests a local meaning of the expression.

The "Our Father" as John the Baptist's Political Prayer

A Ritual Response to the Absence of God's Kingdom

BERNHARD LANG

University of Paderborn, Germany

As can be seen from the combination of baptism and the eucharist as the two main sacraments, Christianity has two founders: John the Baptist and Jesus. In the New Testament, the paramount role of John has been overshadowed by Jesus. However, modern scholarship has occasionally managed to redress the balance by arguing that certain traditions and texts reflect the ministry, ideas, and words not of Jesus but of John and his circle. In addition to his manifest interest in John, whose birth story he recounts (Luke 1), Luke seems to have preserved certain hidden traditions about the Baptist. Relevant passages include the Magnificat (Luke 1:46–55), the Benedictus (Luke 1:68–79), and the cluster of sayings found in Luke 16:16–18.[1] The Gospel of Luke transmits more of the Baptist tradition than the other Gospels. Another early-Christian source that reflects not Jesus but Baptist tradition may be the book of Revelation,[2] and even the Gospel of John may occasionally echo Baptist traditions.[3]

In an all too brief (and generally overlooked) article published in 1973, J. K. Elliott has added one more item to the list of texts to be

---

1. See P. Winter, "Magnificat and Benedictus: Maccabean Psalms?" *BJRL* 37 (1954) 328–47; E. Bammel, "Is Luke 16:16–18 of Baptist's Provenience?" *HTR* 51 (1958) 101–6; idem, "The Poor and the Zealots," in *Jesus and the Politics of His Day* (ed. E. Bammel and C. F. D. Moule; Cambridge: Cambridge University Press, 1984) 109–28; D. Flusser, *Judaism and the Origins of Christianity* (Jerusalem: Magnes, 1988) 126–49: "The Magnificat, the Benedictus and the War Scroll"; W. Radl, *Der Ursprung Jesu* (Freiburg: Herder, 1996) 128–31 (on the Benedictus).

2. J. M. Ford, *Revelation* (AB 38; Garden City, N.Y.: Doubleday, 1975).

3. C. Niemand, "Spuren der Täuferpredigt in Johannes 15,1–11," *Protokolle zur Bibel* 4 (1995) 13–28.

attributed to John: the Our Father. According to Elliott, Luke 11:1–2 can be read to say that in teaching the Our Father Jesus did not teach a prayer *like* John the Baptist but the *same prayer taught by John the Baptist.*[4] To the best of our knowledge, Elliott never went beyond the mere suggestion of this bold attribution. The present paper accepts Elliott's suggestion and tries to establish its plausibility.

We will present our argument in three steps. First we will sketch the essential message of John the Baptist. Then we will show that the Our Father echoes the Baptist's central theological concerns. Finally, we argue that the prayer must be seen as forming part of a comprehensive ritual composed of baptism and recitation of the Our Father.

The Ministry of John the Baptist

The Baptist movement saw John as a new prophet Elijah who was expected "to restore all things" (Mark 9:12); this somewhat cryptic phrase refers to the restoration of an independent Jewish state (Sir 48:10). In anticipation of such an event, the movement already sang a song of victory, celebrating God as the one who brings down the powerful—the Romans and the Herodians—from their thrones and lifts up the lowly—the Jewish people. As P. Winter and others have pointed out, the Magnificat (Luke 1:47–55)—originally sung by Elizabeth, John's mother—makes more sense when we attribute it to the circle of the Baptist.[5] It is precisely this political expectation that provides the key to understanding both John's baptism and the Our Father.

---

4. J. K. Elliott, "Did the Lord's Prayer Originate with John the Baptist?" *TZ* 29 (1973) 215. According to H. Schürmann, *Das Lukasevangelium* (Freiburg: Herder, 1994) 2/1.206, the two petitions "hallowed be your name, your kingdom come" echo the theology of John the Baptist. I acknowledge my indebtedness to three scholars who have explored the "baptismal" context of the Our Father, though not going as far as attributing the prayer to John as does Elliott: G. Klein, "Die ursprüngliche Gestalt des Vaterunsers," *ZNW* 7 (1906) 34–50; J. Swetnam, "Hallowed Be Thy Name," *Bib* 52 (1972) 556–63; W. Popkes, "Die letzte Bitte des Vater-Unser," *ZNW* 81 (1990) 1–20. In a recent paper Mell has demonstrated that the Our Father has few if any connections with the authentic Jesus tradition: U. Mell, "Gehört das Vater-Unser zur authentischen Jesus-Tradition?" *BTZ* 11 (1994) 148–80.

5. Winter, "Magnificat and Benedictus: Maccabean Psalms?"; similarly Bammel, "The Poor and the Zealots," 112–13; and Flusser, *Judaism and the Origins of Christianity*, 126–49.

John "baptized," that is, he assembled people and invited them to be immersed in water for a special religious purpose. John's baptism is a ritual cleansing or, more precisely, an inner, spiritual purification made visible in an outer, physical washing. In ancient Judaism, ideas and practices were regularly derived from or justified with reference to the sacred scriptures that were not only studied by specialists but also publicly read (and translated into the vernacular) in the synagogue. Baptism also has a scriptural basis. John seems to have derived the idea from an Old Testament passage found in the book of Ezekiel. The prophet Ezekiel was active among the exiles from Judah in Babylonia in the early sixth century B.C.E., and he proclaimed to them Yahweh's announcement of salvation.

> I shall hallow my great name [says Yahweh], which you have profaned among those [foreign] nations. When they see that I reveal my holiness through you [Israel], they will know that I am Yahweh, says the God Yahweh. . . . I shall sprinkle pure water over you, and you will be purified from everything that defiles you. . . . I shall put my spirit within you and make you conform to my statutes. (Ezek 36:23–27)

For the sake of his reputation—his holy name—Yahweh will redeem his people. He will restore them to their home country, the land of Israel. When this happens, pagans will no longer ridicule the God of Israel who appears to them as a weak, second-rate deity, unable to protect his second-rate people. In the eyes of the prophet, the Judeans deserved to be exiled to Babylonia: God punished them, for they had defiled themselves with sins of idolatry and unfaithfulness. Yahweh has the prophet announce his intervention, and this intervention involves a cleansing of the Judeans. The prophet speaks of the divine cleansing in ritual terms as a lustration, a cleansing done with water.

The idea that God's name or reputation is closely linked to the reputation of Israel is not peculiar to Ezekiel but can be found in other biblical traditions. (For example in the book of Joshua: when the Canaanites prevail over the Israelites and cause their name to disappear, God's great name is also affected; Josh 7:9.) Equally, the idea of ritual cleansing was also not peculiar to Ezekiel; others also refer to it, most notably Deutero-Zechariah, who predicted: "In that day [of redemption] there shall be a fountain opened to the house of David and to the inhabitants of Jerusalem, for purification and sprinkling" (Zech 13:1).

While in Ezekiel and Zechariah the divine cleansing done with water must be seen as a metaphor for God's *invisible* action corresponding
to the giving of a new heart or attitude (Ezek 36:26), John the Baptist
took it literally, as did the second-century Rabbi Akiba, who quoted the
Ezekiel passage in approval of Jews' cleansing themselves in the *miqveh*,
the synagogue's ritual immersion pool.[6] In John's rite of baptism, God
is seen as the one who sprinkles pure water over his people to purify
them from their defilement. Another explanation might be that John
"pre-imitates" the divine action: his baptism "of repentance" invites
God to act himself and purify those whom John has prepared.[7]

It seems that John considered himself a precursor—not of Jesus, as
the later Christian tradition has it, but as a precursor of God himself,
who would complete the work begun by his prophet John. "One who
is more powerful than I is coming," John proclaimed, and the mightier
one was of course a king who with divine help would restore Israel as
an independent state, indeed as God's own kingdom (Luke 3:16).
Therefore the announcement: "Repent, for the kingdom of God is at
hand!" (Matt 3:2) Thus *John's baptism marks the first phase in the drama of
redemption in which Yahweh vindicates the holiness and reputation of his name
by reestablishing the political independence and glory of his people.* For John,
Yahweh's sanctifying of his own name implies the sanctification of Israel; this connection had already been made explicit by Ezekiel (Ezek
36:28).

John's baptism must have involved the invocation of God's own
name; he baptized, we assume, "in the name of God." By doing so, he
marked his followers with a spiritual sign so that they would be recognized as members of the true Israel when that kingdom was reestab-
lished. The coming of the kingdom was preceded by God's powerful
intervention, which would destroy pagan empires (or just that of the
Romans) and also destroy unworthy Jews. "Repent, for the kingdom of
heaven is at hand! You brood of vipers! Who warned you to flee from
the wrath to come? Even now the axe is laid to the root of the trees;

---

6. *M. Yoma* 8:9.

7. It is not clear, though, whether this link to God was expressed in a formula or
simply taken for granted; von Campenhausen thinks that even Christian baptism originally was celebrated as in Acts 8:38—without invocation of the name of Jesus; see
H. von Campenhausen, "Taufen auf den Namen Jesu?" *VC* 25 (1971) 1–16.

every tree that does not bear good fruit is cut down and thrown into the fire" (Matt 3:2, 7, 10). In war and upheaval, the spiritual sign of baptism will serve as a sign of protection: the baptized will be recognized and spared when God's angels come and destroy the Roman Empire. The idea of a protective sign can also be found in Ezekiel, the book on which the idea of baptism is based (Ezek 9:4).

The "Our Father" as a Baptist Prayer

The Gospels give two versions of the Our Father: a shorter one (Luke) and a longer one (Matthew). While the Lucan version is presumably older and reflects John the Baptist's theology in a clearer way than the longer text, both traditions lend themselves to a reading in the context of John's theology. Set in this context the prayer has a natural and obvious meaning. For the sake of convenience, we insert here an English translation of the two versions and then comment briefly on the Baptist background of its petitions. The commentary will use a variety of paraphrases and translations of the biblical text in order to bring out its meaning as accurately as possible. The paraphrase included in *Praying Together: Agreed Liturgical Texts* is particularly helpful.[8]

Table 1. The Two Versions of "Our Father"

Luke 11:2–4	Matthew 6:9–13
Father, hallowed be your name. Your kingdom come. [Some manuscripts add: Your holy spirit come upon us and cleanse us.] Give us each day our daily bread. And forgive us our sins, for we ourselves forgive all who have done us wrong. And do not bring us to the time of trial.	Our father in heaven, hallowed be your name. Your will be done, on earth as it is in heaven. Give us this day our daily bread. And forgive us the wrong we have done, as we have forgiven those who have done us wrong. And do not lead us to the time of trial, but rescue us from evil.

(I) *Our Father … hallowed be your name.*   The first three petitions of the Our Father are distinguished by their making God's name, his kingdom, and his will the subject of actions whose actor remains implicit. As all commentators agree, the implication is that God himself is asked to

---

8. English Language Liturgical Consultation, *Praying Together: Agreed Liturgical Texts* (Norwich: Canterbury Press, 1988) 2.

hallow his name, to bring his rule, and to do his will. Therefore the authors of *Praying Together* are justified when they paraphrase the first petition by saying, "Father, show yourself to be the Holy One!" A more detailed, explanatory paraphrase may run as follows: Restore the holiness of your name by restoring the reputation of those who, through (John's) baptism, bear your divine name! In this context we can understand why the petition "your kingdom come" is in some biblical manuscripts followed by the request "may your holy Spirit come upon us and cleanse us" (Luke 11:2, manuscripts).[9] This second petition simply explains the first one: God restores his kingdom by sending his cleansing spirit. While Ezekiel, on whom the Baptist generally relied, refers to the sending of God's spirit and to cleansing from iniquities, he does not link the two ideas explicitly; however, an Isaianic oracle may have suggested the idea: "Yahweh . . . will cleanse the blood of Jerusalem from her midst by a spirit of judgment and a spirit of burning" (Isa 4:4).

Why is God addressed as "Father"? Ancient Jewish prayer language includes several possible ways of addressing the deity, one of them being "Father," others being God, Yahweh, Lord, and King. Father seems to be the preferred address used in particularly urgent supplications, when the praying group's or individual's life is at stake. The priest Eleazar uses it when the enraged King Ptolemy's elephant brigade advances against the Alexandrian Jews (3 Macc 6:3); Jesus uses it in the Garden of Gethsemane in face of his forthcoming arrest (Mark 14:36). In situations of extreme distress, God is addressed with a kinship term. In a society in which kinship implies solidarity, we can understand why this should be the case: in times of need, people would also ask the help of their kinsfolk. In Hebrew, one can associate Father with Redeemer, a term denoting a kinsman whose task it is to help. A prayer for Israel's national deliverance actually calls God both Father and Redeemer and refers to the Jews as people called by the divine name: "You, O Yahweh, are our father; our Redeemer from of old is your name. . . . We have long been like those not called by your name" (Isa 63:6, 19). Traditional prayer language allows the deity to be addressed as "Father" in an urgent plea;

---

9. For the manuscript reading of Luke 11:2, see Gregory of Nyssa, The Lord's Prayer, sermon 3 = PG 44.1157; R. H. Leaney, "The Lukan Text of the Lord's Prayer," *NovT* 1 (1956) 103–11. Unlike most scholars, Leaney takes the alternative reading to be the original one. For "spirit" and "cleansing" in Ezekiel, see Ezek 36:26, 33.

the address aims at giving the plea for national liberation a new note of urgency.

(II) *Your kingdom come.* "Bring in your kingdom" runs the correct paraphrase in *Praying Together.* We might suggest a somewhat more de-tailed version: Restore the independent Jewish kingdom! The new Jew-ish commonwealth already announced by Ezekiel will be the kingdom of God. "You shall be my people and I shall be your God" (Ezek 36:28). God's royal rule will be exercised by his human representative, a Da-vidic king (Ezek 37:22–24). The expression "kingdom of God" has so often been misunderstood that it is necessary to refer to and refute meanings that have been read into the Our Father. Misconstruing the original sense, Christians have often thought of God's kingdom as a uni-versal empire that will be established after the end of human history as we know it, a commonwealth directly and miraculously ruled by God or Christ, a kingdom not of this world. This is clearly not what John the Baptist and his circle were expecting and praying for. For them, the kingdom of God was a rather small, this-worldly state in the Near East, ruled by an ordinary human person. The second petition echoes the eminently political character of John's preaching and expectations.

The brief—to me, all too brief—second petition reveals a funda-mental characteristic of the Our Father, namely, its elliptical, condensed form. Its meaning is not spelled out in plain, accessible language; rather, it is encoded in short formulaic phrases. Despite all that commentators have said about the intimacy of a prayer directed to the heavenly "Fa-ther," the Our Father lacks immediacy. The formulaic, "restricted" code, as we may call it, was of course not the only one ancient Jews used in their prayers. They also knew the more wordy, direct, and informal "elaborated" code. The difference can easily be seen when we juxtapose certain petitions of the Our Father and a prayer found in the book of Ben Sira (see table 2, p. 246).

Prayers in the elaborated code are wordy and informal; they also aim at graphic clarity, which contributes to an immediate understanding. By contrast, the condensed, restricted code is terse and enigmatic. We sense that the Our Father is not a naïve prayer, born out of a momentary mood; its short phrases betray its origin in learned circles associated with John the Baptist. They produced a short text whose words are pregnant with meaning. "When you are praying, do not heap up empty phrases as the Gentiles do; for they think that they will be heard because of their

Table 2

Our Father	Ben Sira
Our father—your kingdom come.	Have mercy upon us, O God of all, and put all the nations in fear of you. Lift up your hand against foreign nations and let them see your might. Destroy the adversary and wipe out the enemy. . . . Gather all the tribes of Jacob, and give them their inheritance, as in the beginning (Sir 36:1–3, 9, 13, 16).
Hallowed be your name.	Have mercy, O Lord, on the people called by your name (Sir 36:17).

many words" (Matt 6:7). This word of Jesus reflects common sapiential teaching. "Let your words be few" (in praying), teaches Qoheleth, referring to God's heavenly majesty (Qoh 5:1[5:2]). Ben Sira, in a similar injunction, gives the advice to use economical, nonrepetitive speech when praying, comparable to the formal speech used when one speaks in an assembly. Matthew places Jesus' exhortation right next to the Our Father, knowing, it seems, that the Our Father is in the concise, formal style, made up of pregnant rather than "empty" phrases. The Matthean injunction may reflect the pride of those Jews who cultivated the art of writing short prayers in the "restricted" style.

(III) *Your will be done.* "Establish your will" is the paraphrase proposed by *Praying Together.* A more detailed version might be: Cause us to do your will, which is the only law of your kingdom! In the restored divine kingdom, the faithful will of course do God's will, as Ezekiel clearly indicated: "I will put my spirit within you, and cause you to walk in my statutes and be careful to observe my ordinances" (Ezek 36:27; cf. 37:24). The Jewish historian Josephus called John "a good man, who had exhorted the Jews to lead righteous lives, to practice justice toward their fellows and piety toward God."[10] The insistence on God's will may reflect the Baptist's focus on legal and moral preaching and his opposi-

---

10. Josephus *Ant.* 18.5.116; see also Luke 3:10–14.

tion to King Herod Antipas's divorce (which eventually cost him his life). The third petition may be an echo of an ancient synagogue prayer, the Abounding Love: "Our Father, . . . put it into our hearts to understand and to discern, to mark, learn, and teach, to heed, to do, and to fulfill in love all the words of instruction in thy Torah."[11]

(IV) *Give us today our daily bread.*   Give us abundant harvests! If we stay with our Ezekielian reading of the Our Father, we can refer to the prophet's announcement of miraculously rich harvests: "I will summon the grain [says Yahweh] and make it abundant and lay no famine upon you. I will make the fruit of the tree and the increase of the field abundant, that you may never again suffer the disgrace of famine" (Ezek 36:29–30). The land will indeed become "like the garden of Eden" (v. 35). The petition's reference to daily bread echoes a tradition not found in Ezekiel but in the Pentateuch. According to the story of Israel's wanderings in the desert, God fed his people with daily portions of manna, called the "bread from heaven" (Exod 16:4). As in the Old Testament, the heavenly bread is identified as real bread, not as something merely spiritual.

The Magnificat, which I venture to attribute to the Baptist tradition, gives us another glimpse of what the fourth petition has in mind: "He has filled the hungry with good things, and sent the rich away empty" (Luke 1:53). There will be a rich harvest for the hungry.

(V) *Forgive us our sins (trespasses, debts), as we forgive those who sin against us.*   Forgive us our sins of idolatry and apostasy, as we forgive our enemies who have defeated us and continue to oppress us! The meaning of the fifth petition remains obscure as long as the precise nature of the sin to be forgiven is not determined. In keeping with our contention that the Our Father is a "national" prayer, the sin to be forgiven can only be a national sin, or rather, an accumulation thereof. The sins to be forgiven can only be those that led to punishment with the destruction of the monarchy and with the Babylonian exile. As soon as God forgives, he will also restore the exiles to their home country. Interestingly enough, the Old Testament includes a prayer that spells out in detail the meaning the Our Father expresses in an abridged form:

---

11. J. Heinemann and J. J. Petuchowski, *Literature of the Synagogue* (New York: Behrman, 1975) 23–24.

"When your people Israel, having sinned against you, are defeated before an enemy but turn to you, confess your name, pray and plead with you in this house [the Temple of Jerusalem], then hear in heaven, forgive the sin of your people Israel, and bring them again to the land that you gave to their ancestors" (1 Kgs 8:33–34). In a similar vein, Daniel, after enumerating the sins that led to exile, asks God for collective forgiveness: "O Lord, hear; O Lord, forgive; O Lord, listen and act and do not delay! For your own sake, O my God, because your city and your people bear your name!" (Dan 9:19). Daniel's prayer shares with the Our Father the petition for forgiveness and the reference to the divine name; both are stock items belonging to early Jewish political prayer.

A condition for God's forgiving seems to be that the faithful also forgive their oppressors—the Babylonians, Greeks, Romans, and so on. If this is the correct understanding, it has an important implication: John's message is essentially *pacifist*. Although he expects an independent Jewish kingdom to emerge shortly, he does not encourage hostile, let alone military, action against the Romans. A confirmation of this idea is the tradition that even tax collectors, as collaborators with the imperial authorities, found nothing wrong with being baptized and belonging to John's movement (Luke 7:29). Later, Jesus echoed the Baptist's pacifist attitude when he advised against retaliation: "You have heard that it was said, An eye for an eye and a tooth for a tooth. But I say to you, Do not resist an evildoer. But if anyone strikes you on the right cheek, turn the other also" (Matt 5:38–39).

When in the sixth century B.C.E. God had summoned Israel's mighty neighbors to punish his people by destroying their state, he established enmity and hatred between them. When God forgives his people and restores their independence, the enmity between Israel and its pagan neighbors must also end. The seventh petition, "deliver us from evil," seems to envisage universal political peace and harmony. That such an ecumenical, generous vision existed can be shown from an oracle pronounced in a mood of reconciliation: "In that day shall Israel be the third [power] with Egypt and with Assyria, a blessing in the midst of the earth; for Yahweh of hosts has blessed her, saying: Blessed be Egypt my people, and Assyria the work of my hands, and Israel my inheritance" (Isa 19:24–25). This vision of a community of empires that all belong to the encompassing kingdom of God involves the renunciation of vengeance

in an act of forgiveness. Israel must renounce the wish "to execute vengeance upon the nations, and chastisement upon the peoples; to bind
their kings with chains, and their nobles with fetters of iron" (Ps 149:7–
8). The phrase "as we forgive those who sin against us" envisages an important political program.

The new forgiving attitude vis-à-vis the traditional enemies of Israel
seems to be a prelude to if not a "pre-imitation" of divine forgiveness,
just as John's baptism presumably pre-imitates God's purificatory action.
The Greek wording of the petition suggests that the human initiative
must come first: "Forgive us the wrong we have done, as we [already]
have forgiven those who have wronged us" (Revised English Bible).
Once Israel has forgiven her enemies, God "must" also forgive her—
and restore her to her pristine glory! One ancient source about John the
Baptist includes a hint at the proper meaning of forgiveness. John's baptism, reports Josephus, "would be acceptable if they used it, not for putting away of certain sins, but for the purification of the body, the soul
having previously been cleansed by righteousness."[12] First comes the
symbolic purificatory ritual, and then comes God's forgiving of the national sins (the "putting away of certain sins"), which latter act becomes
visible in the reestablishment of the Jewish state. John does not claim
the power to forgive sins; he only prepares people, making them worthy
for this divine, national act.

(VI) *Save us from the time of trial.*   The traditional rendering, "lead us
not into temptation," has been abandoned by recent scholarship. The
New Revised Standard Version of the Bible (1989) translates: "Do not
bring us to the time of trial." A similar understanding can be found in
the Revised English Bible (1989): "Do not put us to the test." The book
of Ezekiel does not seem to provide a clue to the understanding of this
petition. So we must look elsewhere, and the most obvious relevant tradition can be found in the Pentateuch.[13] God repeatedly "tests" the
faithfulness and loyalty of his people by submitting them to hardship
and challenge. Apparently, such a test has three characteristics: the entire
people is involved; there is great distress; and people are tempted to

---

12. Josephus *Ant.* 18.5.117. The New Testament reference to John's "baptism of
repentance for the forgiveness of sins" (Mark 1:4) "Christianizes" John.

13. For the "trial/temptation" tradition, see, for example, Deut 8:2.

commit acts of disloyalty, such as returning to Egypt and worship other gods. While the hardship Israel experienced in the desert is a mere legend, every Jew knew of the Babylonian Exile as such a test: the entire people was involved; they suffered losses and many were deported to Babylonia; many Jews were tempted to forsake loyalty to Yahweh and to turn to other gods. Viewed in this light, the petition can only mean: Do not bring us to another time of trial, for we went through enough national trials.

(VII) *Deliver us from evil.* Deliver us from all our misfortunes! The final petition echoes a phrase known from a prayer text dating from the second century B.C.E., which sums up what God is expected to do: "You rescue Israel from every evil," that is, from foreign domination (2 Macc 1:25). In the form of a petition, similar phrases are frequently appended to Jewish prayers: "Set Israel free, O God, from all her misfortunes!" (Ps 25:22). These misfortunes are of course political ones, and so the last petition of the Our Father is for delivery from foreign domination. Similar requests are appended to other psalms: "Save your people, and bless your inheritance; and tend them, and carry them for ever" (Ps 28:9). "O Yahweh, God of hosts, restore us; cause your face to shine, and we shall be saved" (Ps 80:20[19]). And again: "O that deliverance for Israel would come from Zion, when God restores the fortunes of his people" (Ps 53:6). Since the Our Father, as recorded in the Gospel of Luke, does not have the seventh petition, it may well be an early addition that reflects the style of standard Jewish prayer.

The Ritual Use of the Our Father

If we are justified in attributing the prayer to John the Baptist and his circle, we may consider the meaning of fasting as practiced by John's disciples. According to Luke, they "frequently fast and pray" (Luke 5:33). Fasting and praying belong together and form one public ritual response to a situation of crisis caused by nature (like drought) or people (like pagan oppression and persecution).[14] It may well be that John and

---

14. On communal fasting in first-century C.E. Judaism, see A. H. Baumann, "Fasttage in der Darstellung des Josephus," in *Begegnung zwischen Christentum und Judentum in Antike und Mittelalter* (ed. D.-A. Koch et al.; Göttingen: Vandenhoeck & Ruprecht, 1993) 41–49.

his disciples promoted this particular ritual response to the absence of God's kingdom. Like baptizing, both praying the Our Father and fasting aimed at speeding up the coming of a great reversal in the history of Jewish political existence. Even if John did not frequently hold public prayer assemblies, he would no doubt have considered private fasting as part of a communal ritual, ideally to be practiced by all Jews. Widely practiced individual devotion would constitute a collective act and bring the same result one expected from assemblies: delivery from oppression and the coming of the kingdom.

Baptism and praying also belong together and form an established ritual sequence: baptism cleanses and thus prepares the individual for participation in the kingdom, and then the newly baptized person joins—or may join—the group in its prayer for the coming of the kingdom. But who is this group? Here a hint given by Origen seems to be relevant. John, he reports, seems to have taught his prayer "secretly" and "not to all who came to be baptized, but to those who became his disciples in addition to being baptized."[15] In other words: there was a wider circle of the merely baptized and a narrower, "esoteric" circle of the actual disciples. These disciples, it seems, practiced the full ritual sequence of fasting, being baptized, and praying for the coming of the kingdom. The "esoteric" quality of the Our Father can still be felt by us in the twentieth century. As a prayer with a rather complex scriptural and ideological background, it betrays its origin with the learned and highly motivated religious elite. It is a prayer not for the masses but for the few.

As we can see from a second-century source, the Didache, the ritual sequence of baptism and recitation of the Our Father was also practiced in the early Christian community.[16] This practice seems to predate the second century; in the first century, the New Testament seems to presuppose it. According to Paul, the newly baptized address God for the first time in the Aramaic idiom as Abba, "Father" (Gal 4:6, Rom 8:15).

---

15. Origen, On Prayer 2.4 = GCS Origenes 2.302–3.

16. For the sequence of baptism and recitation of the Our Father, see Didache 7–8 (ca. 110/160 c.e.) = SC 248.170–74; relevant secondary sources include W. Rordorf, "The Lord's Prayer in the Light of Its Liturgical Use in the Early Church," *Studia Liturgica* 14 (1980–81) 1–19, esp. 4; Popkes, "Die letzte Bitte des Vater-Unser." For a biblical text suggesting the sequence of baptism and prayer, see Luke 3:21.

This invocation appears to represent the first word of the Our Father, for psalms and prayers (as well as other ancient Jewish texts, such as biblical books) were often referred to, not by a formal "title," but simply by their first word. Another echo of the Our Father can be detected in the account of Jesus' baptism by John. After having been ritually cleansed by washing, Jesus prays and hears God's voice calling him his "beloved son" (Luke 3:22). If we can take Jesus' baptism as reflecting the pattern of baptism practiced in Luke's community, then we can conclude that the ritual changes the candidate's status from stranger to son. As a son, he may address God as the Father. Now if the first two Christian generations, that of Paul and that of Luke, knew the sequence of baptism and reciting the Our Father, then we may be justified in attributing this sequence to John. In other words, the central ritual practiced in the Baptist community, baptism followed by the recitation of a special prayer, has been preserved in Christianity. Jesus himself, during the time he baptized and proclaimed the closeness of God's kingdom, may have used both the ritual and the text recited in conjunction with it.[17]

Summing up our argument we can say that the Our Father was originally used as a prayer in ritual assemblies in which John the Baptist announced the reestablishment of the Jewish state (termed God's kingdom) and contributed to its coming by baptizing its citizens. At the center of the promise was, of course, a renewed Jewish state. According to John, both the ritual cleansing with water and a newly devised prayer—the Our Father—would serve as a promising invitation of divine intervention and could indeed help inaugurate the new era of divine blessings. In brief paraphrase: "Our Father in heaven, fulfill for your people Israel all you have promised through your prophets!" In its Matthean form, the one generally used today, this one political petition is repeated seven times, in order to underline its urgency.[18] Just like the Benedictus and the Magnificat, the Our Father is a liturgical text echoing the political hopes and expectations entertained by John the Baptist

---

17. On Jesus as baptizer, see John 3:22. On the historical relationship between John the Baptist and Jesus, see J. Murphy-O'Connor, "John the Baptist and Jesus," *NTS* 36 (1990) 359–74.

18. The Christian (Jesuanic) appropriation and reinterpretation of the Our Father as "the Lord's Prayer" is discussed in my *Sacred Games: A History of Christian Worship* (New Haven: Yale University Press, 1997) 89–94.

and his circle. To be sure, these political hopes were no longer shared by those who compiled the Gospels in which the Our Father is transmitted. However, as is often the case with poetry: its words transcend and survive the context in which they originated. Just as the Old Testament Song of Deborah permits a view into early Israelite tribal life, and as certain Arabic poems echo pre-Islamic culture, so a number of early Christian liturgical texts open a window into a religious world of which only a few traces have survived.

Index of Authors

Index of Scripture

New Testament

Deuterocanonical and Pseudepigraphical Literature

Rabbinic Literature